Timbuktu, where are you?

Enjoy
Russel & Penny

2 *Map: World*

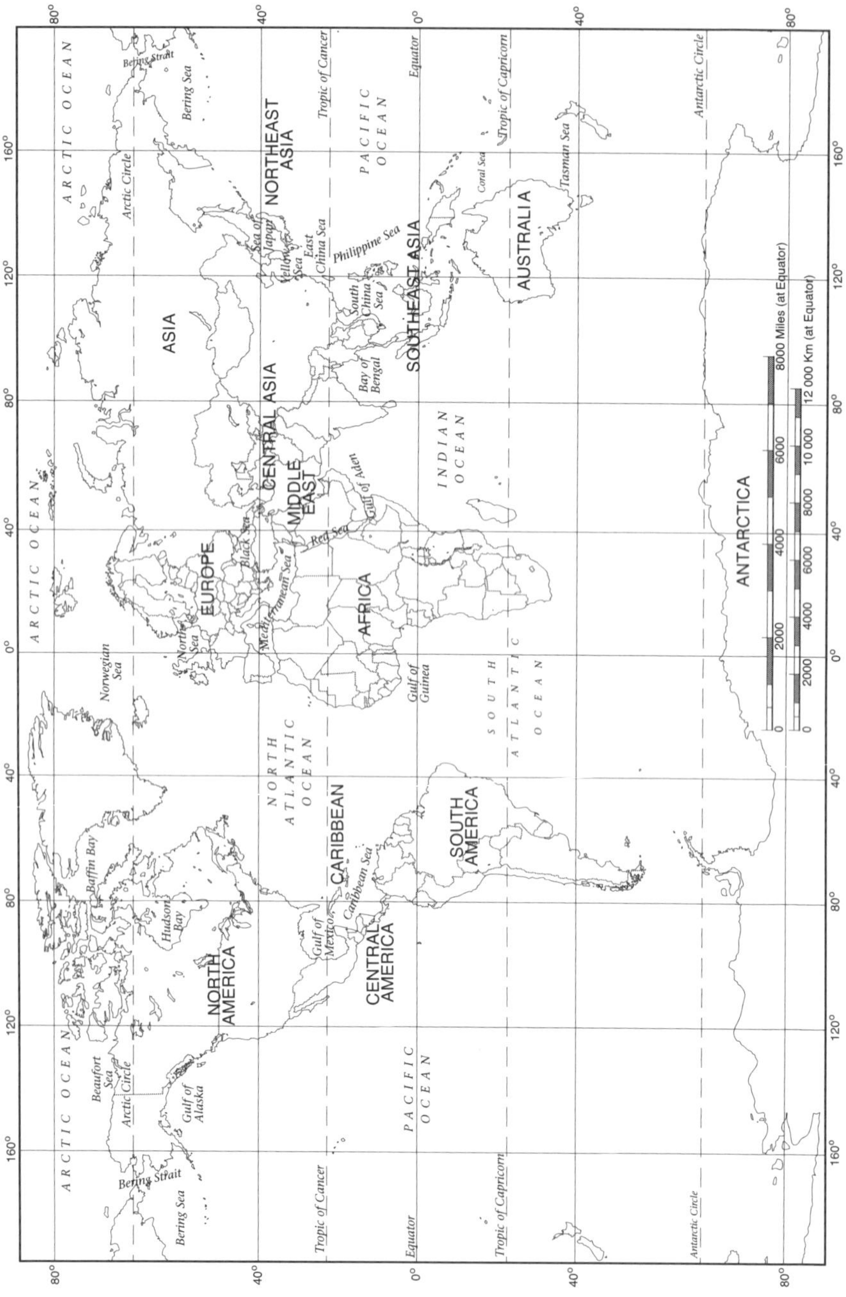
ARCTIC OCEAN
Bering Strait
Bering Sea
Arctic Circle
Tropic of Cancer
Equator
Tropic of Capricorn
Antarctic Circle
PACIFIC OCEAN
NORTHEAST ASIA
Sea of Japan
Yellow Sea
East China Sea
Philippine Sea
South China Sea
SOUTHEAST ASIA
Coral Sea
Tasman Sea
AUSTRALIA
ASIA
CENTRAL ASIA
Bay of Bengal
INDIAN OCEAN
MIDDLE EAST
Gulf of Aden
Red Sea
Black Sea
EUROPE
Mediterranean Sea
AFRICA
North Sea
Norwegian Sea
Gulf of Guinea
SOUTH ATLANTIC OCEAN
NORTH ATLANTIC OCEAN
ANTARCTICA
CARIBBEAN
Caribbean Sea
SOUTH AMERICA
Baffin Bay
Hudson Bay
NORTH AMERICA
Gulf of Mexico
CENTRAL AMERICA
Beaufort Sea
Gulf of Alaska
8000 Miles (at Equator)
12 000 Km (at Equator)
0
2000
4000
6000
8000
10 000
80°
40°
0°
160°
120°

Timbuktu, where are you?

Russell and Penny Jennings

OPEN ROAD PUBLISHERS
Vancouver, BC, Canada

ISBN 978-0-9691363-5-4

First edition, 2008

Library and Archives Canada Cataloguing in Publication

Jennings, Russell, 1943-
Timbuktu, where are you?: there and back in 40 stories / by Russell Jennings; in collaboration with Penny Jennings.

ISBN 978-0-9691363-5-4

1. Jennings, Russell, 1943- – Travel.
2. Voyages and travels.
3. Backpacking.
I. Jennings, Penny, 1941-
II. Title.

G440.J45A3 2008 910.4092 C2008-901751-X

Publisher
Open Road Publishers
3316 West 8th Avenue
Vancouver, BC, V6R 1Y4, Canada

Fax: +1 604 734 1586
Email: jennings@worldweatherguide.com
Web site: www. worldweatherguide.com

Cover photo: Author at Timbuktu, Mali
Printed in Canada

CONTENTS

Acknowledgements

We are particularly grateful to Julie Lees, Lamont Mackay and Dot Wills for critiquing our manuscript and offering suggestions.

Special thanks go to Mark Hoffmann who worked on the cover and arranged the page layout and prepress preparations (mhoffmann@babblefishdesign.com).

Thanks go to Dinesh Sharma for his attention to detail in preparing the route maps.

About the maps

The maps show the tracks laid down by Russell Jennings when travelling solo, journeys with acquaintances he met along the way, and travels with his wife, Penny.

The heading of each story includes a map reference so the reader can pinpoint where an event took place.

Stories from some areas, such as South America, are not included in *Timbuktu, where are you?* They can be found among the forty stories in *Around the World in Sandals*. See back pages.

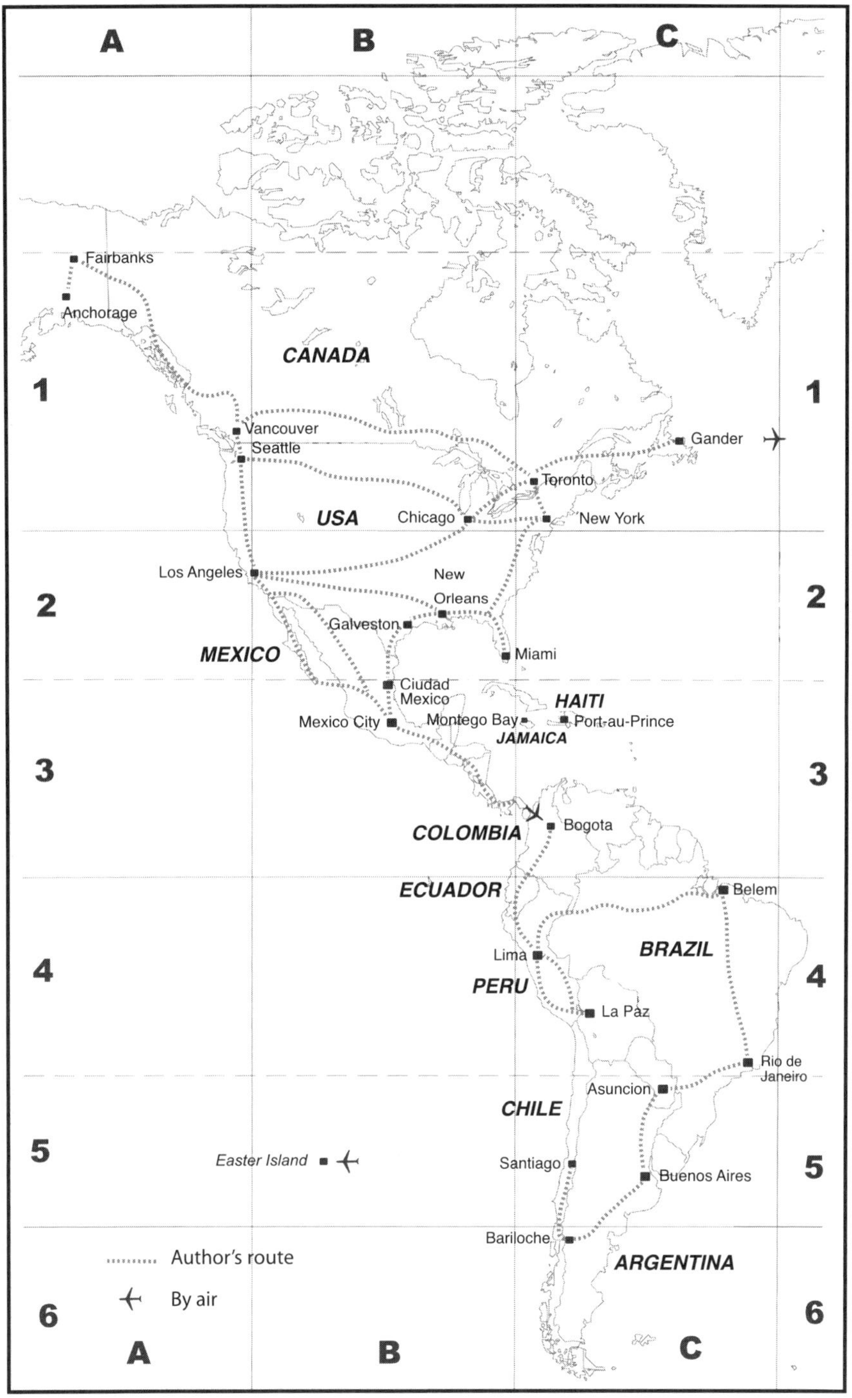
A
B
C
1
2
3
4
5
6
Fairbanks
Anchorage
CANADA
Vancouver
Seattle
Gander
Toronto
USA
Chicago
New York
Los Angeles
New
Orleans
Galveston
MEXICO
Miami
Ciudad
Mexico
HAITI
Mexico City
Montego Bay
Port-au-Prince
JAMAICA
COLOMBIA
Bogota
ECUADOR
Belem
BRAZIL
Lima
PERU
La Paz
Rio de
Janeiro
Asuncion
CHILE
Easter Island
Santiago
Buenos Aires
Bariloche
ARGENTINA
Author's route
By air

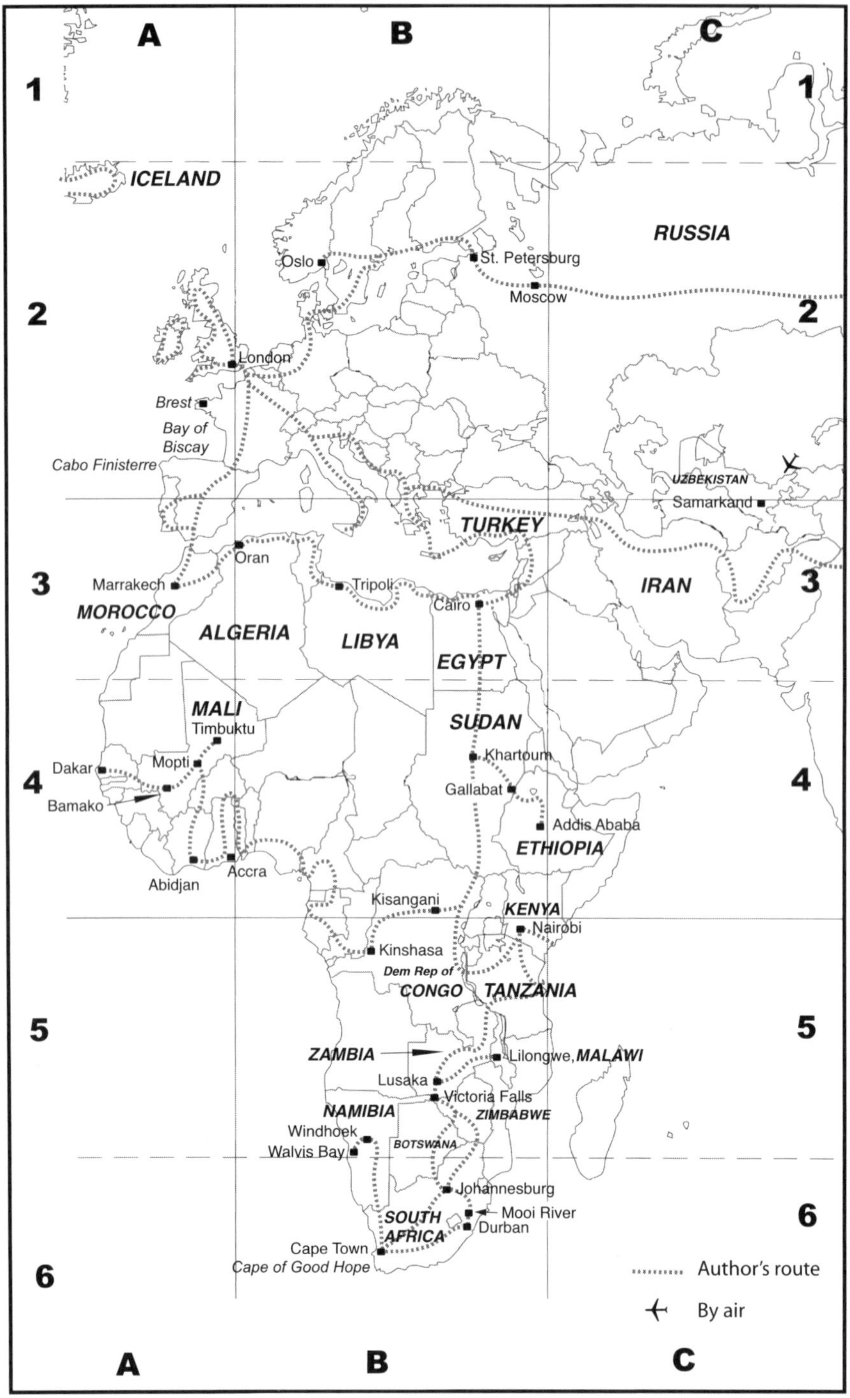
A
B
C
1
2
3
4
5
6
ICELAND
RUSSIA
Oslo
St. Petersburg
Moscow
London
Brest
Bay of Biscay
Cabo Finisterre
UZBEKISTAN
Samarkand
TURKEY
Oran
Marrakech
MOROCCO
ALGERIA
Tripoli
LIBYA
Cairo
EGYPT
IRAN
MALI
Timbuktu
SUDAN
Khartoum
Dakar
Mopti
Bamako
Gallabat
Addis Ababa
ETHIOPIA
Abidjan
Accra
Kisangani
KENYA
Nairobi
Kinshasa
Dem Rep of CONGO
TANZANIA
ZAMBIA
Lilongwe, MALAWI
Lusaka
Victoria Falls
NAMIBIA
ZIMBABWE
Windhoek
Walvis Bay
BOTSWANA
Johannesburg
SOUTH AFRICA
Mooi River
Durban
Cape Town
Cape of Good Hope
Author's route
By air

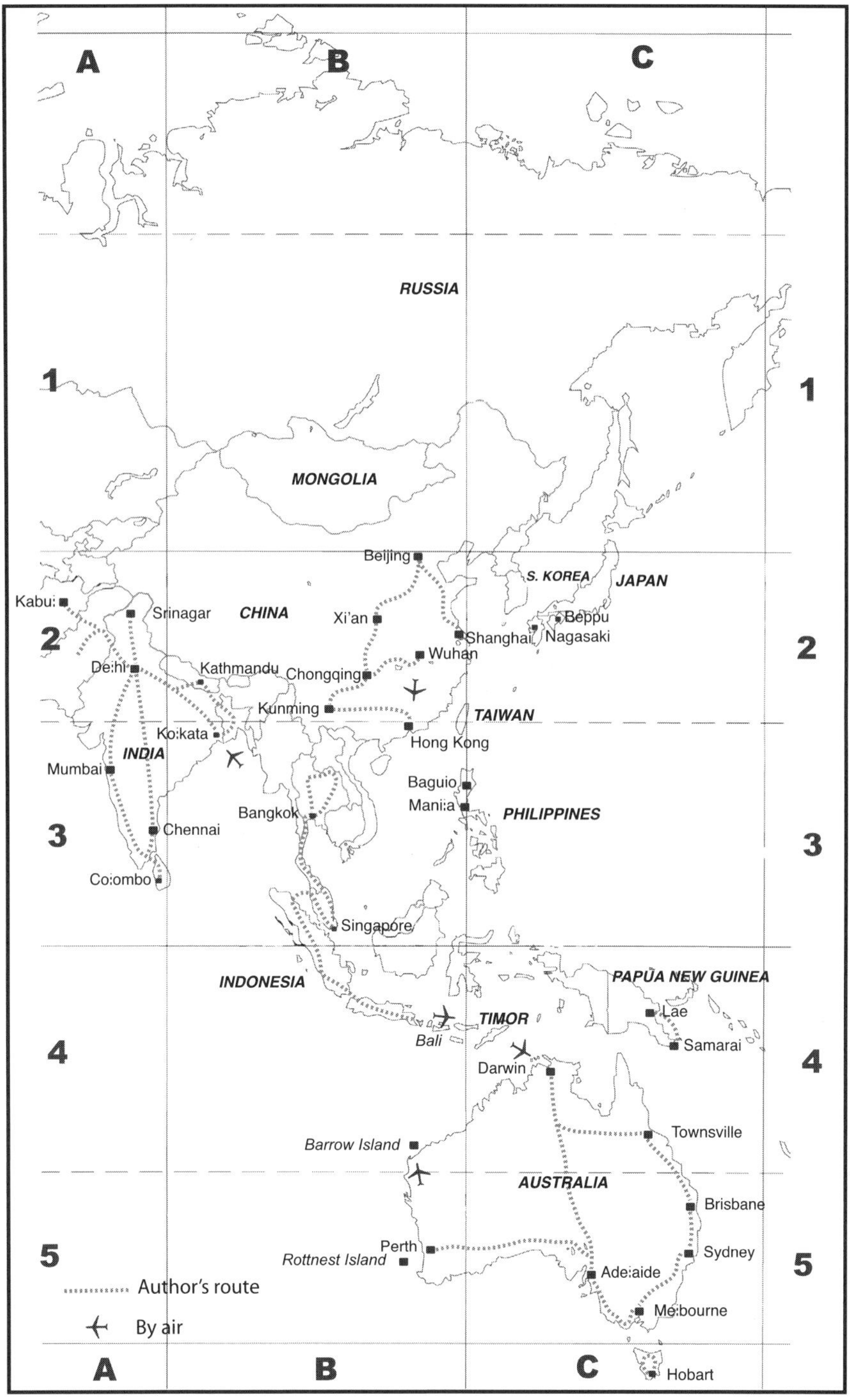
A
B
C
RUSSIA
1
MONGOLIA
Beijing
S. KOREA
JAPAN
Kabul
Srinagar
CHINA
Xi'an
Beppu
Shanghai
Nagasaki
2
Wuhan
Delhi
Kathmandu
Chongqing
Kunming
TAIWAN
Kolkata
Hong Kong
INDIA
Mumbai
Baguio
Manila
PHILIPPINES
Bangkok
Chennai
3
Colombo
Singapore
PAPUA NEW GUINEA
INDONESIA
Lae
TIMOR
Bali
Samarai
4
Darwin
Townsville
Barrow Island
AUSTRALIA
Brisbane
Perth
Sydney
5
Rottnest Island
Adelaide
Author's route
Melbourne
By air
Hobart

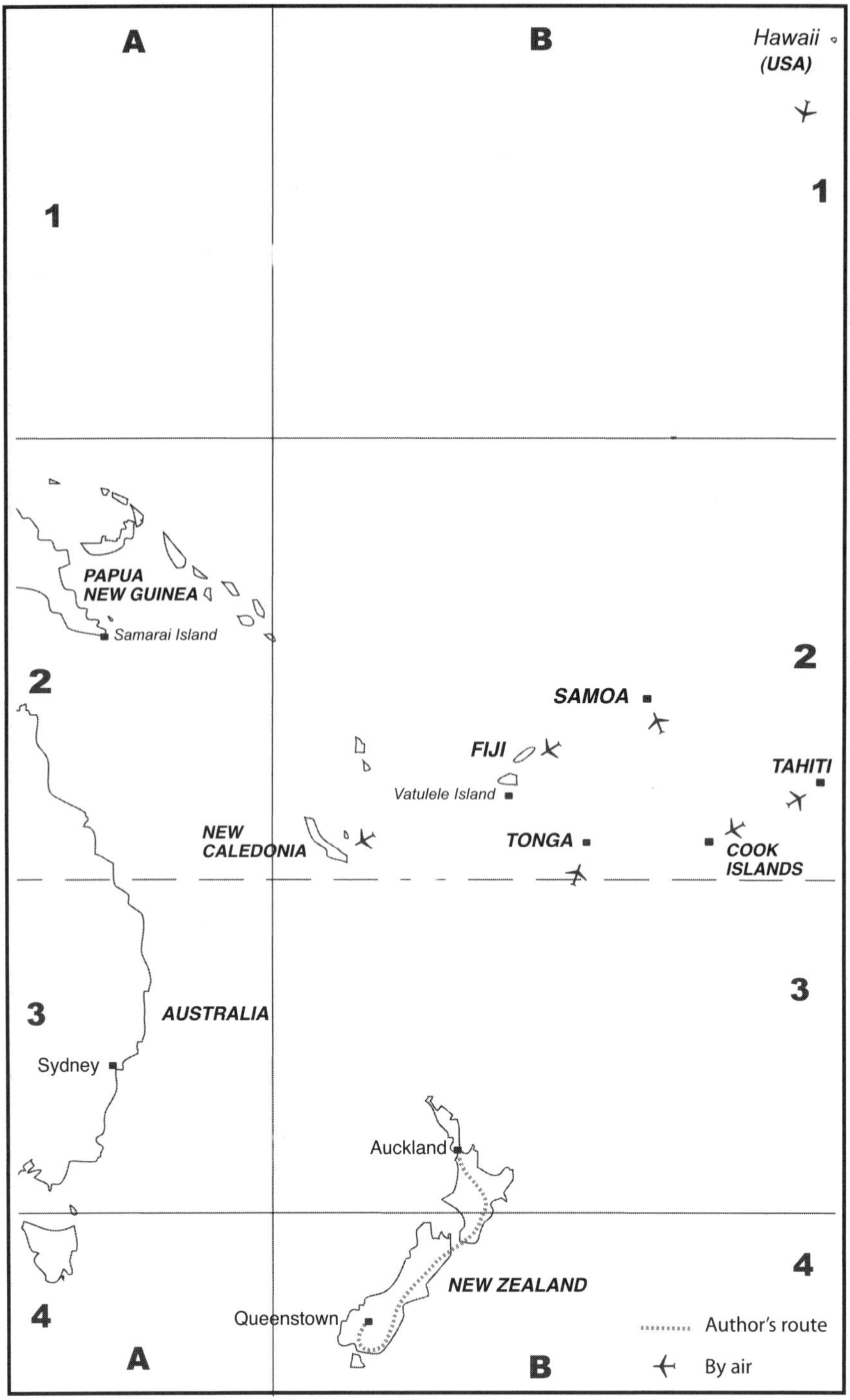
A
B
Hawaii
(USA)
1
1
PAPUA
NEW GUINEA
Samarai Island
2
2
SAMOA
FIJI
TAHITI
Vatulele Island
NEW
CALEDONIA
TONGA
COOK
ISLANDS
3
3
AUSTRALIA
Sydney
Auckland
4
NEW ZEALAND
4
Queenstown
Author's route
A
B
By air

Introduction

What the reader needs to know

My first recollection of wanting to see the world goes back to when I was about nine years old. I took a world atlas, a notebook and a pen and started to write. When my mother asked me what I was doing, I replied: "I'm writing down all the countries and cities I want to visit. But I can't find Timbuktu."

"That's because it doesn't exist," my mother said.

I never questioned her answer until some years later, when I learned Timbuktu *did* exist, but was spelt Tombouctou on most maps. I made up my mind to go there one day.

To pursue my dream I had to make money. I earned diplomas in Sales and Marketing, and Accountancy, the latter of which enabled me to find work easily in Johannesburg, London, Melbourne and Samarai Island in Papua New Guinea.

When I travelled I carried a backpack, hitchhiked and used public transportation, stayed in hostels, no-star hotels and under the stars.

I wrote copious notes in my journals which enabled me to recount my experiences accurately.

Often the highlight of travel is not the destination but the journey to get there, and the people one meets along the way. In the following pages you'll meet some interesting characters.

The most important person I met was Penny, a petite blue-eyed blonde with sparkling eyes and a warm smile. I met her in Vancouver on a blind date when I was hitchhiking from Alaska to South America. We teamed up, and over the years travelled extensively, leaving our footprints on six continents. Many of our experiences can be found in our book, *Around the World in Sandals*.

Prior to meeting Penny I spent ten years working and backpacking. Those travels provided tales for *Timbuktu, where are you?* – a book on which we collaborated in writing. Penny deciphered my scribbled anecdotes, breathed life into the characters and crafted sentences to make the stories readable. In both books the tales are told in the sequence they occurred.

Want to join me in my search for Timbuktu?

Slip into your walking shoes, and let's go!

Papua New Guinea

Forgetful Jack

Marooned on Logeia Island, near Samarai, March 1967

See map, page 13, C4

Samarai Island, a hilly emerald speck surrounded by a dead coral reef, lies at the southeastern tip of Papua New Guinea. This particular Sunday morning the tide was out. Broken coral, empty shells bleached by the sun, and marooned sea urchins with sharp, black spikes lay scattered over the mud flats. In the middle of this wasteland stood Doris, a bronzed, dark-haired woman, daughter of a Greek trader and a native Papuan woman. She was about to drag an 18-foot dinghy across the mud to the water. I trudged through the muck to give her a hand.

"Where're you going?" I asked. "Fishing?"

"Yes, Jack lent me his boat for the day. Wanna come? I've got rods and bait."

"Sure. Is the tank full?"

"Jack was here. He checked everything."

That was good enough for me. Jack was reliable, most of the time. He had lived all of his life on the island but, as he got older, he was becoming forgetful. Of the two motorboats on the island, Jack owned one of them.

"Just give me five minutes to get my hat, snacks, and water," I said to Doris.

To go anywhere on Samarai doesn't take long. You can walk around it in twenty minutes. I had been working on the island for two years as a shipping clerk in the office of a South Pacific Islands trading company.

A day of fishing sounded like a fun diversion. I looked forward to hooking a kingfish, the most prized table fish in these waters.

We slid the boat into the water. I yanked the starter cord and the outboard motor sputtered to life. I pointed the boat towards the neighbouring island of Logeia. A light wind blew, just enough to make the sea choppy.

Doris perched in the bow while I continued to man the tiller which was attached to the engine. I navigated the boat parallel to Logeia's coast, until we spotted a few village huts along the shoreline.

"Let's visit the village," I bellowed to Doris over the roar of the engine. She nodded eagerly. I pulled sharply on the tiller. Something snapped and the engine cut out.

"The tiller broke off in my hand," I yelled to Doris, waving it above my head. We started to drift aimlessly only about 200 yards from shore.

"I'll grab an oar," Doris yelled. "We have to watch out for changing currents."

Because of the islands sprinkled in the area, the currents flowed in different directions. They could sweep a disabled boat out to the open sea.

"Where's the other oar?" I asked.

"I guess Jack forgot to put it in."

"Thanks, Jack," I mumbled. While Doris used the only oar as a paddle, I leaned over the other side of the boat and paddled with my hand. It was hard work, fighting the current, straining my little-used arm muscles.

As we neared the shoreline about thirty young children, some naked, others in T-shirts, bounded out of the village to greet us. Smiling teeth gleamed white against the chocolate brown of their carefree faces.

With the boat bobbing in the shallows I checked the tiller. To my dismay it had corroded because of long-term exposure to salt water. I jammed the broken tiller back in place and pulled the starter cord, but the motor refused to turn over. I desperately fiddled with the motor for another hour but it still wouldn't start. Four men from the village emerged from the nearby coconut palms and helped us beach the boat.

After thanking them for their help, Doris and I sat on the sand and munched the Spam sandwiches I had hastily put together earlier.

The young boys and girls from the village were playing, splashing in the water. We joined them in order to cool off and mull over our next move. "If we don't return by evening our friends will be worried," Doris said anxiously. "They won't know where to start looking."

The only way on and off Samarai Island was by motorboat. With only one other vessel available to search for us, the chance of being found quickly seemed remote.

We decided to make a courtesy call on the village headman. Children showed us to his hut which, like the others, was built on stilts about six feet above the ground. The walls and roof were covered with thatched coconut palm leaves. The floor was made of split bamboo.

A possum was tethered to a post by a cord of coconut fibre. I bent down for a closer look. The size of a squirrel, it had a grey back and a white front with short, woolly fur. Doris crouched beside me. "Isn't it cute?" she said as she tickled its belly. "Oh! It's a female. You can see the nipples. And here's her pouch where she keeps her babies."

I looked closer. The pouch was like that of a kangaroo, but much smaller of course.

"It's rare to see a possum," Doris said, "because they're nocturnal. Must be someone's pet."

The headman, a small muscular fellow, came down the rough-hewn wooden steps of his hut. I told him about our predicament with the boat and the possibility of being marooned in his village. I asked how he made contact with the outside world.

He spoke a mixture of English and the local language, Motu, a language Doris was more familiar with than I. He told us there were no phones or two-way radios. He continued with more grim news. There was no regular boat service to the island. The boats the villagers owned were dugout canoes with an outrigger on one side. They weren't designed to cross the choppy sea between Logeia and Samarai.

When the villagers wanted a boat, like a coastal trader, to stop and pick up passengers or cargo they would flash mirrors at the boat. The sun had to be shining and be at the proper angle to reflect off the mirrors. Someone on the boat must see the flashes and the skipper must be willing to change course. It could be a week or more before a boat would stop.

That was not what we wanted to hear.

As the afternoon progressed, the village women, who wore grass skirts and nothing else, honoured us by offering us a meal. We perched on the trunk of a fallen coconut palm. It was an idyllic setting – palm trees swayed and gentle waves lapped the shore while the women busied themselves with the preparations. I tried to put our situation out of my mind.

A platter-sized banana leaf heaped with breadfruit, yams, native cabbage, and a small roasted animal was placed in front of us. I was alarmed to see the meat and had my suspicions as to its origin. Animals were scarce on the island, and the serving of meat was restricted to special occasions. We picked at the bland food with our fingers until the banana leaf was empty. The women smiled with delight.

Later, we ambled along the curving beach. Under the dome of blue sky the turquoise sea rolled into the shore, breaking into strands of white necklaces. Leaving the beach we strolled towards a grove of coconut palms. The headman's hut stood ahead of us.

We confirmed what I had suspected – the possum was missing. It was now in our bellies. I felt sick to my stomach.

Putting aside visions of the possum, I focused on our predicament and the concern we'd be causing our friends back in Samarai.

My thoughts propelled me into action.

"I'll try to start the motor again," I said to Doris.

We dragged the boat back into the water and I started fiddling again while Doris walked along the beach with the children. All of a sudden the motor roared to life. Doris turned, bounded along the sand and jumped into the boat.

"Let's go," she said, almost out of breath.

I had to grip the tiller tightly and hold it in its socket so the engine wouldn't cut out. Doris waved to the men, women and children lined up along the beach. They waved back. I dared not take my hands off the tiller or move it. Because it was broken I couldn't steer. The boat veered away from Samarai instead of towards it. Doris grabbed the oar, thrust it into the water beside the boat and plied it as a rudder. The boat responded slowly. We turned in a wide arc until we faced Samarai.

The wind whipped my face. The sea became choppier. The engine raced at full throttle. The boat seemed to leap up and over the swelling waves.

I shouted over the roaring engine: "Are there any life jackets?"

"I'll check the locker...No, nothing here. I guess Jack forgot."

As each wave rolled towards us, the boat rose to meet it, cut through the crest, crashed down into the trough then pranced around until the next wall of water crested. I feared being swamped by a rogue wave. I dared not throttle down for fear the engine would cut out.

In the tropics when the sun sets, darkness comes quickly. Already the sun was falling towards the western horizon, turning the sea from blue to gold to sombre grey. The hillocks of Samarai were painted in shades of orange and purple. It was nearly dark when we arrived at the reef and the calm waters around Samarai.

A lone figure stood in the shallows. Jack.

He waded towards us.

"Where have you been?" he called in an agitated tone. "Did you bring me back a kingfish?"

I held up the broken tiller. "We're lucky to have brought ourselves back!"

"Uh, oh!" he said. "Didn't I replace it? I guess I forgot!"

Papua New Guinea

Pigeon soup

By trading boat, Samarai to Lae, April 1967

See map, page 13, C4

The *Fortunate Treasure*, a 190-ton coastal trading ship, sat low in the water. It was tied to the wharf at Samarai Island on the southeastern tip of Papua New Guinea. The trading ships that plied these waters created work for the local islanders, as crewmen and stevedores.

The hold was full of building materials and canned food destined for the mission stations and coconut plantations in the region. When the engine started, the ship vibrated. I stood on the forward deck, watching the stevedores on the wharf as they loosened the ropes around the bollards. The ship's crew hauled the ropes aboard and we pulled away. I had mixed feelings about this trip as it could be the last time I would sail between the islands.

The sky was blue this morning but, because this was April and the start of the wet season, the sky would be grey by afternoon with the promise of monsoon rains. Beside me stood Tobias, the Papuan skipper, a jovial, robust man. I had worked in a shipping office on the little island of Samarai for two years and had known Tobias for most of that time. It had been a rewarding experience for a twenty-three-year-old, but it was time to move on.

Freighters arrived from Australia, Europe and North America and unloaded cargo at Samarai. Coastal trading ships, like the *Fortunate Treasure,* then delivered the goods to neighbouring islands and along the coast. At the coconut plantations the ship's crew picked up sacks of copra – the dried, rancid-smelling white meat of the coconut. It would eventually be exported to be used in the manufacture of margarine and soap.

When my employment contract on Samarai expired I booked my passage with Tobias for the five-day voyage from Samarai to Lae (pronounced Lay). The *Fortunate Treasure,* being a cargo boat, didn't normally carry passengers. Tobias gave up his cabin for me. "I'll bunk with my crew," he said agreeably. He had a crew of six.

The boat pitched and rolled gently. I felt mildly nauseous. The wind picked up in the late afternoon and the sea grew grey and violent. As I stood on deck with Tobias, checking the sky, the heavens opened and rains lashed our boat. We climbed the wooden steps to the wheelhouse. The helmsman breathed a sigh of relief when the skipper appeared.

The monsoon rain was so heavy it reduced visibility to 300 yards. Tobias became so concerned about colliding with another boat, that he ordered the helmsman to steer into a cove and drop anchor for the night. The cove, surrounded by tall trees, gave us some protection from the howling winds but still the sea was rough.

Above the wail of the wind I heard the banging of a spoon against a pan: the dinner gong. The dining room was located midships, next to the galley. I groped my way along the railings, following Tobias, from the wheelhouse to the dining room. The rain continued to lash the pitching, rolling boat with full fury. I staggered into the dining room with water cascading off my brown plastic poncho. Tobias and four crew members were already taking their places on the two benches that flanked the long dining table.

The cook entered and plopped down pots of boiled yams and cabbage. The cook, a bulky man with a big grin that exposed his yellow chipped teeth, told us he had a terrible time cooking because the pots skidded around the stove top and almost catapulted over the guard rail.

We spooned the food onto our tin plates and sprinkled salt liberally to spice it up and make it palatable.

The next morning, under a cloudless azure sky, we motored

along the coast and discharged a cargo of building materials at a Seventh-day Adventist mission station. We stayed tied up at their small wharf for the night.

The morning dawned fair and fresh. As the crew untied mooring lines a trio of seagulls whirled, screeching farewell. Farther along the coast we stopped at the small port that served Popondetta, a town located fifteen miles inland. Another coastal trader was berthed at the wharf, taking on sacks of copra. Because there was room for only one boat at a time, we dropped anchor in the bay to wait. The other boat was still loading copra the next day, and the day after, being Saturday. The missionaries had taught the local people that Sunday was a day of rest so it stayed idle all day Sunday as well.

I saw a wave of concern pass over Tobias's face.

"We've gotta move and find some food," he said. "Our stock is getting low with all this waiting around."

"You've got a hold almost full of canned goods," I said.

"We can't eat our cargo – except as a last resort. We have to find our own food."

"Like hunter-gatherers," I said.

Tobias nodded, then he yelled to a couple of crewmen relaxing on the forward deck: "Up anchor."

To another crewman he bellowed in his bass voice: "Start the engine."

He turned to me. "We'll sail to a nearby island with a coral reef. We should be able to spear some fish, just you and me."

"Sounds great." This plan really enthused me.

Within five minutes, glistening waves were glancing off the bow as we chugged northeast towards a low, dark island that seemed to float in the grey-green sea.

We dropped anchor and Tobias divided the crew. Four were to go to the island: two with the shotgun to shoot pigeons and two with baskets to collect coconuts. The remaining two were to stay on board while Tobias and I would drop overboard with goggles and home-made spearguns. Each speargun consisted of a four-foot wooden shaft. Sharp prongs made from wire coat hangers were attached with thin wire. A rubber strap cut from the inner tube of a bicycle tire was tied near the prongs.

Tobias explained the primitive speargun: "Pull the rubber strap along the shaft, holding it firmly as you do so. When you release the rubber strap, the shaft shoots forward."

Tobias and I donned goggles, flippers and snorkels and lowered ourselves over the side of the ship into pleasant, warm water. I swam over the reef, peering through my goggles. I held my speargun at the ready. I didn't see any fish, and the reef was without colour. The landscape below me was an expansive wasteland of bleached coral, in varying shades of grey, with mysterious black shadows. It was like looking at an underwater desert on a black-and-white television set. Any evidence of colourful algae, which normally live with coral, had disappeared. The coral had been left to turn white and die. I dove deeper looking for crabs and sea urchins and anything else that moved, but came up with nothing. Tobias's head broke the surface beside mine. We agreed that the reef was dead and waded ashore.

"A rise in water temperature may be the cause," Tobias suggested.

We followed the route of the other crewmen into the mangroves – a natural world of interlocking roots and limbs that surrounded the island. I heard a shotgun blast and saw a flock of pigeons scatter above the treetops. Presently, the hunter-gatherers returned with big grins. One of them boastfully held a basket of pigeons above his head. He was joined by another who had a basketful of coconuts.

Back on board the cook prepared pigeon soup for dinner. By the time he had plucked and gutted the birds, and picked out the shotgun pellets, there wasn't much meat to add to the pot. The pigeon soup, with a strong salty taste, was barely edible. It was served with boiled yams in coconut milk. Thanks to the yams we had full bellies.

Our arrival in Lae was four days late. Tobias wasn't concerned. He had a full cargo of copra.

The next morning we stood on the deck together, under a turbulent sky. We watched a flock of pigeons fly just under the layer of grey cloud, within shotgun range. Tobias followed their flight path with interest.

"Tobias," I said, "don't even think about pigeon soup for lunch. I'm buying you a steak."

Australia

Buscapade

'Borrowing' a bus on Rottnest Island, February 1968
See map, page 13, B5

Dave shouted: "Everyone out and push."

Within moments two dozen partygoers filed off the bus into the balmy night air to push the bus while I revved the engine. The rear wheels spun in the dry, soft sand but the bus didn't budge. Dave and I could be in big trouble. We had borrowed the bus for our personal use – without permission.

Two weeks earlier, beneath a blue sky with puffs of white cumulus cloud, I stood on the dock at Rottnest Island and watched the morning ferry approach with a hundred or more holiday makers. From Perth, on the mainland, to the island, known locally as "Rotto," the distance was about 20 kilometres.

Rotto, only 11 km long and 5 km wide, is a vacation spot that attracts day-trippers as well as visitors with more time to spend. Its attractions are the numerous pristine sandy beaches, woodlands, grassy plains and salt lakes.

Beside me on the dock stood my travelling companion, Dave, who wore a perpetual devilish grin. We had been hired by the Rottnest Island Board for two weeks' work. Our official job description was 'General labourers.' It included sawing low-hanging branches off tea and pine trees that arched over the sandy, winding roads.

We also provided a meet-and-greet service. Dave transported luggage in a truck while I drove visitors in a bus. When the ferry berthed, it discharged a colourful horde of day-trippers who streamed onto the dock with towels, bathing suits and plastic coolers containing food and drinks. Others carried suitcases or backpacks. They were the overnighters – our clients. Dave and I hoisted their bags onto the truck while they boarded the 25-seater bus.

We both carried notebooks to record the cabin numbers of vacationers whom we felt would enjoy a party at the single men's quarters of which we were the sole occupants.

The hotel on the island, a colonial-style mansion, was affectionately named Quokka Arms, after the small marsupial indigenous to the island. 'A kind of rat as big as a cat' is how the seventeenth century Dutch explorers described the *quokka*. Officially, the Quokka Arms was the Rottnest Hotel.

On most nights after the bar closed in the hotel we invited the patrons to bring their bottles of *Swan Lager* and *Emu Bitter* to our quarters, otherwise known as Party Central. One eventful night a few sailors were drinking at the Quokka Arms. They heard Dave announce an invitation to Party Central. Five Fijians, an Englishman and a Spaniard arrived with other revellers to liven things up. When the party was over the sailors headed back to their seismic survey ship anchored in the bay.

Within an hour I heard knocking at our door. I crawled out of bed and found seven soaked, shivering crewmen. They had boarded their dinghy and were one-third of the way to their ship when someone rocked the dinghy and it sank. All could swim, except the Spaniard. One of the Fijians saved the Spaniard's life by holding his head above water until they reached shore.

Our single men's quarters held a dozen empty bunk beds with plenty of blankets. It wasn't long before the men had stripped off their wet clothes and climbed under the blankets. The next day their fellow crewmen came looking for them and took them back to the ship to face the captain's wrath.

To celebrate the last night of our working holiday on Rottnest Island, a group of regular visitors to our nightly parties arranged a farewell for us. It was to be held at their cottage located in a remote part of the island. Because of the distance, I offered to pick up partygoers and take them to the cottage in the company bus.

Dave and I were unfamiliar with the sandy road as we still hadn't been to that part of the island to trim the overhanging branches. Getting there was going to be a challenge in the semi-darkness.

After I picked up the guests I crawled along the sandy trail in first gear. I hoped there would be enough space for the bus to pass under low-hanging branches. Just as I spotted the lights of the cottage in the distance, a scraping, screeching sound of tortured metal made me sit bolt upright and stomp on the brake. A sinking feeling hit my gut as the bus came to an abrupt stop. The roof had collided with an overhanging branch.

That's when Dave shouted, "Everyone out and push." But while the rear wheels spun, the bus stayed put in the soft sand.

Dave yelled to me, "I'll let some air out of the front tires to lower the height of the bus."

There was a loud hissing sound. I rammed the bus into reverse. The passengers heaved against the sides but the rear wheels continued to spin.

Dave bellowed, "I'll let some air out of the four rear tires." More hissing. More pushing. More revving. The spinning wheels dug deeper into the sand, up to the axles. Things were getting serious. We simply had to get the bus out.

Six party hosts from the cottage appeared out of the darkness to investigate the commotion. Someone suggested that extra weight might lower the bus. About thirty people climbed aboard, but that didn't work either.

I poked my head out of the driver's window. "Dave," I yelled, "I think there's a storage compartment at the back of the bus. Maybe you'll find a shovel."

He checked and I heard an excited shout. "Two shovels!" With willing helpers he shovelled sand from under the front wheels to lower them so I could drive out from under the branch. We dug trenches behind the front and rear wheels and laid small branches and twigs to give the wheels traction in the sand.

Finally, with preparations complete, I shoved the gear stick into reverse and gently depressed the accelerator pedal. Thirty helpers, in front of the bus and beside it, dug their feet into the sand and pushed the bus backwards. The bus lurched back as it cleared the branch. The rear wheels spun in the trenches and we started to climb out.

Everyone cheered and boarded the bus. I drove at a tortoise-like pace until we reached the cottage. I told the passengers we had to check over the bus, and if we didn't come back they would have to find their own way home.

Dave and I took the bus back to the compound, near the single men's quarters. The bus had to be ready for the next morning's meet-and-greet service by two new employees. We found a foot pump and spent the next hour or more pumping up the six tires.

We fell into bed exhausted.

We missed our own farewell party!

Australia

The foreman from Texas

Labouring on Barrow Island, March 1968
See map, page 13, B4

Sweat trickled down my forehead as the hot afternoon sun, an orb of molten silver in the blue sky, poured down its wrath. I shovelled sand, stones and cement powder into the rotating drum of the cement mixer.

I was working on Barrow Island, a desolate, sunbaked mound of red earth dotted with clumps of spinifex grass, located 50 kilometres off the coast of northwestern Australia. Since the discovery of oil a year earlier, workers from all over the country were travelling to this speck in the ocean to make their fortune. Three hundred men laboured on the island, but no women.

"Women are a distraction," the foreman said. "You are here to work, work, work."

The foreman, with an unpronounceable name, was from Texas. He was known as Tex by most of the workers. Other employees, including me, considered him a mean-spirited character, a reject from the Texas oilfields. We called him anything but Tex. He was a bulky figure with a puffy face. His veins bulged at his temples when he was stressed.

My workmate was Bill Bell, a man with a small build and a round, intelligent face. Like me, he was hired by *Oil Drilling and Exploration* as a roustabout, or general labourer, for a dollar an hour with free board and lodging and a free round-trip flight from Perth.

This was a good opportunity for me to save money to travel.

As I poured the concrete mix into wooden forms for a building foundation, Bill trowelled the concrete mixture until it was smooth. At our job site, Station AA, in the shade of an oil storage tank, we could get some relief from the blazing sun. A three-inch iron pipe snaked across the flat landscape from a distant oil well. It passed under the nearby dirt road to the storage tank.

I glanced down the road and spotted a yellow road-grader trundling towards us. Its massive, curved blade levelled the rough, gravel road. Because of constant use all the roads were deeply corrugated. All of a sudden I heard a loud clang. The grader had hit and ruptured the buried pipe. Oil spurted skywards like a fountain. Bill and I were covered with the slime. Because the oil was crude, mixed with natural gas, it was volatile. If the wind blew the fountain of oil towards the road-grader the gas would ignite over the hot engine and blow the machine and the driver sky-high.

I hollered at the driver, "Cut the engine and run." As I dashed from the pipeline I looked back to see the driver following me. Bill was running in the opposite direction. I guessed he was headed for a wellhead where he could possibly shut off the oil supply.

Bill obviously didn't find the right shutoff valve because he lingered for only a few moments before running farther along the pipeline. For another ten minutes the oil continued to gush at the powerful pressure of 500 psi, the same pressure at which it came out of the ground. Then it subsided. Bill had found the correct shutoff valve.

Someone must have radioed base camp about trouble at Station AA because within 15 minutes Tex arrived. He immediately focused his wrath on the grader driver.

"I've got a list of qualified drivers waiting to get your job. Another mistake and you'll be off the island."

There was no use in arguing. Tex always had the last word. He took Bill and me off the job at Station AA until the cleanup was finished.

In the afternoon my new job was to tow a concrete mixer and a compressor behind a Land Rover to a distant station. The bumps in the road had not been scraped flat by the grader. Bill, in the passenger seat, looked back continually to be sure the equipment rode as gently as possible over the corrugations. At a particularly high bump, the mixer bounced into the air, the connecting shaft twisted, the mixer tipped over and either broke or bent some of the metal parts. The compressor went adrift and turned on its side. I was horrified.

With trepidation I drove to base camp and reported the accident to Tex. His face almost exploded as his veins bulged at his temples. He rolled his eyes at my incompetence and ordered a salvage crew to retrieve the two machines. He had long ago lost his sense of humour or compassion for the new guy on the job.

The next task Tex unwisely entrusted to me involved the cutting of two-inch diameter pipes. The job required learning new terms: couplings, nipples, plugaroos and reducers. I worked with Phil, a thick log of a man. I was cutting threads into a pipe when it fell from the machine and hit my knee, leaving an inch-long gash. The pain was excruciating; blood poured from the wound. I couldn't believe I could be so clumsy. Phil rushed me back to base camp in the Land Rover.

The medic, a young guy with bright red cheeks, said he could either stitch it or simply bind it tightly. "If stitched, it would heal better," he said. I agreed to be stitched. He left for a few minutes, came back and looked at the gash again. "I think I should bind it. If I stitch it, it would need three or four stitches and the local anesthetic would really sting."

I assumed he couldn't find his How to Stitch book so I agreed to have my knee bound. I shuddered. How would he handle himself in a real emergency?

The medic signed a sheet of instructions stating I should have a day off. I needed to stretch out my leg in order to allow the gash to knit together. He also said that I should be on light duties for a week. I dreaded having to tell Tex, and when I did he responded as expected: his veins bulged at his temples.

A week later I was walking, albeit stiffly, and was assigned by Tex to a team of twenty men. We were to build a 2,000-barrel storage tank using prefabricated sheets of steel that required 10,000 bolts and the corresponding number of nuts and washers. Hour after hour I poked bolts through pre-drilled holes and screwed on nuts until I could stand the boredom no longer. I applied for a change and joined the crew who operated the Work-over Rig.

Armed with his list of who was where, Tex inspected the job sites and discovered I was missing from the storage tank construction site. His paperwork hadn't kept up with my movements. He was livid. His bulging veins receded when he found me working at the Work-over Rig, an oil rig that was deployed when an existing well was having trouble producing. If sand was blocking the flow of oil we would be sent to pump the sand out. I noticed with some concern that of the six guys I was working with, two had lost fingers.

"The job has its dangers," said John, a big man with a florid face who was missing the little finger from his right hand. "Be careful of the clamps," he advised.

The clamps were attached to the ends of steel cables that hung from the overhead derrick. My job was to attach the clamps around the drilling pipes to raise or lower them in the well. As was my luck, I was on the rig platform when a set of clamps dangling at the end of a steel cable swung directly towards me. I tried to duck but the clamps sideswiped my hardhat and almost knocked me off the platform. Fortunately I was only dazed.

After ten weeks on the job I felt I should leave for new challenges before anything worse happened to me. I was lucky. I still had all my fingers intact, I was now walking normally despite the gash in my knee, I had a fistful of dollars for future travels and Tex was off my back!

Australia to Norway (Part one)

Luck of the albatross

By freighter, Sydney to Cape Town, August 1968

See map, page 13

High waves and wind gusts buffeted the freighter in the waters off southern Australia. The veil of dusk descended as I stumbled across the deck to the crew's quarters.

I opened the door to a passageway and saw José, the second cook. For his work on the ship he wore a long-bladed, two-edged knife in a sheath on his belt. A cord tied to the bone handle ensured he wouldn't misplace it. José was squatting on his haunches in the passageway of the crew's cabins, picking up a few coins he had dropped.

The second officer approached – a six-foot-two Norwegian with yellow hair, powerful arms, blue eyes flaming and the arrogance of a bully. He kneed José in the ribs, sending him sprawling. Startled, José, the normally docile Spanish seaman, jumped to his feet, fire in his eyes. His muscles swelled with rage. The officer laughed. José fumbled for his knife, grabbed it and lashed viciously at the air. The officer backed up against a cabin door. José attempted a thrust which could have skewered the Norwegian to the door but the officer dropped, rolled, leapt to his feet and ran like a rabbit. José wheeled and sprang at him like a wildcat, but the long-legged Norwegian was too fast. He darted to the safety of the officers' quarters.

I watched in disbelief. I was working my passage from Australia to Europe and wondered what sort of crew I was sailing with.

I had always wanted to work on a ship, but I didn't have seaman's papers. I was told that Norwegian ships sometimes employed non-union labour.

My chance came when I located the Norwegian freighter, *Triton,* docked at Melbourne. It was painted black with a white stripe along its side from the back to the pointy end. I strolled up the gangway and found the captain. A short, lean man, he was gazing down from the bridge into a hold where bales of wool were being loaded.

"Excuse me, Captain."

He turned. His navy blue cap shielded his deeply-tanned, middle-aged face.

"I want to go to Europe. Can I work on your ship?"

Without answering he looked away. He watched the crane swing more bales of wool into the hold then turned to me. "I need more bales than those 5,000 to break the record and win the bet."

What that had to do with my request to work on his ship I couldn't figure out, but the man obviously had a competitive spirit. A man willing to gamble? On me, perhaps?

"Have you worked on a ship before?" he asked.

A leading question! My heart sank.

"No," I said, but added cheerily, "I'm a good worker. You won't be sorry."

"Yes," he said in a friendly, no-nonsense tone, "you may come."

It seemed too easy. Did he understand me? Yes! He scribbled a note to the Norwegian Consulate saying he was giving me a job as a 'workaway' – one who works his passage, often without pay. I had a spring in my step as I made my way to the Norwegian Consulate.

I spent an hour at the Consulate filling out an application form. A consular official drew up a seaman's contract, a *hyrekontrakt*, which stated I was to be paid a weekly wage of one kroner (about ten cents).

"A wage has to be stated in the contract to make it legal," he said. He added that the *Triton* was a freighter of 5,414 tonnes unloaded, or 10,000 tonnes loaded, and carried a crew of thirty-five officers and men. It would carry thousands of bales of wool in its holds and a deckful of sea containers.

As I stood to leave he handed me my contract and a Norwegian Seaman's identity card. "Meet the ship in Sydney in a month's time when it will leave for Europe," he said. "Until then it'll be sailing to Hobart, Brisbane and Newcastle to pick up cargo."

A month later I boarded a bus in Melbourne, my home town, for the 14-hour trip to Sydney. I arrived energized by the thought of working on the ship. I felt more knowledgeable about shipping jargon, having studied a list of nautical terms over the past few weeks.

Under a blue sky with puffy white clouds I walked to Sydney's Glebe Island docks and found the *Triton* at Number 4 wharf. I strode up the gangway. Each step propelled me closer to the world of shipping of which I knew virtually nothing.

I stepped onto the ironclad deck, largely covered with sea containers. I said "Hi" to seamen painting the white railings and asked for the bosun, the man in charge of the crew. The bosun, whose face bore grey stubble and deep lines, touched his cap in salute, then led me to the crew's quarters at the stern.

He pushed open the door of a cabin where a young seaman was relaxing on the bottom bunk. About seventeen, I guessed. Seven years my junior. "His name is Markus," the bosun said. "He's been with us for three months. He doesn't speak any English." Markus stood up – a small, muscular man, clean-shaven, long fair hair hiding his ears. He shook my hand, grunted a greeting, then left the cabin. We would be sharing the cabin for the next six or seven weeks. I anticipated a quiet trip.

When the bosun left I opened my backpack and placed my clothes in the chest of drawers, the only furniture apart from the two bunks and two lockers. A porthole let in some light. As I unpacked, I heard someone pad along the passageway tapping on doors, but without any response. Then a soft rat-tat-tat on my door. I opened it to a young woman with a pasty face, tousled brown hair and tattoos of dragons on her arms.

"I want to show you my new tattoo," she said as if we were old friends. She stepped boldly into the cabin, shoved the door closed with her shoe and raised her red skirt. "It's on my thigh." I glimpsed a blue and red rose, but before she could show me more, I eased her out of the cabin. She continued to tap on doors while I set off to explore the ship.

On the deck a man approached and introduced himself as Roy – a fair-haired Australian of medium build, with a bright smile. "What are you doing on this ol' tub?" he asked. I told him how I got the job as a workaway.

"They call me the ship's carpenter," he said. "I was working on a ship at the Cockatoo Docks when I heard of the vacancy on the *Triton*. The Norwegian carpenter had jumped ship." Roy added that he had been on the ship for a month as a paid seaman.

"Who's the strange bird in the red skirt?" I said.

"She stowed aboard in Brisbane and has been keeping the crew company. She'll have to get off before we sail."

Roy filled me in on the *Triton's* motley crew: five Spaniards, two Chinese, two Swedes, a Finn, a Chilean and about twenty Norwegians.

Departure day, July thirtieth, arrived.

In the morning the third mate gathered the crew in the *dag rum* (day room) and told us to stay put while officers searched the ship for girls, checking under beds and in lockers. Our next port would be Cape Town and the captain didn't want stowaways. Later, from the deck, I watched the red-skirted girl wander the wharf towards the ship docked next to the *Triton*.

There was work to be done. The bosun shouted orders and pointed to where crewmen should get started. I helped lower the derricks with an electric winch, batten the hatches, fold tarpaulins, coil ropes and raise the accommodation ladder which hung over the ship's side. Wow! This was exhilarating.

I watched the crew slacken the fore and aft manila ropes so the stevedores (or wharfies as they are colloquially called in Australia) could unwind the ropes from the wharf bollards. The crew then hauled the ropes aboard and coiled them on the deck. By releasing the brake on the electric winch, crewmen allowed each of the two spring lines – metal ropes – to slacken so the wharfies could free them by lifting them over the bollards.

I felt elated on this first day of new adventures. At 16:45 the ship pulled away from the dock. The bosun told me they always used the 24-hour clock.

As the *Triton* nosed its way to the open sea the bow cut a swath, forcing foam-tipped waves to roll sideways. Even though the ship rolled softly and pitched gently, my stomach felt queasy.

After the earlier activity, I felt a little lost for something to do. But not for long. An officer approached.

"Have you seen the bridge?" he asked in a thick, throaty – but not unpleasant – accent.

"Yes," I said, remembering I had met the captain on the bridge one month ago in Melbourne.

"Good. Go and steer."

I stood rooted to the spot, puzzled. Must be a communication breakdown. I had steered a motorboat once, with a disastrous result. I snapped off the steering lever of the outboard motor when I turned too sharply. The damage I could inflict on a ship, I loathed to imagine.

Nevertheless, I climbed the steps to the bridge. In the adjoining chartroom I met the chief mate, a barrel-chested man with a pleasant, ruddy face. My cabin mate Markus was already on the bridge. In a gravelly voice, the officer issued our orders for the voyage: "Stand the middle watch from midnight to oh-four-hundred and the afternoon watch, midday to sixteen-hundred. Have two spells of one hour each at the helm, on each watch. At night, the person not steering is to stand on the forecastle deck – at the bow – and watch for lights of other ships." During the afternoon watch, while Markus steered, I was to swab decks and paint the superstructure.

After the officer gave these orders to me in English, he briefed Markus who already knew the drill.

Darkness had closed in when I returned to the crew's quarters. It was there that I had witnessed the Norwegian officer knee José, the Spaniard, in the ribs then run from his knife.

I mentioned the altercation to Roy. He told me the second officer was a bully who harassed crew members when he was drunk.

A few days later we passed Albany on Australia's southwest

corner and steamed along the thirty-fifth parallel. We sailed into the influence of the notorious Roaring Forties, the wild winds near the fortieth parallel, that cause monstrous storms.

Markus and I clambered up the steps to the bridge to start our middle watch at midnight when a storm struck. The third mate, the officer on duty, was visibly perturbed. "Turn the ventilators," he bellowed.

Markus and I donned oilskins and struggled up the ventilator ladders in the pitch blackness, watching each other in case one of us fell off a ladder and disappeared overboard. The winds grew violent. They half-groaned, half-screeched, tore at our faces and hands and tried to throw us onto the deck. The work became dangerous; we couldn't hang on. We slid down the ladders and dashed to the safety of the bridge. From behind its protective glass windows we watched a smooth, shining, jet-black wall of water leap over the bulwarks and thud onto the deck. Close behind, towering above us, loomed another high, black, mountainous ridge. It, too, crashed onto the deck, its foam looking like an avalanche of tumbling snow. Climbing ventilator ladders was not my favourite chore.

Suddenly, the door to the bridge swung open and the captain appeared, shrouded in yellow oilskins, dripping wet. He strode immediately to the chartroom to confer with the third mate. I stood at the helm and tried to hold a westerly course as I was ordered. The mate directed Markus to the starboard wing of the bridge to look out for storm-tossed ships that might cross our path. The captain emerged from the chartroom to say that storms were raging all the way between Australia and South Africa. I was to steer northwest to go beyond the storms so we could resume our westerly course in relatively calm seas.

Lights appeared on the Australian mainland. "Cape Leeuwin," the mate said. The captain told us that our radio operator had picked up a signal from the *Tallyrand* which, like our ship, belonged to the *Wilhelmsen Line*. It had just left Fremantle, near Perth, and would attempt the direct route to Cape Town, through the storm. Our captain grimaced and explained that he didn't agree with the *Tallyrand's* skipper so he challenged him to a race to Cape Town.

The other captain agreed. Our skipper rubbed his hands together, confident of a win.

The ship pitched and rolled violently as I finished my watch and started to leave the bridge. Over the sound of sheets of rain pelting the windows I heard loud clangs coming from the hold. The captain heard them too. "Go see what it is," he said to me.

In the hold, a tall gate of iron bars protected a cargo of expensive vintage wines. The gate was unlocked, swinging to and fro with each roll of the ship. After I reported to the captain an officer appeared in his pyjamas to lock it.

With that problem taken care of I headed for my cabin via the officers' galley where I intended to stop for an illicit slice of cake or a wedge of pie – delicacies that were not served to ordinary seamen. I included this stopover as part of my regular route from bridge to cabin at the end of the middle watch. Tonight the galley floor was a disaster. The rocking of the ship had forced open the fridge door and spilled its contents. Broken eggs lay in a puddle of tomato and soya sauces. A custard pie floated in a sea of green pickle juice and milk sloshed over mounds of peas and carrots. I gagged. Almost threw up! I didn't want to be caught in the galley where I wasn't supposed to be, so I quickly left the mess behind and retreated to my cabin.

The sea varied from slate to emerald-green as we sailed into calmer waters. While the storm raged in the south I sat on the poop deck and watched albatrosses glide in wide sweeps over the ocean then hover just six feet out of my reach. The huge birds, with their brown and white plumes, boasted wing spans of eight to ten feet. They wheeled and dived and emitted joyous squawks. They skimmed to and fro over the ship's wake, searching for fish.

My mind churned up schoolboy memories of Samuel Coleridge's epic poem, *The Rime of the Ancient Mariner,* and the crew's respect for the graceful albatrosses. Over the centuries, when albatrosses were sighted far out to sea, sailors believed that they were a good omen because their appearance indicated land was relatively nearby. Coleridge alluded to the birds being a good omen in his epic poem, and also noted that the killing of an albatross, as the ancient mariner had done, would bring bad luck.

It occurred to me that maybe an albatross would bring the *Triton* and the captain good luck. Had he noticed the birds circling overhead, following our ship?

I was on my way to the bridge when I thought of the *Tallyrand*. I assumed their radio operator was keeping our captain informed of their progress.

"Big trouble for the *Tallyrand's* captain," our skipper said with a smirk, as he came onto the bridge. "The ship is fighting storms all the way. We are winning."

Our ship maintained a steady fifteen knots, its propellers acting like a ploughshare, leaving a furrow in the sea. The green water flowed into the moving valley of the wake. Sparkling bubbles were illuminated by the soft evening light. As the sun descended, the cloudy western sky became streaked with red and orange and the sea turned amber.

At midday, on August twentieth, just as I was taking over at the helm, we rounded the Cape of Good Hope and steamed towards Cape Town Harbour. Because the Suez Canal was blocked with sunken ships following the 1967 Six-day War in the Middle East, the number of ships stopping in Cape Town had multiplied. We had to wait four hours for a pilot to dock the ship.

The door to the bridge burst open. The captain stood smiling. He spoke in English, probably for my benefit. "We beat the *Tallyrand* by three days and if we pick up enough bales of wool in Cape Town we will break the record for cargo."

Then the captain peered up at the sky as if to say 'thank you.'

Did he believe in the luck of the albatross?

Australia to Norway (Part two)

The drunken sailor

By freighter, Cape Town to Oslo, September 1968

See map, page 12

The *Triton* pulled away from the Cape Town dock a few minutes after midnight. The captain was elated, grinning from ear to ear, having just won a bet. He'd been successful in loading a full cargo of shipping containers on the deck and filling the holds with a record number of bales of wool. Some of his officers had bet it couldn't be done. They lost.

The dark harbour waters sparkled with lights of other freighters at anchor.

The captain took his place on the bridge to direct me between the freighters. He truly was a gambler to let me steer out of the busy harbour.

The second officer switched on the radar and stayed glued to the monitor, watching for vessels of any size that would show as a blip on the screen.

Markus, the apprentice seaman with whom I shared a cabin, stood at the bow. Beside him hung a warning bell. He was to ring it three times if we were on a collision course.

The captain peered through binoculars into the darkness to choose a route to the open sea. I stood at the helm and waited for his orders.

"Two-hundred and ninety degrees," said the captain in clear English.

"Two-ninety," I said as I turned the helm slightly.

"Hold the course," said the captain as we passed between two ships.

Then he gave me a new course: "Five degrees starboard for course three-twenty-three."

I turned the helm to the right until the rudder was angled at five degrees from the centre line on the Rudder Indicator. I held the rudder at five degrees while the ship slowly turned from 290 degrees to 323. This course took us safely past three ships and into the open sea. Phew! What a relief. And Markus didn't have to ring the warning bell.

I reflected on my good fortune of working my passage from Australia to Europe on the *Triton*. One kroner a week, about ten cents, was to be my pay when we arrived in Oslo at the end of the voyage. Not enough to celebrate with but it would be enough to buy a daily newspaper!

As we sailed north from South Africa we experienced calm seas and were able to maintain a speed of 15 knots. Ahead, the imaginary shipping lanes were spread over a broad expanse of the South Atlantic Ocean, so spotting another ship was rare.

Occasionally I met with the *Triton's* Australian carpenter, Roy, in the day room to play cards, have a beer and listen to a seaman's shortwave radio for snippets of news from the BBC and VOA (Voice of America).

As the days passed I noticed Markus was isolating himself from his shipmates. He would become belligerent and want to fight after drinking a few bottles of beer. As his roommate I was able to see other ways he was changing.

One night I was relaxing on my bunk reading a *Time* I picked up in Cape Town. Markus, mumbling to himself in Norwegian, yanked open the bottom drawer of the dresser. He had stashed two or three of his slept-in blue bed sheets there instead of putting them into the laundry basket. He raised his eyebrows as if to say: What do I do with these?

Why ask me? He knows the laundry room is down the corridor. Nevertheless, I said, in English, which he didn't understand: "Put them in the laundry basket." As a joke I pointed to the porthole as a place to store the sheets. Then I rolled over to continue reading. Moments later a blast of fresh sea air filled the cabin. I sat bolt upright and caught Markus ramming his last sheet through the porthole. I was flabbergasted. "Idiot," I said, as I rolled my eyes and shook my head. Was he suffering from cabin fever?

The day we crossed the equator the quartermaster provided complimentary drinks to celebrate. The dining tables were well stocked with *Frydenlund* beer and aquavit, the powerful Norwegian spirit distilled from potatoes. Throughout the evening we raised our glasses of aquavit, said *Skal,* and with our heads tilted back, tossed the firewater to the back of our throats, then chased it down with sips of beer.

I wished the celebration could have included a special meal. Boiled potatoes twice a day, every day, had become rather boring. And dried or frozen fish (dead for a long time was how one crewman described them) had grown monotonous. A piece of pie or cake, as served regularly to the officers, would have been a treat. The celebration continued almost to midnight when Markus and I were scheduled for the watch.

After I'd steered for an hour I expected Markus to relieve me but he was a no-show. I left the helm in the hands of the officer-on-watch to search for him. He lay sprawled on his bunk. He'd had a beer too many. This wasn't the first time I had found him in this state.

I didn't relish steering for four straight hours. I told this to the officer who marched to the cabin and coaxed, pushed and dragged Markus upstairs to the bridge. The fresh air woke him up and he was able to take over the helm. When he finished his hour on duty, I took over and he disappeared. He didn't return for his second hour. Again I checked the cabin but failed to find him. Where would I hide if I were Markus? On top of a shipping container at number five hatch! I had seen him loiter there before.

I was right. I poked, prodded and pushed but couldn't budge him. Nor could another officer who came to help. For me, it was back to the helm. I couldn't believe anyone so irresponsible was seriously training to be a seaman. I wondered if his sailing days were numbered.

Days passed.

I was about to leave the bridge after my turn at the helm when I spotted a ship in the darkness, off our port bow. It was steaming towards us, flashing dots and dashes. I called the officer from the chartroom who lugged his signal lamp to the port wing of the bridge. For the next ten minutes dots and dashes of Morse Code flashed back and forth between the two ships. I looked at the officer and asked what was happening.

"The ship is on its way from Antwerp to Canton," he said. "The signaller warned me of dense fog in the Bay of Biscay."

Soon after, we experienced pitch-black nights, no stars or moon to navigate by, only radar. We passed the light at Cabo Finisterre and nosed into a veil of thick fog, the colour of pewter. I imagined the *Triton* a ghost ship gliding above the waves. It was an eerie feeling. No one spoke. Our foghorn sounded every ninety seconds to conform with shipping regulations. Our journey through intermittent fog ended after twenty-four hours, when we sighted the light at Brest.

As we sailed along the Dutch coast I rested in the dark on the top bunk, awaiting a call from a crewman to stand by for the midnight watch. All of a sudden the door burst open, a hand reached in and switched on the light. I jumped. Four bodies converged at the doorway. Two of them were officers, their white shirts bloodstained. They panted heavily as they dragged Markus into the cabin and, with the help of an oiler from the engine room, tossed him onto the bottom bunk. A loud moan rose from his inert body. Blood oozed from facial cuts. It must have been quite a fight. I had no sympathy for him. I wasn't sure who started the fight, but I bet it was Markus. One thing I was sure of – he wouldn't be on watch at midnight. I would have to do his stint at the helm.

After this altercation, Markus, I felt sure, would suffer another black mark against his work record. He had become belligerent with his shipmates and, in particular, the officers. How long would they put up with his antics?

The next day the captain reprimanded him.

Roy, my carpenter friend, was kept busy almost every day hammering and sawing, but he was able to join me when we had shore leave. We disembarked together in Rotterdam to check out the cluster of sailors' pubs near the docks.

We visited *Kapabana*, patronized by Greek seamen, and the *Norge Bar*, full of Norwegians, including Markus. Next was the *International* with its sprinkling of many nationalities, including English-speaking sailors.

Similar to it was the *Neutraal* where, just after midnight, we saw half-a-dozen policemen converge on a group of revellers – ten British seamen from the *Canberra Star* – who'd had an altercation with a German sailor. The result: one German sailor, dead from a fractured skull. I was stunned. I wondered whether cabin fever contributed in some degree to the fight, or was it just booze?

The *Triton's* second officer happened to be near the scene, buying beer. He told us later how he checked the man's rapidly dropping pulse rate. He made a statement to the police and understood the British seamen would be detained. The officer described how the German sailor's face had been slashed by the sharp end of a broken rum bottle.

I began to wonder about the life of a seaman. It seemed rather dangerous, not only on the high seas but on shore as well. I decided six weeks as a seaman would be enough for me!

We eventually sailed from Rotterdam. Most of the crew would have been sleeping when, in the predawn, I heard yells and scuffles from the day room, along with the sounds of furniture being tossed around. I looked down at Markus's bunk. Empty. I could hardly believe it. Another fight! The sounds of scrapping bodies spilled into the passageway, stopping at my closed door. Fists smacked against flesh until there was a loud groan, and then silence. I opened the door and found a bloodied Markus on the floor in the fetal position. I dragged him inside the cabin and heaved him onto his bunk.

I imagined Markus's employment file growing thicker by the day with misdemeanors. Later in the morning the captain fired Markus. He would leave the ship in Oslo. At seventeen his shipping career was finished.

Three weeks after leaving Cape Town we sailed into Oslo Fjord. Lights blinked from the surrounding hills. The city stood at the head of the fjord where the two towers of City Hall dominated the skyline.

After we docked in Pipervika harbour most of the crew went ashore. From the main deck I looked down onto the dock. A lone figure, head bowed, a duffel bag over hunched shoulders, shuffled away from the *Triton*. The drunken sailor.

Roy and I went to the paymaster's office, Roy to collect about six thousand kroners for his work. I was envious. I put out my hand to receive my hard-earned six kroners.

The paymaster laughed. "You should be paying us for the onboard entertainment! Be glad you survived the drunken sailor."

I'm still waiting for my kroners!

Russia

An encounter with the KGB

Befriending a political dissident in Moscow, October 1968

See map, page 12, B2

Harry's shoulders sagged. A look of desperation washed over his round, freckled face. Roy and I watched helplessly as this Russian acquaintance was ordered from our Moscow hotel room by a burly agent of the Committee for State Security, the dreaded KGB *(Komitet Gosudarstvennuy Bezopasnosti)*.

We sat in shock, powerless to help. So ended an evening of political discussion with a student dissatisfied with the Soviet Government.

Earlier in the evening, before meeting Harry, I felt a chill in the air as the Moscow night grew cold and crisp. The clouding sky promised snow by morning. With me was Roy – thin, angular, sandy-haired – my travelling buddy in Russia. We were headed for the Hotel Bucharest with our coat collars upturned to ward off the gusts of wind and dust. The drab stone buildings of the capital merged with the sullen black and grey clouds.

I looked forward to getting into the hotel, out of the cold. But I spotted someone leaning against a lamp post, observing us.

A figure in a long coat, raven-dark against the dim grey light, approached. "Do you speak English?" a male voice asked.

We said "yes" together. I looked into a freckled face with strong boyish features and deep-set eyes. There was a wariness in his manner.

"You're a student who wants to practise English. Am I right?" I said matter-of-factly, but I was only guessing.

"Yes. My name is Igor but call me Harry, my name in English. I am a university student, in economics. It is a cold night. Will you come to a bar for wine and ice cream?"

Wine and ice cream? An interesting combination. I checked my watch. Nine o'clock. I looked questioningly at Roy who nodded. Sure, why not?

We descended into the bowels of the earth to a Metro station, its platforms spotless and decorated with bronze statues, marble busts and backlit stained glass panels. The ride was brief, only four minutes.

The wine bar, dimly lit, smelt of booze and cigarettes. There were about ten tables of dark, varnished wood, each with four wood-framed chairs, partly filling the cavernous room. Its planked floor was swept and smooth. It was about two-thirds full of people in their 20s and 30s, some of whom had brought their radios to listen to pop music broadcast by Radio Luxembourg. The government frowned on Western pop music. The people here were obviously snubbing their noses at the lawmakers. My thought was that where dissidents gather, informers follow.

When we slipped into our seats Harry leaned forward in a conspiratorial manner, looked intently at us in turn and whispered: "I don't know who to trust in here. If either of you see anyone come near our table, scratch your nose as a signal for us to stop talking."

We discussed politics, the Vietnam conflict and the 1968 invasion of Czechoslovakia by Soviet forces. There was an undercurrent of opposition among university students to the action but there could be no open discussion about it.

Harry warned us about Russia's secret police, known the world over as the KGB. "They frown upon students fraternizing with visitors from the West."

"What could happen," I asked, "if someone reported that you were seen talking to us?"

Harry looked around the room before he answered. "If I was often seen speaking to foreigners, the government might consider me a threat and reduce my education allowance or expel me from university. If I ever tried to defect to the West my family would suffer."

"How would they suffer?"

"My father could be prevented from advancing in his job. Or my family could be transferred to a smaller apartment."

Harry stopped and looked directly at us. "Tourists can also be trapped in the web of the KGB. For instance, the KGB could remove the loose-leaf visa from your passport and keep it for a few days to teach you a lesson. You'd have to pay the hotel for the extra nights they forced you to stay."

Roy looked pensive. "That's a subtle punishment," he said. "We should remember that."

When we finished our wine and ice cream, a pleasant combination, the clock was showing eleven. Time to leave. I invited Harry back to the Bucharest for a couple of beers. He accepted but suggested we not go directly to the hotel in case someone in the wine bar was an informer who intended following us. "We will take the Metro," he said.

We descended a stairway to an underground station. A train hurtled into the station so fast that I thought it was an express. I doubted it would stop at the platform. But it did, and we jumped aboard. At the next station, at Harry's urging, we leapt out and dashed across the platform to take a train just pulling in. It took us back the way we had come. "If anyone is following us we will have lost them," said Harry gleefully. We stayed on board through two stations and jumped out at the next, but before the automatic doors closed we leapt on again. After our exercise for the night we arrived at the Hotel Bucharest.

The clock on the wall in the lobby had already struck midnight when Roy, Harry and I climbed the stairs to the third floor. On each floor of the hotel a woman sat at a desk keeping track of who came and went. It was with her that we left our keys when we went out of the hotel. We thought of these keepers-of-the-room-keys as in-house spies. I approached the desk and, as I took the key from her outstretched hand, noticed that the woman, middle-aged and stout, was casting quizzical looks from me to Roy and Harry and back to me. She must have realized Harry wasn't a tourist. I glanced at Harry. He didn't appear concerned. I felt uneasy as I ushered him into our room for more political discussions.

The room appeared tired. The beige carpet was scuffed and dirty and the paint on the beige walls was peeling. From the top of the high window a curtain of dark-green velvet hung limply, keeping the room in darkness day and night. The place was not one to inspire free thinkers. Furnishings included two beds, a free-standing, dark-brown clothes closet, a small table with a black phone and four huge vinyl-covered armchairs. This was our abode for four days.

Roy snapped the caps off our room-temperature beer and we sank into the chairs.

Harry asked if he could change some rubles for dollars. We had enough rubles, I told him, having changed some in the street earlier in the day. He gently persisted so Roy exchanged two dollars for six rubles.

At that moment the telephone rang. The ring startled me. Who could be calling? Roy lifted the receiver and listened for a few moments then turned to me. "It's a woman speaking Russian." Roy responded in English and the caller hung up.

"Wrong number, I guess," Roy said.

Five minutes later someone knocked firmly on our door. I rose and opened it to an unsmiling woman with wisps of grey-blonde hair straggling from under a knitted wool *babushka*. She scanned the room, spotted Harry, tapped her watch and muttered something to me in Russian and left.

It was obvious to me that she was saying our guest shouldn't be here. I looked at Harry who was sipping his beer. "Everything's all right," he said. "Don't worry."

I felt apprehensive. Harry's laid-back attitude surprised me. After all, he was the one who had us leaping on and off trains to lose anyone who might be following us.

A few minutes later the door vibrated with loud, heavy thumps. I glanced at Roy who shrugged and grimaced. Harry's body stiffened. I strode to the door and opened it a few inches. Four stern faces stared at me. Everything was not all right! They must have just come in from the cold because each man was wrapped in a heavy charcoal-coloured overcoat with large lapels. There was no mistaking who they were. I had seen enough caricatures in Western newspapers to recognize them as agents of the KGB.

The KGB had a worldwide reputation for its efficient spy network and its propensity for detaining, interrogating and eliminating dissidents considered undesirable citizens of the Soviet Union.

The agent in charge, a short, broad-shouldered creature with a dominant jutting chin, looked beyond me and barked something. Harry jumped. Blood drained from his face; he trembled as he shuffled past me to the door. I wished Harry had left the room earlier when the phone rang or after the *babushka's* visit. Now it was too late.

The four men hovered around him like vultures about to rip apart a carcass. Each one fired questions to which Harry mumbled answers. When the barrage slowed, Harry turned to us. "They said they have come to control me. I've told them I am your cousin and that I've come to visit you. Will you agree with my story?" His words were more heavy breathing than sound.

I felt helpless. "I'm sorry," I said. "We can't do that. When we entered Russia we signed a form saying we don't have relatives in the Soviet Union."

Harry's shoulders sagged. His one hope of saving himself had been dashed. He looked defeated. We watched three of the security agents escort him to the elevator. Head bowed, Harry never looked back. The men nudged him into the elevator, the door slammed shut and he was gone.

The fourth agent looked at us with a flat expression and beckoned us to follow him. We passed his shuffling bulk as we strode to the stairs. He barked *Nyet* (No) in a bass, booming voice. We stopped abruptly. He was going down to the lobby by elevator and obviously we were to go with him.

In the lobby he jabbed a pudgy finger at two empty chairs. We were to sit and wait. The clock on the wall chimed half past midnight. Fifteen minutes passed before he returned with an interpreter who asked both of us separately, slowly and deliberately: "Do you have relatives in the Soviet Union?"

We shook our heads. What else could we do? Then they left.

Roy and I sat in silence, not knowing whether they wanted to question us further. Roy looked ill at ease. "I'm worried about the two dollars I gave Harry in exchange for his rubles. I broke the law by not changing them at a bank. If they search and question him they'll learn the money came from me."

"Let's go to our room," I said. "If they want us they'll have to come and get us."

Safely inside the room, I inserted the large key in the big, brass lock and twisted it so no one on the other side could insert a key to unlock the door.

I slept fitfully until six. I half-expected to hear someone rap on our door, but no one did. It was our day to leave Moscow for St. Petersburg. We held tickets for the night train scheduled to depart at 11:55 p.m.

Our passports were locked in the hotel safe. We didn't want the KGB to beat us to them. They might remove the loose-leaf visas and delay our departure to "teach us a lesson."

To be one step ahead we leapt down the stairs two at a time and hurried to the reception desk. The receptionist was a different woman who probably knew nothing of the previous evening's activity. This was good! When checking out we showed our train tickets with today's departure date. She handed back the tickets but not our passports or the loose-leaf visas. *"Nyet,"* she said. "Too early."

I wasn't going to rest easily until we got our passports and visas.

We stepped out of the hotel into a light fall of snowflakes. A beautiful sight but the air was a grey, damp cold. We took a cab to the train station where we stashed our backpacks. Because of the snow we chose to take refuge indoors at the Historical Museum.

The museum featured wars Russia had been involved in. Garish paintings of battles from the two world wars hung on the walls. Little old ladies of retirement age wearing *babushkas* cared for the exhibits. One of them followed us around.

Roy turned to me. "She probably wants to practise her English."

Then added with a smile: "Just joking."

Hearing Roy speak a language other than Russian must have given the lady in the *babushka* confidence to vent her anger about the Soviet Government's incursion into Czechoslovakia. For our benefit she pointed to the hapless country on a wall map, made battle sounds like bang-bang and boom, shook her head, contorted her face.

I looked at Roy and raised my eyebrows. "Another dissident," I said.

"Let's leave," said Roy. "I'm sorry, I can't face another one!"

Snowflakes continued to fall so we stayed in the warmth of the museum and mulled over Henry's fate. Hopefully, in the KGB files they would just flag his name as a person to watch, and not do anything drastic like reducing his education allowance.

Our passports and visas concerned me. "We'd better head for the hotel," I said.

In the late afternoon darkness we hailed a cab to the Bucharest. In the gloomy light from a street lamp the hotel appeared peaceful. No furtive student dissidents lurked in the bushes.

In the lobby no one looked like a KGB agent. As we approached the front desk the clerk turned her back to us.

Trouble?

No! She was kneeling at the safe to retrieve our passports – and our loose-leaf visas!

Russia

A pocketful of rubles

Socializing in St. Petersburg, October 1968

See map, page 12, B2

Roy and I wove an erratic course between throngs of office workers and shoppers who cluttered the late afternoon sidewalks. They strode homebound along Nevsky Prospekt, a main thoroughfare in St. Petersburg. Roy was my travelling companion – a thin, fair-haired guy with a square jaw and warm, bright, hazel eyes.

As we wound our way we overtook two local girls chatting as they dawdled. Roy and I glanced at them; they smiled.

"How are you?" Roy said.

They didn't understand. Instead, they stopped walking. I thought they must want to meet and speak with foreigners.

Much to my chagrin I realized they had stopped to catch a fast-approaching, fume-belching bus.

Before the girls boarded the bus Roy quickly pointed to his watch, and using sign language, indicated we should all meet at this bus stop the same time tomorrow. I made an eating motion with my hands, to tell them we would like to take them to a restaurant for dinner. They seemed to understand because they pointed at our watches to confirm that they'd be at the same spot at 6 p.m. the next day. They boarded the bus, waved to us, and were gone.

"Whaddayaknow," Roy said as we walked back to our hotel. "If they understood us, we may have dates for tomorrow."

We would have to exchange some dollars into rubles to take out the girls. We had been changing dollars into rubles with unauthorized money-changers on the streets because their exchange rate of three rubles for a dollar was better than the State Bank's one ruble. As we approached our hotel a man strode towards us. Speaking in Russian and pointing to his cigarette, we guessed that he needed a match. I shrugged and said, "Sorry. We don't smoke."

"That's okay," he said in English. "What I really want to do is change money." I looked around. There didn't appear to be anybody within earshot who would report us or him to the authorities.

After exchanging some dollars Roy and I walked away with a pocketful of rubles. The money-changer would use his dollars to buy western goods either for himself or to trade for profit.

At 6 p.m. the next day we stood at the bus stop waiting for our dates. I scanned the crowd of office workers on the sidewalk and finally spotted the girls coming towards us, wearing big smiles. We introduced ourselves and learned their names. Tania was a petite blonde and Lillya, also petite, a brunette. Both were in their early twenties, like we were. I said we would like to take them to a restaurant.

The Russian word for restaurant is the same as in English. I thought they would pick up on that but it seems they didn't. Tania responded in Russian but Roy and I didn't understand a word. We all laughed. Then Roy and I spoke a few Russian words to break the ice. N*yet* (no), *da* (yes), *dacha* (cottage). They conferred and responded with "Mother, one, two, three, thank you.

Conversation was painfully slow. I wished we had a Russian-English dictionary. Nevertheless, we set off along Nevsky Prospekt, said to be the longest street in St. Petersburg. When we passed a restaurant I pointed to it but the girls both shook their heads. A little farther on Roy spotted a sign on the other side of the road saying *Pectopah*, the way Restaurant is spelt in the Cyrillic alphabet. Again they shook their heads. We continued our stroll along the street clogged with thousands of bustling pedestrians. We pursued our conversation in English with a lot of hand movements. They responded in Russian. It was like playing a game of charades.

An hour passed. I assumed we were heading to their favourite restaurant. At about 7:15 p.m. the girls stopped at a public telephone and Lillya made a call. She appeared crestfallen. Her mother had told her to be home soon. Lillya pointed at my watch to the number 8. We deduced she had to be home by 8 p.m.

Our night out was ending much sooner than we anticipated. Roy showed our disappointment by sketching unhappy faces on a scrap of paper. They held our hands as if to say sorry. This appeared to be the end of our date. We all hugged each other. Lillya pointed to an approaching bus. I said "taxi," a word common to both languages, indicating with signs we would send them home by cab. But *nyet*, they would go by bus.

Once again the girls got on a bus, waved to us and were gone.

Roy turned to me and shrugged. "That was an interesting experience," he said philosophically. "Now what do we do? The night is young and we both have a pocketful of rubles to spend."

Because we had obtained the rubles on the black market we couldn't change them back into dollars as there was no official record of the transaction. We were leaving Russia the following night so we needed to spend them fast.

"Let's splurge on dinner at the Astoria," I said.

Half-an-hour later we stood at the entrance to the dining room. A waiter led us to an empty table for four. Almost immediately a third man was brought by the waiter to be seated with us. He was a short, thin man with dark inset eyes and a shock of black hair over his forehead. He looked distressed. We greeted him in English; he responded in Russian and called the waiter for a bottle of vodka and half a dozen bottles of beer. "He's here for some serious drinking," I said to Roy. The waiter put down six glasses, three for vodka and three for beer. I realized he wasn't planning to drink alone. He poured each of us half a glass of vodka, beckoned us to stand and raise our glasses in a toast.

"Lenin!" he said.

"Lenin!" we repeated, then threw our heads back and swallowed. The spirit burned my throat. Our new acquaintance filled our glasses with beer. We followed his example by sipping the beer chaser.

Who was this guy?

On my paper napkin I drew a stick man to represent him then added another stick person to represent a possible wife. He got the idea. He took my pen and added two small stick figures, his children. To describe his occupation he drew a needle and thread. A tailor? I repeated his action, pretending to mend an imaginary hole in my shirt.

"Nyet," he said as he shook his head.

On the napkin, he sketched a carpenter's saw then rolled up his sleeve and pretended to amputate his arm.

"Surgeon," I said.

"Da," he answered gleefully.

He poured more vodka and Roy and I stood with difficulty to propose another toast. It was my turn. I had to think of a word we all understood.

"To surgeons," I said. We drank our half glasses of vodka and followed them with beer.

A dancer swirled and swooped like a bird between the tables, coloured ribbons streaming from her long sleeves. But she was only a blur.

Roy and I kept putting rubles on the table to cover our share of vodka and beer. The toasts continued, to Communism, Stalin and comradeship.

Much later, as I rose from the table, the dining room spun around me. I couldn't remember whether or not I had eaten dinner, but one thing I knew for sure, I had spent my pocketful of rubles.

Algeria

A place to stay. Cheap.

A steamy night in Oran, January 1969

See map, page 12, B3

The waiting room of the Bureau of Social Aid in Oran, Algeria, reeked of despair. Women with dark, troubled eyes and hollow cheeks held children whose skinny limbs and distended stomachs screamed hunger. Gaunt, tight-skinned, sallow-faced men with spent bodies lolled on the benches. They were waiting for the overworked bureau official behind the desk, at the end of the room, to offer them a place to sleep.

A powerful feeling of guilt surged through me. Chuck and I should not be here seeking free accommodation.

Chuck, a Canadian in his twenties, with a muscular build, dark intelligent eyes and a black beard was my hitchhiking buddy during this journey across North Africa. An hour earlier we had rumbled along rough roads in the back of a truck, into the 1000-year old coastal city of Oran. Cars, trucks and buses filled the air with a continual honking of horns and belching of the residue from heavily-leaded fuels. The city sucked the truck into a maelstrom of motion along the winding, narrow, hilly streets of the old part of Oran, near the harbour.

Hundreds of pedestrians clogged narrow sidewalks. Half of the people were dressed in Western-style clothes. Some men wore the *djellabiah*, the traditional hooded caftan. Virtually all the women, whether they dressed in Western-style clothes or a traditional shroud, wore a loose headscarf that could be pulled across the face as a veil.

We clambered down from the truck into the throng. It was time to take stock of where we were.

A young man, dressed in a loose-fitting *djellabiah*, emerged from the chaos with a "Can I help you?" The man introduced himself as Hadj-Aissa Si Mohammed, a student teacher eager to practise his English.

"We're looking for a place to stay. Cheap." I said. To travel for an extended period with meagre funds, seeking low budget accommodation was always a high priority.

Mohammed knew of an *Auberge de la Jeunesse* (Youth Hostel). He walked us there but it was boarded up. Undaunted, he led us to a police station and asked the officer at the desk if we could stay overnight in a cell. A novel idea, I thought. The officer rolled his eyes, shook his head and told Mohammed to take us to the Bureau of Social Aid, about six blocks away, where free lodging was provided to the homeless.

Shadowy alleyways were lined with sand-coloured apartment buildings. Street-level shops sold fruit, groceries and bread. The roads climbed and dipped around the hilly terrain. I worked up a sweat carrying my backpack. Chuck, Mohammed, and I strode through the open door of the Bureau of Social Aid and found ourselves in the middle of the waiting room. I gasped. Benches were crammed with homeless, poverty-stricken men, women and children.

The official behind the desk called to us in English: "What do you want?" The greeting wasn't friendly; the tone was that of a man struggling with too much work.

"We are looking for accommodation," I said.

His eyebrows shot up like window blinds. His face reddened with rage. "Why don't you stay in a hotel?" he bellowed. He waved an angry arm towards the room full of people with broken spirits. "These people are desperate. You're not!"

His outburst almost blew me over. I had never felt so small in my life. I backed away, embarrassed.

On the sidewalk, we regrouped. Mohammed refused to be beaten;

he had another idea. "The public bath house," he said, "is about eight blocks away. It has small, cheap rooms for people to relax overnight after a bath. But you must pay for a bath."

So we followed Mohammed, wondering what would happen next. I relished the thought of washing away the day's sweaty grime.

The bath house, a red brick building, stood at the edge of a residential district.

"It is used by people who don't have running water in their homes," Mohammed explained. "There are thousands of such people. Not all are poor."

Chuck and I gave the equivalent of a dollar each, the normal price of a bath, to the desk clerk. This provided a small room just big enough for two mattresses on the floor, use of the sauna, plus two towels each.

At this point Mohammed said he must be going home. "I have classes tomorrow." Then he added "*Salaam aleikoum* (Peace be with you.)"

I offered *baksheesh* (a tip) for his education, but he declined. "You need it for your journey," he said.

Chuck and I sat in the steamy, hot, sauna room with about thirty local men, and perspired. The grime picked up from our travels in the back of the truck seeped out of our pores. After cooking our bodies for twenty minutes, we staggered, exhausted, to our little room and collapsed on the mattresses.

Thanks to Mohammed, we got what we asked for: A place to stay. Cheap.

Libya

The box motel

Desert 'digs' near Tripoli, January 1969

See map, page 12, B3

The dry heat of the early afternoon sun bore down from the dark blue sky, blistering the desert around us. Chuck and I stood by the roadside on the outskirts of the Libyan capital, Tripoli. I felt as if we were standing in front of a hot oven.

Chuck, dark-haired, lean and affable, looked pensive. "We've been standing here for two hours and there's been hardly any traffic. Why are we punishing ourselves?"

The same question had crossed my mind. Two weeks earlier we had started to hitchhike across North Africa from Morocco to Egypt. Progress had been slow.

I tried to sound cheerful. "We're past the halfway point and only have 2,000 kilometres to go. We should reach Egypt in about a week."

The dun-coloured desert floor extended endlessly from the road. There wasn't a date palm or anything else to provide shade.

Gusts of wind whipped up dust as we waited for signs of anything on wheels.

"I'm thinking," Chuck said, wiping his brow with his dirty handkerchief, "about how great it would be to sleep in a bed with clean white sheets tonight."

I agreed. "You never know your luck."

As I spoke I saw a vehicle taking shape on the horizon. Hot

air shimmered above the blacktop. The car appeared to float towards us.

We crossed our fingers and raised our thumbs. The car veered onto the shoulder and stopped.

What a relief!

A fair-haired, ruddy-faced man greeted us with a cheery hello. We heaved our gear onto the back seat next to a carton of beer. I got a sudden thirst. A cold beer would be a godsend.

We sat up front with the driver, a tall stringbean of an Englishman who introduced himself as Simon. He was an engineer with an oil drilling company.

Simon gunned the car along the ribbon of blacktop, swerving occasionally to avoid potholes that varied from the size of a car wheel to shallow holes the length of a car. Sand blew across the road, slowing us down. After three hours, the sky gradually faded into pale blue and pink pastels.

"I'll be turning off soon," said Simon, "and heading south into the desert to the oil field where I work. I'll drop you at the turnoff." Then he added with a wry smile: "You can live it up tonight at the box motel." Chuck reacted immediately. "That's great. A bed for the night."

Simon laughed. I wondered why.

Half-an-hour later large wooden boxes, some big enough to hold a car, loomed beside the highway.

"It's a good place to stay overnight," Simon said as he stopped. "The boxes were used to transport cars and machinery on flatbed trucks. There are about fifty. No one wants them." As the sun fell, the boxes cast long shadows across the grounds of a compound enclosed by an eight-foot high chain-link fence.

Simon told us to look for a gap in the fence. "It's on the western side and is big enough to crawl through. Near the gap you'll find a large box with plenty of room for sleeping."

It all sounded a bit bizarre. Simon reached into the beer carton on the back seat and handed us a couple of cans of *Ottakringer Vienna*. They weren't cold but they would quench our thirsts anyway. We thanked him and watched as he pointed the car's nose south. The car lurched forward and bounced on the gravel road deeply corrugated by heavy trucks. He disappeared into a purple sky.

We crawled through the chain-link fence and found the large box, high enough to stand in and long enough to sleep in. Thankfully we wouldn't be sharing the desert floor with scorpions.

We weren't the first to take advantage of this 'box motel.' The room was littered with empty beer cans, cigarette packets, old newspapers, magazines and white wax from melted candles.

Half-a-dozen travellers had written their names on the walls for posterity. 'Alf was here' was prominently scrawled in large letters. I wondered where Alf and the other travellers were from, and how they heard about this place.

What the 'box motel' lacked was heat. The cold desert breeze acted like an air conditioner that we couldn't turn off. I shivered.

The box wasn't the Ritz. But it served a valuable purpose: our motel in the desert.

Egypt

'You can only get there by horse'

A gallop from Giza to Saqqara, February 1969

See map, page 12, B3

Clouds of dust billowed from the stony Egyptian desert as the four white Arab stallions surged forward and broke into a gallop. For a moment I was in the lead; then, from my left and right the other horses hurtled past. The ground below me was a blur as I bounced in the saddle. I felt exhilarated and at the same time terrified. I leaned forward, the reins in my hands, and grasped the saddle to stop myself from crashing to the ground. The horses continued their breakneck speed. Hot wind blasted my face. Froth from my horse's mouth spattered back along its head and dark patches of sweat showed on its neck. The earth rumbled beneath the pounding hooves.

Just half-an-hour earlier I had been standing with two companions, Colin and Chuck, on the plateau of Giza, near Cairo, awestruck by the massive size of the famous pyramids. My thoughts were interrupted by a local man hurrying towards us from a horse corral. He wore khaki-coloured trousers and a once-white shirt that whiffed of a horse barn.

"My name is Ahmed," he said, displaying a salesman's grin from ear to ear. "I rent horses."

Quick to reply was Colin, a lanky man with long dark locks that framed his oval face. He was used to riding horses, having been raised on a sheep station in Australia.

"Where can we ride to?" he asked.

"To King Zoser's pyramid – the oldest one in Egypt. It's also called the Step Pyramid. It is at Saqqara, two hours' ride across the desert." Then he added emphatically: "You can only get there by horse."

My other companion was Chuck, tanned and lean with bushy black hair. We both had ridden horses but couldn't class ourselves as accomplished riders. Colin said he would teach us the basics of riding if we all decided to rent horses.

We agreed on a price to pay Ahmed, provided he came to show the way.

Colin gave us a quick practical lesson. "Mount the horse on its left side. To move the horse forward, press your legs against its flanks. To turn the horse to the right, pull on the right rein and press the left rein against the left side of the horse's neck. To turn left, pull on the left rein and press the right hand rein against the right side of the horse's neck. To stop the horse, pull back gently on the reins so the horse feels the pressure of the bit in its mouth. If you're galloping and the horse won't stop, pull on one of the reins as hard as you can to turn the horse's head to the side so he can't see where he's going. Then he'll stop."

Willing to take a chance, we rented three muscular-looking white stallions. Before mounting, I stroked my horse's head, talked calmly but firmly and hoped he got the message that I was in charge. We followed Ahmed and cantered across the barren, stony desert. Its dry surface was burnt like the crust of an overbaked pie.

We headed to where the distant horizon met the pale blue sky. I pulled gently on the reins to stop my horse from surging forward of its own will. Ahmed suddenly rocketed ahead and raised his arm, motioning us to gallop after him. With Colin's instructions crammed into my head I hoped I would remember what to do. I loosened the reins and dug my heels into the flanks of the white beast. That's when all hell broke loose!

We raced neck and neck over rocky ground and up and over sand dunes. Hot wind enveloped me and fine particles of sand and desert dust blasted my face. My eyes watered. We galloped for about a mile at this frightening speed. I was gaining on Ahmed when he started to slow down. I pulled on my reins but my steed twisted and turned, aching to continue the wild gallop. I gripped the reins tightly until he calmed down.

I was elated that I had galloped this far without tumbling off. I had to thank my horse for not tripping in one of the many invisible, sand-filled depressions on the desert floor.

Two hours after leaving the corral I saw a bump on the horizon and felt a jolt of excitement.

"The Step Pyramid of King Zoser," yelled Ahmed.

If visiting the Step Pyramid by horseback was the only way to see it, as Ahmed told us, I assumed there would be very few people at the site.

We trotted closer and the pyramid loomed higher. Then I started to doubt Ahmed's words. Near the pyramid I saw vehicles taking shape. Tour buses! I called to Ahmed.

He turned in the saddle, shrugged and grinned. I knew then that we'd been deceived into renting horses. He didn't show any guilt. He probably delivered the same spiel every day to get customers. I realized he was only trying to make a living and that he was reliant on ill-informed foreign visitors for some of his livelihood.

Ahmed explained that the site was called Saqqara, and the Step Pyramid was the oldest major stone building in the world, built about 4,700 years ago. Saqqara was also the cemetery for Memphis, an old capital two miles east, which was almost devoid of ruins.

We dismounted to explore the pyramid. Many stones and bricks had dislodged and cracked. Some had been reduced to powder, only to be blown away in desert sandstorms. The four-sided pyramid rose in six giant steps to about 200 feet.

"There's a burial chamber underneath it," said Ahmed, "but you can't go inside. Too dangerous. I'll take you to the Serapeum."

"What's that?" I asked, realizing how little I knew.

"It's the part of the cemetery where the sacred bulls were embalmed, and buried in granite sarcophagi." I hadn't heard about the embalming of bulls before, and the fact we were about to see their coffins added an unexpected bonus to our adventure.

We descended into underground corridors hewn out of

rock. Lanterns placed on the floor by the caretaker created a haunting light. Our shadows danced on the walls as we passed the now-empty sarcophagi lined up along the passageway. I tried to transport myself back in time to imagine the sacred bulls being placed inside these coffins. Ahmed told us one sarcophagus weighed 70 tons. Because Saqqara served as a cemetery I wondered what else lay undiscovered under the desert sands. Archaeologists continue to excavate the site.

After we spent a couple of hours clambering over rocks and exploring dusty corridors, Ahmed was ready to return to his stable at Giza. We mounted our trusty steeds and galloped back towards the three famous pyramids at Giza. Eventually we saw them silhouetted against the pale blue and mauve of the late afternoon sky.

Back at his corral we tipped Ahmed generously for the experience. His eyes sparkled. He switched on his salesman's grin and blurted: "Would you like to visit Memphis tomorrow? You can only get there by horse."

Egypt

The Palestinian Resistance

Meeting the PLO in Cairo, March 1969

See map, page 12, B3

"The Egyptian police picked me up at the Suez Canal and accused me of spying for Israel. One of the policemen said I must be a spy because I looked like one!" Colin, a lanky Australian with long brown hair that rested on his shoulders, was relating his experience to Chuck and me as we walked through busy El Tahrir Square in Cairo.

Chuck, a dark-haired bearded man, and I, had arrived in Cairo after travelling across North Africa from Morocco by a mix of bus and hitchhiking. We had met Colin previously near the pyramids.

"They marched me to the police station," Colin continued, "and questioned me for hours, asking the same questions in different ways, obviously trying to trip me. They said I should sympathize with the Palestine Liberation Organization. One of the policemen said the PLO was advertising for volunteer fighters to take back their lands from Israel. I told them I knew nothing about the Organization, and that I was neutral about the conflict in the Middle East. Nevertheless, they locked me up overnight and released me in the morning."

"Wow, what a story," Chuck exclaimed. "I've seen posters in Arabic glued to power poles and buildings. Probably the PLO advertising for recruits."

Along Ramses Street I spotted a wall plastered with posters. We all stopped and stared. They showed caricatures of guerilla fighters with snarling faces, their lips drawn back tightly across their teeth, the veins in their foreheads standing out like red, angry welts.

Colin looked pensive. "Let's find out more about these guys. But who would we ask?"

A man in a brown and white striped robe, a *gallabiha*, approached. Chuck and I recognized him as the moneychanger who had changed our dollars for Egyptian pounds the previous day. He wanted to change more money but I pointed to the guerilla poster and asked if he knew the address of the PLO office. He beckoned us to follow him as he set off along the Ramses Street sidewalk.

I hoped he understood where we wanted to go. He seemed to have a knowledge of English beyond his moneychanging vocabulary. We set off after him.

The road was clogged with buses, trucks and cars spewing foul-smelling toxic fumes. Irate drivers honked their horns. Jaywalkers darted between vehicles, risking life and limb to cross the road. Street vendors thronged the sidewalks selling fruit, peanuts, trinkets and perfume. Shops displayed brassware, leatherwear, carpets, fine silks, cloth, ceramics, robes and veils. Tantalizing aromas of lamb roasting over charcoal burners filled the air, and mingled with the smell of exhaust fumes.

After half-an-hour of tagging along behind the moneychanger, I started to doubt he knew where he was going even though he was consistent in his gait. Finally he stopped in front of an old stone building that displayed a faded sign that announced in pale blue letters: Bel-Air Hotel. The building looked tired. Its yellow paint was peeling off the outside walls and dirt and scraps of paper swirled around the steps that led to the open front door. The moneychanger told us this was the building we wanted and, taking a final opportunity asked, "Wanna change money?"

"No thanks." Chuck spoke for the three of us.

At that moment a smiling policeman appeared, exchanged pleasantries with the moneychanger, and beckoned us into the Bel-Air.

The high walls of the lobby were lined with recruitment

posters, Palestinian flags, a map of the Middle East and a large, framed portrait of President Gamal Abdel Nasser. Its days as a hotel were obviously over. The policeman yelled for some attention. A thin-faced man with a sharp nose and a bushy mustache appeared from a back office. After a few words with the policeman, he led us into an office of dark, wood-panelled walls, a large desk piled high with magazines, and a scattering of wooden chairs. The man motioned that we sit down, then he left.

An elderly, stooped little man wearing striped pyjamas – popular in-house daytime wear – entered and served thick, black coffee. Another mustached man came in and asked in reasonably good English what he could do for us. Chuck explained we were curious about the PLO and wanted to find out about its purpose.

The man attempted a short discourse on the subject, but quickly realized his English was too limited to be informative. He telephoned someone to arrange an interview with a representative who could explain it better.

We settled down to wait. The little man in pyjamas served more coffee and carried in Palestinian publications in English, French and Arabic, for our perusal. We flipped through them. Stories and artwork glorified acts of sabotage against Israel. Egypt had been defeated a couple of years previously in a war against Israel so I understood there would be people seeking revenge. What sort of organization had we stumbled on?

Half-an-hour later the door swung open and three men in dark suits strode into the room. They introduced themselves as PLO representatives, having just arrived from the Organization's offices a few blocks away.

I was confused. "What place is this?"

"The office of the General Union of Palestine Artists, our publicity section," one of them explained, then added, "Let me see your passports."

After we had shown our passports and assured them we were not spies they offered to take us to the PLO office to meet the regional leader.

To exit the building we marched along a corridor, past

half-a-dozen rooms full of posters and magazines in foreign languages – evidently the work of Palestinian artists to promote the PLO – and through a door that opened onto an alley.

We followed the three men along a labyrinth of narrow lanes that smelled of donkey dung, urine, dust and rotting garbage. We turned into an alley and flattened ourselves against the wall as a young boy in a dirty blue robe led a lame donkey pulling a cart of garbage.

Other narrow streets were almost impassable, being used as unofficial parking lots. We dodged between parked cars and finally halted at the rear door of a multi-storey building. The stucco exterior was crumbling; holes pitted the walls. A pile of old newspapers, sugar cane stalks and orange peels were strewn in the lane, providing a haven for rats. Inside the doorway, a guard lounged on a chair with a Sten gun, a 30-inch long British submachine gun from the Second World War, nestled in his lap.

He greeted us affably and led our party of six up two flights of stairs to an office. Inside the doorway stood a man in his forties with sculpted cheekbones, a neatly clipped mustache and an aquiline nose that thrust itself eagerly into the humid, smoky air. He welcomed us in fluent English. "Educated in England," he said, "and now the regional leader of the PLO." Also inside the room were about fifteen young men who sat smoking. Recruits, I assumed. They found chairs and gave us cups of coffee. One of the men tapped *Cleopatra* cigarettes out of a packet but we declined. The room was already blue with smoke.

"Please be seated," the regional leader announced to the group, and looked toward us. "I have heard you're interested in our Organization, so I will be pleased to give you some information."

He explained that the PLO was started five years earlier, in 1964. "It was comprised of various groups of freedom fighters," he said, "and included political factions, the largest one being Al Fatah."

I shifted uncomfortably in my seat. Were they expecting us to become recruits?

"The purpose of the PLO," he continued, "is to free our homeland. To do so the PLO may have to destroy the economic, military, social and political structure of Israel, as well as bring world attention to the rights of the dispossessed, uprooted and displaced Palestinian people."

I was sure the Israelis would call the freedom fighters something different, like rebels, terrorists or reactionaries.

"The PLO is not operating against any particular faith," the speaker said. "Palestine, the region now known as Israel, has consisted for centuries of people belonging to the Muslim, Christian, Jewish and other faiths. Harmony always prevailed between these groups in Palestine. The struggle of the PLO is against Zionism, not Judaism."

As he spoke, I scribbled furiously, trying to write down as much as possible, because it was all new to me.

He continued: "The Zionist Movement was launched in 1897, its aim to create the National Jewish Home, be it in Palestine or a region carved out of another country. Zionism not only led to the establishment of a Jewish state, but also to the expulsion of Palestinian Arabs to make room for more Jews. Zionism is a political doctrine which threatens Arabs; Judaism is a religion with which we can come to terms. The Palestinians demand that the Zionists give up statehood and permit the country to be run by Palestinians. In other words, we want an independent Palestine."

I interrupted him to ask how they hoped to achieve an independent Palestine. "Hopefully," he said, "by diplomacy. If that does not work we will continue our guerilla warfare. Our commandos will make hit-and-run rocket attacks on Israeli army patrols and set off bombs in the cities to terrorize the people."

I could hardly believe I was sitting in a room listening to a plan to destroy a country. The speech was given in a matter-of-fact tone, as if the plan would be executed very soon and that there was no doubt as to the outcome.

"A lot of innocent people will be killed," I said.

"I am sorry about that."

"It is a pity," Chuck said, "that Palestinians won't know what it's like to live in peace. Your young men and women will be drilled for war, to be taught only to destroy. What sort of a life is that?"

"Is life worth living without freedom?" he countered. "We have nothing to lose. We shall continue to fight until we win."

"If you win back your land," Colin said, "will you then live in peace?"

"Insh'allah," he said, then added the English equivalent, "If God wills it."

Insh'allah seemed to be a signal to the other men that the meeting was winding down because they started to chat, and scrape their chairs on the floor as they stood up. I nudged Chuck and Colin. We walked up to thank the regional leader. He accompanied us downstairs to the main door and we reconnected with the familiar sounds and aromas of Cairo.

"I don't know what you guys think," I said, "but I predict a bleak future for the Middle East."

"I agree," Colin said, "especially when there are Palestinians who want to fight forever for what they believe is right, against Israelis who will fight for what *they* think is right."

"We should talk to some Israelis," Chuck said.

"But the border is closed," Colin said. "I don't want to go anywhere near the Suez Canal again."

"Psst. Wanna change money?" A familiar voice interrupted our conversation. Our guide to the PLO was making another effort to do some business.

We all changed a few dollars as a way of saying "thank you."

Sudan

Encounter with armed tribesmen

Forty-kilometre night hike, Basunda to Gallabat, Mar. 1969

See map, page 12, B4

A blood-curdling howl pierced the cool night air. It came from the dark grove of trees ahead of us. Ben and I stopped. We leapt off the trail. We grabbed sticks for self-defence and crouched behind a bush. The muscles in my arms and legs stiffened.

Ben, a trim, athletic man with a jaunty air, and I were trudging along a narrow trail through the hills of eastern Sudan, heading towards the Ethiopian border. Two other travellers, Rob and Clem, who were slow walkers, lagged about fifteen minutes behind us.

A few hours earlier we had all met by chance in Basunda, a dusty town on a scrubby plain in eastern Sudan. We decided to travel together as we had the same destination, Ethiopia, and we all knew there was safety in numbers.

Basunda's police commander told us there was no public transport to the border, forty kilometres away.

"Occasionally," he said, "a Land Rover or Bedford truck belonging to the police makes the journey and you could go for free. But I don't know when the next trip will be made."

There was no alternative; we had to walk. Unfortunately, the temperature was over 40 degrees Celsius.

"Leave when the sun starts to go down," the policeman suggested. "It will be cooler."

In the late afternoon I heard the sound of an approaching vehicle and turned to see a Land Rover, not a police Land Rover but a private one. A Union Jack flapped from the aerial. It stopped beside us. Six Britons jumped out to stretch their legs.

"I guess you're heading for the border," I said to the driver.

"Yes."

My hopes rose. "Can you give us a lift?"

The driver answered in a plum-in-the-mouth voice: "Sorry chaps. We're already heavily loaded with our own gear." Then, in a conciliatory tone added, "We can take your backpacks to the border and leave them at the police post."

We four discussed the pros and cons. Would the Land Rover crew look after our bags as if they were their own? At the police post at the border would the staff be vigilant in minding our luggage until we arrived? Theft was always a possibility. To part with my luggage was not something I would normally do but when faced with a forty-kilometre hike it seemed like the only answer. We decided to accept the offer. With trepidation, I handed over my worldly possessions. The others did the same. After the luggage was tied onto the roof rack we watched the Land Rover kick up a swirl of dust as it roared away, bucking wildly over the potholes and wheel ruts.

We filled our water canteens at the police station and hit the road. It was five-thirty p.m. The track ahead across the plain looked like a line of scribble that petered out in the distant blue and purple hills. The first fifteen kilometres proved quite easy; we simply followed wheel ruts. But when we reached the hills, difficulties arose. The wheel ruts descended into a dry, boulder-strewn riverbed where, in the half-light, we tripped over football-sized rocks.

Twilight engulfed us while the half-moon floated low in the eastern sky. We followed the curve of the riverbed and almost stumbled into a black bull nibbling grass on the edge of the river bank. The bull raised its head, displaying a threatening set of long horns. The horns spelled trouble if the bull was rankled. We backed away. Slowly.

When out of sight of the bull, we scrambled up the riverbank away from the wheel ruts and discovered a narrow footpath that snaked through stunted trees and scrub. Rob and Clem stopped to rest while Ben and I marched onwards. By splitting up we were doing exactly what we had agreed not to do when we had met in Basunda.

Ben had an insatiable thirst for water, his own as well as mine. Soon, both our canteens had dwindled to a few drops.

The trail continued to rise, skirting heavily timbered hillocks. The night remained quiet except for the rustle of leaves in the trees and the snap of dried twigs beneath our sandals.

It was while we were hiking briskly in this tranquil setting that we heard the blood-curdling howl of the mysterious beast. Whatever made the noise, it howled again as it crashed through the undergrowth and bolted across the trail about thirty metres ahead of us. We guessed it was somewhere between the size of a bull and a boar but we couldn't identify it in the darkness. Still crouched behind the bush, we listened as the sounds faded into silence.

With the danger over, I wondered about Rob and Clem who had fallen behind. Two hours had passed since we had seen them. I felt guilty for having left them. We shouted their names into the darkness. Our calls reverberated through the trees. Almost immediately we heard dogs bark from farther up the trail. We tried to ignore the distraction while we listened for a response from Rob and Clem behind us. A muffled yell wafted up through the trees but we couldn't distinguish the words.

Ben stood and pondered out loud. "I hope they're saying they're all right. Anyway, there must be a village ahead. They can meet us there. And we can fill our canteens."

Narrow shafts of moonlight penetrated the heavily treed track. The dogs continued to bark, signalling our approach. We felt threatened as more dogs lent their lungs to the commotion. Twigs and small rocks littered the trail, and trees with low branches hung across the pathway, slowing our progress. The barking continued, sounding closer and louder with each step.

I was relieved when we eventually emerged from the dark trail into a clearing where the half-moon was throwing white patches of light. Suddenly I froze. Immediately in front of us stood a dozen tribesmen armed with spears, clubs and knives. They, too, stood motionless as they scrutinized us. As tall as Harlem Globetrotter basketball players, they were lean coal-black warriors wearing loincloths and T-shirts. No one moved. Their scrawny barking hounds circled us. They snarled and snapped. They whined and growled. My legs trembled and my heart pounded against my ribcage. I dreaded being bitten by a rabid dog. I hoped the dogs weren't aware of my fear.

I raised my right arm slowly to avoid exciting the slobbering curs and greeted the men with *Salaam aleikoum*. (Arabic for "Peace be with you.")

They grunted and came closer.

I pointed to my nearly empty water canteen and forced out a whisper, "*Moya*." It was the local word for water.

To my relief they grinned, showing toothpaste-white teeth. They gabbled and gesticulated amongst themselves and beckoned us to follow. We strode across the moonlit clearing surrounded by our friendly captors. Because they bristled with weapons I assumed they had come in search of the wild animal we had heard, or whatever else it was that had disturbed their dogs.

The tribesmen led us through the trees to their village, located on a flat, cleared area. I quickly estimated about twenty *tukuls* – circular huts of mud and sticks with thatched roofs. In the middle of the clearing sat a camel, tethered to a stake. The animal was munching cut grass, its legs beneath it, folded up like a collapsed lawn-chair. Outside the huts children slept on reed mats. In front of another hut a calf was lying with two children cuddled up to its belly to keep warm. The children were naked and black as lava. I guessed there were others inside the dark huts. The six or so dogs, thankfully, had lost interest in us. They had rolled over and gone to sleep.

Half-a-dozen women, bare-breasted and wearing only loincloths, perspired as they stirred the contents of iron pots over open-air fires. Orange flames licked at the underbellies of the pots. A porridge for making the sour, pancake-like flat bread they called *injera* was bubbling inside two of them. The dough was made from fermented teff flour, teff being tiny round grains, the smallest grain in the world. Two other pots contained *wat*, a stew to be eaten with the *injera*. We were familiar with the food, having eaten it in Basunda.

A villager approached us, said *moya* and pointed to our water canteens. We handed them over and followed him to a hut where he poured water from a hairy goatskin bag into Ben's army canteen and my one-gallon plastic jerrycan. The floor of the hut consisted of a mixture of mud and cow dung which had hardened through constant foot traffic. The cow dung, an antiseptic, prevented bugs from burrowing up through the ground.

Presently, a tall skinny man emerged from a hut. He spoke rapidly in an authoritative voice and waved his arms to indicate a circle. Judging from the way the other villagers deferred to him, he seemed to be the headman of the village. The tribesmen sat in a circle on the ground. The headman motioned that we join them. A boy passed around a goatskin of water.

As I drank my fill I visualized Rob and Clem groping along the dark trail with their tongues hanging out. I looked towards the headman and caught his eye. Raising my hands, I rubbed my index fingers together, sign language in the region that meant friend. At the same time I said, "*Inglezi*." Then I pointed towards the trail. His eyes brightened when he understood my sign language that our friends were coming along the trail. It was easier to refer to Rob and Clem as *Inglezi* (English) because that was the only word I knew to describe them.

After a quick verbal command from the headman, six of the gentle giants loped away into the darkness to bring them in. Ten minutes later I heard voices jabbering excitedly along the trail. Into the clearing burst the warriors, gripping the wrists of two captives the colour of bakers flour. Clem gasped with relief when he saw us. Rob was hyperventilating; his nerves were obviously shot. They both rubber-legged their way towards us and collapsed on the ground.

"I was petrified," Rob said, shaking all over. "I thought my number was up. They came out of the bush like shadows, not saying a word. They grabbed our wrists and didn't let go until we got here."

"Don't worry," I said, patting him on the shoulder, "they're all friendly. We shouldn't have split up."

Rob started to regain his composure, although he still shook.

"You need water," I said, "you're dehydrated."

Someone brought a goatskin of water, then the headman clapped his hands to get everyone's attention. A tribesman leapt into the centre of the circle. We watched with amusement as the man, an entertainer, danced with floppy arms and rubbery legs. The village men laughed at him and shouted encouragement; the women rushed from the cooking fires to watch the dance spectacle. Their upper torsos heaved and quivered as they laughed.

The dancer revelled in the attention and gyrated crazily. He repeatedly leapt into the air and collapsed on the ground like a rag doll. I quickly realized our entertainer was dim-witted. One often found an imbecile in a village because of the age-old custom of permitting intermarriage between first cousins. Although the custom had largely died out in the big towns, it still prevailed in rural areas.

The buxom women placed wooden platters of *injera* and *wat* on the ground in front of the men. The *wat*, a thick, generously spiced beef stew, had been poured on top of the *injera*, a flatbread about 20 inches in diameter. We ate with our right hands as is customary, using our fingers to break pieces of bread and scoop up the *wat*.

The entertainer sang a sentimental song, accompanying himself on a guitar-like instrument. As he shuffled closer to Rob, whose face was plump and cherubic, the singer warbled a love song.

"He likes you," laughed Ben.

Rob's arms and legs shook. He still hadn't gained control of his nerves.

The singer bent low over our cherub-faced friend. Rob elbowed himself backwards across the ground and out of the circle.

"Goddammit," he blurted.

The circle rocked with laughter at his outburst.

The whole scene was bizarre. On this moonlit night, in a village of strangers, in the middle of nowhere, we laughed while our friend was being wooed. I felt guilty about laughing at Rob's predicament. The poor guy was suffering from exhaustion and needed rest to recharge his batteries.

Suddenly a flash – the glint of moonlight on shiny metal. A knife. My body tensed. The singer advanced towards Rob. Now in a sweat, Rob eased back a little farther. The man stepped closer. Then, Rob surprised us; he put his hand out for the knife. The singer handed it to him willingly then stood back and grinned, saliva dribbling from his open mouth. He simply wanted to show Rob his homemade knife. I relaxed. Rob admired the knife with "oohs" and "aahs." He passed it to us so we could admire it, then handed it back to the proud owner who carried it to his hut.

How easily it had been to misconstrue the man's intentions.

I checked the luminous numbers on my watch. Almost midnight. To reach the border before sunrise we'd have to leave now.

I looked at Ben. "Ready to go?"

"Sure."

"And you, Rob? Clem?"

It was Rob who replied. "No, Clem and I will stay overnight. We'll catch up tomorrow. We're both dog-tired."

"You're splitting the team," I said. "Not only that, you're crazy. You'll cook in the sun."

"I need to rest," Rob said. "Besides, there's a wild baboon out there."

"How do you know?"

"I saw it crash through the bushes."

I looked at Ben. "Must've been the animal we heard howling. Hopefully it's long gone."

When the headman saw Ben and me rise to leave, he picked one of his men to guide us towards the border.

As we collected our full water canteens, I watched the villagers stoke the fires and lay down their sleeping mats. Our guide came to us, pointed towards a track and indicated we follow him. I looked back and saw our two companions being given reed mats to sleep on.

Our guide, a friendly daddy-long-legs, forged ahead at a loping gait. Ben and I jogged behind him on a trail that plunged into an overgrown forest, dark and primeval. Our path curled and twisted through tangled undergrowth. I was glad we didn't have our backpacks as we lurched and stumbled through the bush. I hoped our bags were at the police post.

We puffed and panted.

Ben glanced at me. "How're you feeling?"

"Tired. I feel as if I could drop dead."

Finally, our guide halted. We were gasping and wheezing when we caught up to him. We had reached the road that led to the border. The warrior pointed the direction we had to go, uttered a few unintelligible words, clasped our hands, smiled, turned around and loped into the darkness that swallowed him whole.

"Well," said Ben. "Forward, ho!"

"I'm beat," I said.

"We have to press on," he coaxed. "We must reach the border before sunrise." I checked my watch: four o'clock. We'd been on the move for ten hours.

After a few quick swigs of water we started along the road, walking on the flat ground between the wheel ruts. I trudged behind Ben with my head down, my feet dragging. Everything was quiet in the surrounding trees and scrub. Even the animals and birds were asleep. Sleep would be wonderful.

"Ben," I croaked. "I can't go on. I need forty winks." I slumped on the dirt and knew no more.

I don't know how many winks had gone by before I woke up suddenly with something sharp poking into my back. I opened my eyes. I had rolled onto a sharp twig. Ben didn't stir. Birds chattered in the trees, welcoming the first hues of daylight before the sun rose. I stood up stiffly and prodded Ben in the ribs with my sandal and whispered, "It's time to go!"

He flipped open his eyes. "I needed that sleep," he admitted.

As we marched eastwards, the morning sun pierced the sky with its golden arrows of light. The rays shone through the trees and scrub, creating a weird play of shadows on the road. We passed a few isolated *tukuls* where villagers were lighting their cooking fires. Roosters crowed and donkeys brayed. The road curved around a scrubby hillock and emerged above the border town of Gallabat.

Already the sun was rising rapidly, producing dry heat.

Quickening our pace, we headed downhill directly to the police station. When nearly there I heard the sound of a vehicle approaching from behind. I turned and watched a police truck crawl down the hill. It stopped, and out of the back jumped Rob and Clem looking well rested and fit.

"We slept well," Rob said. "A man guided us to the road, then fifteen minutes later the truck came by."

I was envious but thankful they had caught up with us. Ben and I wouldn't have wanted to leave Sudan without knowing where they were. A bond, however loose, had formed between all of us.

Together we strode to the police post to locate our luggage. I glimpsed the short, one-truck-at-a-time concrete bridge that crossed the sluggish river, the border between Sudan and Ethiopia.

The police officer behind the desk beamed as we entered; he was expecting us. I felt relieved to see four backpacks tied together with rope, stashed in a corner of the office. We happily hoisted them onto our backs and marched onwards to the bridge. We were a team again.

Zambia to Zimbabwe

Prohibited immigrant

Crossing the Zambesi River bridge, May 1969

See map, page 12, B5

The train rumbled and clattered over the bridge that spans the Zambesi River – the river that determines the border between Zambia and Zimbabwe. I gazed out the window towards Victoria Falls. The early morning rays of the sun glinted off the clouds of spray that billowed out of the chasm. The spray fell like rain against the windows of the train.

Having travelled overland from North Africa to Zambia by bus, boat, train, truck and foot my plan was to go through Zimbabwe (or Rhodesia as it was known then) to South Africa to find work.

I had a major problem – money. Not enough of it. Zimbabwe wouldn't admit anyone who couldn't show either an air ticket to their home country, or the funds to buy one. I only had US$110. A ticket would cost $600.

Despite my meagre funds, I decided to try to cross the border and bought a 35-cent train ticket from Livingstone, Zambia, to the town of Victoria Falls in Zimbabwe. I hoped my arrival by train would give the immigration officials the impression I was affluent. My thinking was naive, but what were my choices? If I walked across the bridge they would know I was travelling on the cheap, and would definitely check my funds.

When the train rolled into Victoria Falls station twenty minutes later, uniformed officials climbed aboard to check passengers' travel documents. I feared they would ask how much money I was carrying. I heard compartment doors open along the corridor and the officials requesting, "Passport, please." My pulse quickened. They were getting closer.

I nervously thumbed through my travellers cheques. One hundred and ten dollars. If I counted them twice I'd have two hundred and twenty!

Eventually an official reached my compartment. A man with a reddish-face and short-cropped fair hair poked his head through the doorway. "Passport, please." I held my breath and handed it to him.

Then the dreaded question. "How much money do you have?"

"Over two hundred dollars, American," I said, hoping he wouldn't ask to see it.

"Let me see it."

He flipped through the cheques, which took all of five seconds.

"There's only one hundred and ten."

"Oops! I must have counted twice," I said sheepishly. He wasn't amused.

"Get your luggage and come with me," he commanded.

He led me into an office in the train station, filled out a form and handed it to me.

The heading read NOTICE TO PROHIBITED IMMIGRANT. He had ticked the box next to paragraph C of subsection 1 of section 5 of the Immigration Act.

I looked up from the paper. "What does this mean?"

"It means you're a P.I., a Prohibited Immigrant. We can't let you in because you don't have enough money to buy a ticket home."

"What happens to me now?" I felt deflated.

"We'll drive you to the Zambian border, then you're on your own. When you have a minimum of $600 you can try again."

I clambered into a police Land Rover and sat behind the driver and the immigration official. We drove back onto the bridge that carried rail, road and pedestrian traffic high above the Zambesi River. White water raged far below. We stopped at the halfway mark. Spray continued to fall like rain.

"This is where you get out," the official said.

"But it's raining. Can't you drive me to the other end of the bridge?"

"See the white line across the middle of the bridge?" said the driver. "That's the border. We have to stop here."

Through the spray I dashed to Zambia. Three Zambian soldiers greeted me. They stood in the guards' hut, rifles slung over their shoulders.

I hitchhiked the seven miles to Livingstone, scribbled a short note to the custodians of my bank account in Melbourne (my parents) and asked that they wire $600 to the bank in Livingstone. I anticipated a wait of about ten days.

Meanwhile, I hitchhiked back to Victoria Falls to camp under the stars. I found a flat, grassy area beside some bushes and unrolled my sleeping bag.

African sunsets never ceased to amaze me. I watched in awe as the large golden orb approached the horizon. It illuminated the sky with shades of red and orange. The waters of the mile-wide Zambesi reflected the sky, transforming the river into a wavy pane of orange glass.

When the sun dropped out of sight, the sky darkened. Floodlights, installed for night-viewing of the falls, shone on the lip of the Eastern Cataract. They lit up the foaming water, making it appear to tumble out of the black sky. As spray soared hundreds of feet, the white light from the floodlights reflected off the myriad of droplets, tinting the mist a pale green.

The local people called the falls *Mosi-O-Tunya* (the smoke that thunders) – an apt name to describe the smoke-like mist. The sound of the water thundering over the falls lulled me to sleep. In the morning I awoke to a spray-soaked sleeping bag, a drawback of sleeping under the stars.

I needed a better place to stay overnight, preferably cheap and dry. I ambled through a campground which appeared deserted except for a lone caravan parked near the only building – the public washroom. I stepped into the men's section and found the expected urinals, shower and toilet cubicles. At the far end I discovered a small bathroom with a bath tub. This place had accommodation possibilities! I stashed my backpack beside the tub, bolted the door on the inside, climbed over the low wall into the adjacent shower cubicle then left the building, confident my belongings would be reasonably safe.

I hitchhiked back to Livingstone to while away the time at the museum with its display of sorcery dolls and rattles, tribal dance costumes, clubs and spears and some personal effects of Dr. David Livingstone, the medical missionary after whom Livingstone was named.

Back at the campground I saw a young black man wandering near the public washroom.

"Hello!" I said. "Who are you?"

"My name is Joseph. I work here. I make fire to heat water tank for showers and bath. You want hot water?"

"Yes, please," I said enthusiastically. I relished the thought of soaking in the bathtub. No one else was around. I discovered the caravan was vacant after having knocked on the door.

Joseph was an attentive, non-smiling 15 year-old in forest-stained khaki shorts and shirt. In bare feet he searched for fallen tree branches to stoke the water boiler. He lit a match and within half-an-hour hot water was gurgling through the pipes. Joseph was a handy person to know. After a two-hour soak I slept in my sleeping bag on the bathroom floor.

Over the next few days I killed time at Betty's Bakery and Restaurant, and the Dairy Den. Some of the local shopkeepers thought I was a new resident because they kept seeing me walk up and down Mainway, the section of highway that ran through the town.

Was my money on its way? Back to the bank to check again.

It had arrived! Elated, I converted the money into travellers cheques, then in the late afternoon, hitchhiked back to the falls. The next day would be Saturday. I looked forward to rising early to cross the bridge into Zimbabwe.

In the morning, while the dew-laden grass and leaves were glinting in the early sunlight, I left my 'washroom hotel,' headed towards the bridge, and jogged through the mist in my waterproof poncho.

The same immigration official who had prohibited my entry a few days earlier flipped through my travellers cheques, shrugged, and sighed. I sensed something was wrong.

"You have to pay the security bond in cash. I need to walk to the bank with you so you can change your travellers cheques into cash."

"I can go to the bank by myself," I said. "It'll save you time."

"No. I must accompany you as you are not officially in Zimbabwe until you've paid the security bond. Without supervision there is a chance that an unscrupulous P.I. would keep walking and not return from the bank to pay the bond."

"Okay. Do I get a receipt?"

"Yes, you do. And when you leave Zimbabwe at the South African border our customs office will refund the bond money. There'll be no problem with that. But the problem right now is that today is Saturday, the bank is closed so you cannot change money. You'll have to come back on Monday."

My jaw dropped. I felt as if I'd been punched in the stomach. "Isn't there something you can do? I don't want to go back to Zambia *again* and hang around for another two days."

"Sorry. Rules are rules."

Thwarted again, I humped my backpack over the Zambesi River bridge through the familiar shower of spray, greeted the Zambian border guards as if they were buddies and headed back to the 'washroom hotel.'

Monday morning arrived. A tranquil blue sky with wisps of white clouds greeted me. I ambled confidently across the bridge. The falling spray tasted refreshing as it hit my face. I was in high spirits.

For the third time I met the reddish-faced man with the short-cropped fair hair who had originally classed me as a P.I., thirteen days earlier. In a friendly tone he said, "Ready for another try?" I showed him my wad of travellers cheques.

"Great. I'll take you to the bank."

Over the next half-hour, events occurred swiftly. I cashed my travellers cheques and handed over $600. The immigration official thumped an entry stamp into my passport and reversed my Prohibited Immigrant status with the stroke of a red pen.

I sat in the sunshine and watched a train from Livingstone rumble into Victoria Falls station.

Perhaps with another P.I.?

Zimbabwe

Saved from the hyenas

Incident near Victoria Falls, May 1969

See map, page 12, B5

To escape the burning African sun I stood in the shade of a tall eucalyptus tree. I was on the outskirts of the tourist town of Victoria Falls, hitchhiking to Bulawayo, Zimbabwe's second-largest city. Most of the passing cars were filled with vacationers, many of whom waved and smiled as they zoomed by. Beside me a signpost warned: WILD ANIMALS. The hairs on the back of my neck prickled as I scanned the bushes around me. I hoped a car would stop soon.

I was still there four hours later as the red orb drifted towards the horizon and smeared the sky with mauve and crimson. Then the trees and scrub blackened into night. Most predators hunted around sunset; I hoped they'd find their pickings far from where I stood.

I wanted to catch a ride at first light the next day. My best chance for that to happen was to sleep under the tree. With the sun having set, the mercury dropped a few degrees. I spread my nylon sheet over the rough ground, crawled into my sleeping bag to keep warm and propped myself against the tree trunk. I felt apprehensive about the warning sign over my shoulder but decided to stay the night.

On the other side of the road, in the grounds of a motel that appeared to be under construction, a man was stoking a fire. He added dead logs until he had a massive bonfire. While scrounging for more wood he saw me and walked over. He was an elderly man with wrinkled black skin and grey frizzy hair. He was dressed in well-worn blue shorts and a green sweater.

"Bwana," he said, "you should not sleep here. It is dangerous. Two weeks ago I found a white man in his sleeping bag under this tree. His head had been chewed off by hyenas. Come and stay by my fire."

In a flash I slipped out of my sleeping bag, packed up and followed him across the road.

"You're a guardian angel," I said.

"I am the night watchman," he replied. "My job is to guard the building materials at the motel. The big fire keeps animals away. Even though there is a wire fence around the property, the fire gives extra security."

He added that the area was home to elephants, leopards, kudus, hyenas and the occasional lion. "A lion killed a man two weeks ago," he said, "just four miles from here." I shivered, and thanked him for warning me.

I perched on a log by the fire and watched the flames lick the dry branches of eucalyptus. The wood exploded into fountains of orange and yellow sparks. While the night watchman patrolled his domain, I felt secure and entertained myself by visualizing faces of wild animals in the embers of the fire.

At about nine o'clock a Toyota pickup bounced into the yard and a gorilla-sized, barrel-chested man with a dark-as-plum complexion emerged from the driver's seat. He called to the two workmen in the back of the truck to bring the pail of *chibuku* – a local beer brewed from maize. The driver introduced himself as Peter, the site boss, and handed each of us a mug of beer. I tried to enjoy its acidic aroma and mild-to-tart taste but the look of the brew – a beige slurry – put me off.

"It's a cheap intoxicant," Peter confided. "It gets stronger with age. We call it the beer of good cheer."

After a few sips, I pointed to the eucalyptus tree I had planned to sleep under. Horror showed on Peter's face. "Don't do that!" he said. "Packs of hyenas roam at night in search of prey. You'd make a perfect meal. If they didn't kill you they would rip open your face. It's happened before."

I felt protected by this group of men. As we huddled around the fire I explained I was a grateful guest of the night watchman.

"You're welcome here. Enjoy the *chibuku*," Peter said.

He nodded towards the unfinished motel. "You should sleep in a motel room tonight. We will do the same."

Then he added, "Beware of snakes. They come out of the bush and crawl along the outside walls. If there's an open doorway a snake will turn into the room. If it comes to a warm body in a sleeping bag it may crawl inside the bag. If disturbed, it could bite."

I felt uneasy. "How do you stop a snake from entering a room?"

"We'll simply put a piece of plywood across the doorway and support it with bricks."

We did the job quickly. For extra security, I stacked additional bricks against the plywood.

I closed my eyes and listened to the steady hum of water crashing over the rim of Victoria Falls, the rustle of leaves, the orchestra of crickets and the welcome sound of the night watchman adding more logs to the crackling fire. Feeling safe from slithering snakes and marauding hyenas, I drifted off to sleep.

The warning about hyenas had touched a sensitive chord. I dreamt vividly. I was lying in my sleeping bag when they came for me. Eyes glowed, fangs flashed, claws reached out to slash and maul. They made no sound as they crept closer, their powerful jaws ready to rip and crunch.

The night watchman stepped into my dream. The pack scattered. I jolted awake. Again he saved me.

South Africa

Ups and downs of ostrich riding

Ostrich farm at Oudtshoorn, east of Cape Town, June 1969
See map, page 12, B6

The ostrich bucked like a wild bronco, trying to throw me off its back. It leapt into the air, twisted, turned and bounced up and down as if it were on a pogo stick. Then, abruptly, it stopped in its tracks. I pitched sideways off its back into a mushy mixture of mud and manure. I had been on its back for only three quick seconds!

Just fifteen minutes earlier I had arrived at the ostrich farm at Oudtshoorn and had seen spectators grouped at a corral. I dashed over to them, dodging puddles from the previous night's rain, not wanting to miss anything. Four ostriches were milling around an ostrich keeper, a wiry, jockey-sized, dark-skinned man who was speaking to the crowd.

"...has a brain no bigger than its eye," I heard him say. "The plumes of females are dull brown while those of males are black and white."

The man spoke articulately and his talk was well rehearsed.

"Ostriches are the largest birds in the world but cannot fly because their wings are not strong enough to lift their bodies. Males can weigh more than 140 kilograms, or 300 pounds. Each foot has two toes, of different lengths. The longer one has a sharp nail. If aggravated, an ostrich will lash forward with its foot with enough force to crack a man's ribs or break a leg."

I chuckled. Who in his right mind would want to aggravate

an ostrich?

He continued. "These four ostriches here with me, are males. I have ridden each of them. They are tame. Would someone like to ride one?"

I looked at the dark chocolate, muddy ground, spattered and streaked with white ostrich droppings. The last thing I wanted to do was wallow in it.

I looked around for a raised hand. No volunteers!

I'm usually content to let others do the volunteering but this time, no one did.Why not me? I had nothing to lose. Nervously, I raised my hand. The next thing I knew I had climbed to the top of the corral fence, had mounted the ostrich and, within three seconds, had fallen into the slush.

I dragged myself up from the mess amid the laughter and cheers of the spectators.

I realized my mistake. I should have gripped its wings tighter. I called for another ostrich, hoping it was not aware of my inexperience.

The ostrich keeper picked up his long pole with a hook at one end and stealthily approached another ostrich. He hooked it by the neck and slowly drew the ostrich towards the fence where I teetered, waiting to mount. There were no saddles for ostriches; bareback was the only way. I lowered myself gently onto its feathered back. The ostrich gave a quick start but the pressure of the keeper's hook against its neck prevented it from leaping away prematurely. I grabbed hold of the shoulders where the bony wings joined the body, placed my legs ahead of the ostrich's thighs and tucked my knees snugly under the feathered armpits. I felt fairly secure.

"Are you ready?" the keeper shouted. I hesitated for a moment then said, "Ready."

When the keeper released the hook from around the ostrich's neck the bird sprang forward and jumped up and down as if it were bouncing on a trampoline. It tried desperately to catapult me into the air by charging towards the corral fence then stopping short, expecting me to rocket forward over its head and over the fence. But I stayed on.

It jerked its body left and right. I gripped its wings as tightly as possible and pressed my legs against its flanks. My leg muscles cramped as I held on. Below me was the slush. I didn't relish another mud bath! As the crazed bird dashed around the compound in circles and figures of eight I bounced around on its back. The spectators were just a blur but I clearly heard their screams and laughter.

As the bird leapt up and down, its long thin neck wavered and jerked right before my eyes. Suddenly it lowered its head! I lurched forward and before I could regain my balance I slid, headfirst, down the long neck and into the slush, facefirst.

I curled myself into a ball and prayed the big bird wouldn't kick me.

When I raised my mud-streaked face I saw the ostrich prancing around the corral – declaring itself the winner!

South Africa

Experiencing apartheid

The quest for motor oil, June 1969

See map, page 12, B6

On a sunny, windy morning on the northern outskirts of Cape Town, I stood by the roadside, left arm horizontal, thumb vertical.

A shiny, new, blue Volkswagen sedan slowed as it passed. Two brown faces scrutinized me. The car glided to a stop, then reversed. My senses shifted to the alert mode.

The driver rolled down his window and asked: "Are you carrying a pistol?"

His question didn't surprise me. I surmised the men were concerned about giving a ride to a hitchhiker who might hold them up and steal their car.

South Africa was experiencing government-induced racial disharmony which officially started in 1948 – the year *apartheid* was introduced by the ruling National Party.

Under *apartheid* the population was divided into Black, White, Indian and Coloured. According to the policy, people of different racial backgrounds were banned from travelling together in trains, buses and cabs, and could not use the same public beaches, swimming pools, cinemas, libraries, restrooms, water fountains, ambulances, hospitals or hotels. And marriages between the races were prohibited. Distrust permeated the population.

Apartheid is an Afrikaans word, pronounced a-part-ate, which means apartness or separateness. Afrikaans is the language that developed from Dutch, the language of the first settlers. When the Dutch language changed significantly over the years by the addition of native words, it came to be called Afrikaans. The white descendants of the mostly Dutch settlers called themselves Afrikaners. Descendants with a mix of white and non-white blood were called Coloureds. Their skin colours ranged from almost black to almost white.

Of the two men, the driver was almost black, and the other almost white. To the question about a pistol I answered no.

"Are you prepared to be frisked?" the driver said.

I didn't want to lose the chance of a ride in an area where traffic was sparse so I agreed. The two men looked like friendly, everyday Joes; I didn't feel threatened.

"We won't frisk you," the driver said. "Hop in."

I learned that both men, Nolan and Peter, taught English at a school in Cape Town. Like most Coloureds, their first language was Afrikaans. They were on their way to my destination – Windhoek, 900 miles north – for the school holidays. It was not uncommon to see hitchhikers along the road, they said. They explained that they had agreed to pick up a hitchhiker as long as he agreed to being searched for a pistol.

The trip was frightening at times when Nolan occasionally drove at excessive speeds. By looking over his shoulder I saw the speedometer touch 95 miles per hour more than once. Too fast for the condition of the road. After passing through Citrusdal the engine grumbled. Nolan stopped the car and checked the dipstick.

"We're out of oil!"

I looked around. We were in the middle of a sandy, desert region sprinkled with spindly trees and low bushes. No one spoke.

After a few seconds Nolan, who owned the car, broke the silence. "We should keep going. Maybe there's a farm where we can get oil." Nolan nursed the car slowly for a couple of miles then stopped at the driveway of a farm. A sign on the fence announced 'van der Merwe.' Nolan and Peter exchanged a few quick words in Afrikaans, then turned to me with furrowed brows. Nolan spoke in a concerned tone: "We need your help but it could be dangerous."

I leaned forward to catch every word.

"We have to ask a white farmer, an Afrikaner, for engine oil. Many Afrikaners don't allow uninvited Blacks or Coloureds onto their property. I can't go to the farmhouse because of my dark skin. If I did go the farmer might boot me off his land or shoot me for trespassing. It's better if Peter goes because he looks like a suntanned white man, and being with you, the farmer will assume he is being visited by two white men.

"To solve the problem," I said, "I could go by myself."

"No. You need Peter because he speaks Afrikaans. The farmer probably doesn't speak English; most of the farmers around here speak only Afrikaans."

"How do you know he's an Afrikaner?" I asked.

"The Dutch name on the fence," said Nolan.

Peter and I walked the curved driveway that led through a maize field to the farmhouse. I didn't feel good about this bold plan of deception. I could have left Nolan and Peter by the roadside with their oil problem. But they had been good enough to give me a ride so I didn't want to abandon them.

As we approached the farmhouse, a one-storey wooden structure enclosed by a white fence, a blonde-haired woman appeared at the door. She was pleasant-faced, smiling, and in her forties. Peter told her of our need for engine oil. The woman extended her hand, invited us into her living room and offered tea. From a glass-doored cabinet she removed delicate cups and saucers, obviously her best china. As she poured the tea she told us her husband would be home soon and that he had oil. She spoke only Afrikaans which Peter translated for me.

We had been accepted by the woman but what about her husband?

Within half-an-hour the door swung open and a big-boned, sandy-haired man filled the doorway. He extended a muscular arm and pumped my hand vigorously, almost crushing it. He seemed pleased to have us as visitors. Peter shook hands and explained our need for oil. It may have been my imagination, but I thought I detected a quizzical look on the farmer's face as his eyes flashed from me to Peter and back again.

Afrikaners are well-known for their hospitality and generosity. The farmer offered to carry the oil to the car and tinker with the engine. I saw a look of concern pass across Peter's face.

The farmer couldn't understand English so on the walk along the driveway Peter quickly explained to me that when the farmer saw dark-skinned Nolan he could realize he'd been duped. What the farmer might do then was unpredictable.

"We'll refer to Nolan as our driver," Peter said.

When we arrived at the car Nolan was still in the driver's seat. Peter put his finger to his lips to indicate to Nolan that he mustn't speak.

Peter explained to the farmer that Nolan was our driver. The farmer grunted, poured the oil, then barked at Nolan to switch on the engine. Nolan obeyed without uttering a word.

The ruse seemed to be working. But the engine wouldn't turn over.

The farmer said something to Peter who immediately translated.

"He suggests we return to the farmhouse and call a tow truck. I'm worried. We'd be going back onto his property. He may have realized we tricked him and he wants to get back at us."

"We have to go," I said. "We need to use the phone. If we don't accept his offer he may wonder why. Let's take a chance that everything's okay."

I wondered, in my naiveté, whether my suggestion was a good one.

We walked back to the farmhouse. Peter telephoned for a tow truck and the farmer left to go back to his fields. I felt relieved.

My Afrikaans was confined to just a few words but I was able to farewell the farmer with *Baie danke*. (Thank you very much.)

He turned and acknowledged my thanks with a wave. The words were easy for me to remember because they were pronounced "Buy-a-donkey."

Back at the car, Peter told me that if he had been recognized as a Coloured, the farmer would probably have shot him because he had drunk out of the best cups in the house, and had shaken hands with both the farmer and his wife.

"He'd be charged with murder!" I said.

"Yes!" Peter replied. "But he would plead 'not guilty' and say that I'd been trespassing. He would be released, thereby getting away with murder."

I shook my head, finding it hard to believe. But, having read articles in the major daily newspapers I realized that these injustices really did happen.

The tow truck arrived and hauled us into Citrusdal, but the mechanic there wasn't familiar with Volkswagens. Nolan telephoned a friend in Cape Town to come the following day to tow them home.

By this time it was twilight. Lights came on in the town. We sat in the car and talked about our day's experience. We discussed the *apartheid* policy and decided that we weren't going to let it spoil a friendship by dictating we go to separate hotels. Instead, we decided to sleep in the car.

I curled up on the back seat in my sleeping bag while Nolan and Peter wrapped themselves in blankets in the front.

I mulled over the bizarre situation. What would happen if a policeman passed by the car and peered through the window? Would we all be accused of breaking the law designed to keep us separated?

I woke up at first light when the sun's rays played on the car windows. As I corkscrewed out of my sleeping bag I saw Nolan and Peter stir. I whispered "Good morning." Both men, still half-asleep, emerged from under their blankets.

"I want to make an early start hitching north," I said, and thanked them for the eventful ride.

We all got out of the car and shook hands warmly.

I stared at the disabled car, shook my head and said, "Buy-a-donkey!"

Namibia

Never give up

Overnight in Windhoek, June 1969

See map, page 12, B5

Dusk was engulfing Namibia's small capital city of Windhoek when I arrived by car. I had hitchhiked from Cape Town, 900 miles south. As darkness fell over the city, the facades of the one- and two-storey buildings were silhouetted against the steel grey sky.

The driver coasted along the city's main streets, wide and clean, past a mix of furniture and clothing shops, restaurants and banks. Cool air blew in through the car's open windows. The coolness didn't surprise me; Windhoek was situated in the desert at an elevation of 5,534 feet, and it was the beginning of winter.

Namibia, once called German South-West Africa, was a German colony until the beginning of World War One. There was still a large presence of people of German ancestry. They comprised nearly twenty-five percent of the white population. The remaining seventy-five percent were Afrikaners.

The driver let me off in central Windhoek. I could have stayed in a hotel but I carried a sleeping bag so I had the flexibility to sleep anywhere. All I needed was a roof over my head. Any roof.

I had heard from other travellers that unsavoury characters prowled the Windhoek streets at night, looking for vulnerable victims to rob. I asked a passerby for the police station.

"Go across the street," he pointed, "then turn left, then right, then left again. There's a big tree in front of the police station. You can't miss it."

I found the station, a low, brown brick building, and I met the desk sergeant. He was a big red-faced man with a crew cut.

"I have a sleeping bag," I said. "All I need is a roof over my head. Can I stay in a cell overnight?"

"Sorry. Against regulations," he said.

"Can you arrest me for something?"

"Can't do that. I would have to fill out the charge book and say why I'm arresting you. But you've done nothing wrong."

"There's a big tree outside," I said. "If I laid down to sleep under the tree what would you do?"

He laughed. "If you refused to move on I would arrest you for vagrancy and put you into a cell."

"Why can't you just shorten the procedure and put me into a cell now?"

The sergeant sighed and shook his head.

"Wait here," he said, "I'll talk to my boss."

He returned with his superior officer, a tall, angular, bespectacled man.

I repeated my argument.

The officer listened, looked at his sergeant, shrugged and said: "For one night only."

The sergeant showed me to a cell. He pulled the wooden door closed but didn't lock it. I stared at the profusion of graffiti on the walls. Detainees had scrawled poetry and slogans beside their names, and dates of detention. All were written in Afrikaans or German except one: "Born to Suffer." I wondered about the fate of the man behind those words.

I wrote my name and date of visit and added a couple of my own slogans: "Born to Travel" and "Never Give Up."

Namibia

In the news

Sharing a cell in Walvis Bay, June 1969

See map, page 12, B5

The Mercedes-Benz became almost airborne when the driver, a bulldog of a man, flattened the accelerator to the floor. My body compressed against the black leather seat as the speedometer clocked over 100 miles an hour. I, a humble hitchhiker, held my breath, thankful to be in a car going the full 250 miles from Windhoek via Swakopmund to Walvis Bay, my destination on Namibia's desert coast.

Why Walvis Bay? I had heard from other travellers that pots of money could be earned on the trawlers even though the commercial fishing season was very short.

The 220 miles of road from Windhoek to Swakopmund cut through undulating desert where acacias twisted out of the dry, sandy soil. The sun blazed down, heating the blacktop. The road ahead shimmered, causing the infrequent, oncoming vehicles to appear to hover above the paved surface. At Swakopmund we turned south and followed the coast. Towering sand dunes, painted gold by the late afternoon sun, stood as high as six-storey buildings.

Fierce winds screamed across the road. Sand settled on the blacktop. The driver swerved to miss the drifts without slowing down. I'm not usually a nervous passenger but I was relieved when we literally zoomed into Walvis Bay in the early evening. I asked the driver to drop me at the police station where I hoped to stay overnight.

The driver looked at me quizzically. "Are you sure?" he said.

"It's not a thing I do all the time," I said. "Just when I feel like it. Especially when there is no inexpensive hotel or hostel in town. Police stations don't charge anything. This helps to stretch my travel dollars."

The driver shook his head as I got out of his car. Then his tires spat gravel as he took off.

I ambled along the footpath across the sandy front yard to the office door, knocked and went in. The officer behind the desk – a big-boned man with a blunt face burned coppery-red – looked surprised when I asked if I could sleep in a cell. He refused my request.

I persisted. "I have a sleeping bag. All I need is a roof over my head." The man mellowed and suggested I return later to ask the station commander.

I left my backpack in the office and strolled to the town centre. I had food and a job on my mind. The wide streets were lined with one- and two-storey stuccoed buildings. It took me a few minutes to get used to the smell of the fish factories even though the sea breezes helped carry away the odour. I stopped at the Restaurante Granada. Most tables were occupied. And most customers were sipping Coca Cola. I ordered a Coke.

"Would you like the special?" the waitress asked. Not knowing what she meant, but willing to find out, I said, "Yes, please."

She stepped behind the counter and poured something into my glass. Then she brought it to my table with a can of coke. I sniffed the contents of the glass. Rum! The restaurant was not licensed to sell liquor but that didn't seem to bother the diners, most of whom were drinking the 'special.'

I spoke to the proprietor, Pepe, and told him of my plan to work on a fishing boat.

"Go to the pubs," the restaurateur said, "and speak to the skippers. Try the Atlantic, the Mermaid and the Flamingo."

In the pubs I met four captains, thanks to barmen who pointed them out.

"The town is full of experienced fishermen looking for work," one scraggily-bearded skipper told me. "They would be employed first. If you told me you were experienced, I'd know within five minutes of boarding whether you were or not. You wouldn't even leave port."

I knew my lack of experience would be obvious.

The other captains voiced the same opinions. My chance of finding a job looked bleak.

The clock struck midnight when I walked back into the police station. The station commander, a hearty bear of a man, welcomed me enthusiastically. "This is a novel idea of yours, asking to stay in a police station." His blue eyes sparkled. He seemed pleased that I interrupted his normal routine.

"Have you eaten?" he asked.

"Yes, at the Granada."

"Ah, yes. They serve an excellent Coke." There was a smile on his face.

Good! A boss with a sense of humour.

"You look like you've had a long day," he said. "Would you like a hot bath?"

I jumped at the chance. He showed me to the police officers' bathroom which contained the deepest, longest bathtub I had ever seen. I luxuriated for an hour in the hot water then returned to the front desk.

"I checked our cells," the commander said. "They're all full. Would you mind sharing a cell with some prisoners?"

I stiffened. "What are they in for?"

"Nothing too serious. No one's violent."

"I'm willing. If you think it's okay," I said.

I hoisted my backpack over my shoulder and trailed him along a corridor into a different world, one of wooden cell doors to the left and right. A constable joined us. "In case of trouble," he said. We stopped at a large, heavy wooden door. The commander unlocked it, shoved it open with his foot, switched on the light and boomed "Wakey, wakey. You've got company." Four men lying on the floor on foam mattress pads woke up and groaned.

No one smiled.

I sniffed the unmistakable odour that permeates rooms that are continually occupied – the smell of bed linen, bodies – and feet. In a corner stood the lone toilet that resembled a throne. No privacy here. High up the wall a barred window allowed moonlight to filter in.

The constable laid a foam mattress on the floor and I rolled out my sleeping bag. The two policemen bade goodnight. The key turned in the lock. I felt uneasy being shut in with four jailbirds. To be friendly I apologized for their rude awakening at one in the morning, and explained I was just passing through town. I wanted to find out who my companions were.

"Why are you here?" I asked the freckled-faced man next to me.

"Forging cheques."

"And you?" I said to the younger man whose unkempt fair hair spilled onto the floor.

"I stole 500-rand. But I was going to pay it back."

The third one said he refused to go to court to settle a speeding ticket. The fourth one said he could leave if he wanted, but preferred to stay in jail because he was assured of three meals a day. Obviously he didn't want to tell me the reason for his being there. I hoped he wasn't an axe murderer.

At six in the morning I heard a noise at the door. I looked up and noticed a peephole. Whoever was on the other side could see us, but we couldn't see him. Half-an-hour later the door opened and two policemen entered with breakfast – a mug of black coffee and four thick slices of buttered brown bread for each of us.

After breakfast I rolled up my sleeping bag. A policeman I hadn't seen before returned for the dishes and asked what I was doing.

"Leaving," I said.

"Oh, no you're not." He slammed the door and turned the key.

I was shocked. Before I could decide what to do he returned a few minutes later, and apologized. "I thought you were a prisoner," he said with a smile then added: "The commander wants to see you."

I bade farewell to my cellmates and headed for the front office.

"There's a phone call for you," said the station commander. "It's the press. I told them you were here. They want your story."

That afternoon I read in the *Namib Times* a paragraph on page three under the heading:

AUSSIE IN WALVIS:

> *Mr. Russell Jennings, a 25-year-old Australian accountant who has hitchhiked 15,000 miles through Africa since the beginning of January has finally made it to Walvis Bay. Russell has lived in New Guinea and has hitchhiked thousands of miles in his journey around the world. When asked why he had decided to come to Walvis Bay, Russell said that he had heard reports about the fishing industry and had decided to find work on a fishing boat in Walvis Bay.*

I chuckled. Every skipper who read page three would be aware of an Australian on the prowl for a job on a fishing boat but whose experience was questionable.

I decided to forgo my fishing career before starting it. I retrieved my backpack from the police station and stood beside the road, with my thumb out, to retrace my route through Swakopmund to Windhoek.

After fifteen minutes a Ford Mustang hurtled past me, screeched to a halt and backed up. The engine throbbed noisily; the muffler had a hole in it.

The driver poked his deeply tanned face out of the window. "I'm going to Windhoek," he shouted over the din. I quickly got in and had no sooner flopped into the seat when he floorboarded the accelerator, leaving behind a blue plume of exhaust.

Within minutes we arrived at the first dunes that lined both sides of the road.

Again, powerful winds from the desert buffeted the speeding car and blew sand across the road. When the driver swerved to miss the drifts, the car bounced along the broken edges of the blacktop. The car quivered, pitched and rolled.

Almost sick, I closed my eyes.

I imagined being in a storm-tossed trawler on the high seas. It was something I could do without.

South Africa

Riding the wind

Skydiving at Springs, September 1969

See map, page 12, B6

For many years I had dreamed of jumping out of a plane, with a parachute, and floating down to earth on a gentle wind surrounded by a blue sky.

And here I was standing on the flatbed of a Nissan truck with a skydiving instructor and three other trainee jumpers. The truck crawled at 15 miles an hour over the grassy airfield at Springs, 35 miles east of Johannesburg. I readied myself to jump off the back.

Henry, the skydiving instructor, a tall skinny man in a blue jumpsuit, repeated his orders. "When you jump off the truck, keep your legs together and your knees bent slightly to absorb the shock when you hit the ground, then roll sideways. If you roll forward, you could break your arms and neck and smash your face."

I got the message loud and clear. All four of us leapt off the back of the truck and survived to continue the training the next weekend.

The altitude of Springs is about 5,500 feet above sea level. The air is thinner than at the coast, so when you land with a parachute you hit the ground with a thud, at about 15 miles per hour. This explained why we had to practise jumping off a moving vehicle at the same speed.

The day arrived for my first jump. I looked up at the afternoon sky, a turmoil of grey clouds and sunshine. Above the western horizon a wall of storm clouds swirled, building into a battlement of dark vapours. It was moving towards us. Slowly.

Directly overhead, the sun's rays burst through a break in the grey cover but soon the sunlight was shut out and the temperature dropped a few degrees. The wind picked up, powerful enough to flatten the trousers of my jumpsuit against my legs. I shivered.

I heard the drone of the parachute club's Cessna 182 as it landed after having disgorged four other skydivers. The pilot joined our small group and frowned. "The wind is blowing pretty bad up there. We should cancel further jumps."

My body and mind were keyed up, itching to go. I spoke to my fellow first-timers. They wanted to jump. Today.

"Is it really that bad up there?" I asked. Then pleaded, "Can you make one more flight?"

The pilot looked to Henry for a decision. "We'll try it," Henry said. "If I say it's too windy to jump, we turn back. Okay?"

We agreed, donned our main parachutes and strapped on reserve chutes in case the main chute failed to open. We clambered aboard the Cessna with Henry and sat on the floor behind the pilot, knees doubled up in front of us. The engine revved, we rolled along the grassy airstrip, lifted off and climbed to 2,500 feet above Springs. For first-time jumpers a static line, or cord, was hooked to the plane and the other end attached to the parachute. It pulled the chute open – a safety feature if the jumper forgot to pull the ripcord. It was a comforting thought.

When Henry opened the door the combined howl of the wind and roar of the engine almost deafened me. I looked down at the drop zone, marked by large, orange plastic sheets in the shape of an arrow, a garish blot on the landscape.

"Think you can land on it?" Henry bellowed to me over the motor.

How could I not land on it? I felt confident. Without waiting for my response he yelled to the pilot, "The wind's blowing a gale out there. We can't drop these guys yet. They'll be blown way past the drop zone by the time they hit the ground."

"I know," the pilot yelled back. "I'll fly farther upwind to give them a better chance."

Henry turned to us. "You should be all right."

Did I detect uncertainty in his voice?

Henry looked at me. "Ready?"

I nodded and yelled an exuberant "Yes!"

"Legs out," Henry ordered.

I stepped out of the cabin onto a step and a wheel and grasped the wing strut for support. I was in a spread-eagled position. The wind screamed and clawed at my face. My heart thumped but I wasn't afraid. I looked to Henry for his order to jump.

"Go!" he shouted.

I let go of the wing strut and started to freefall. Exhilaration mesmerized me as I plummeted to earth. Then God or something slowed my fall. The chute had opened automatically – which I was most thankful for.

The parachute billowed. I dangled below it, riding the wind. The chute, a 28-foot diameter sport parachute, had a couple of panels cut out of it for air to escape. This enabled a skydiver to steer by manipulating two cords that hung from the chute. I reached above my head, grabbed a cord and pulled. The parachute responded by turning a full circle. And another circle. I spiralled downward. Like a corkscrew. My heart pounded. I scanned the ground for the big, orange arrow. Spotted it. Lost it. I was running with the wind and would finish up miles from the airfield if I didn't do something drastic. I remembered what Henry had taught us. I pulled the other cord and turned the parachute into the wind. The spinning stopped. The speed of my drift slowed.

I searched the unfamiliar terrain again for the drop zone. Where was it? I could see neat rows of houses, open fields and the airfield. I glimpsed the orange marker, then lost it again. The wind buffeted me, turned me left and right. I looked for the other three divers. Didn't see them. All this time I was streaking across the heavens, the only sound the ruffling of my silk chute.

Who's in control? The wind or me? The wind carried me towards great gashes of gouged earth littered with yellow mounds – the tailings of old gold mines. Demolished houses with caved-in roofs stood nearby. Their high walls leaned precariously. I saw the ground rising quickly to meet me. I was on a collision course with a high brick wall! There was an empty yard around the house. And a perimeter fence of tall, dark green pines. I hoped to clear the trees and drop into the yard without killing myself.

The house and trees loomed large. Suddenly a treetop was almost in my face. My boots snagged the upper branches, my legs got tangled. I fell into the tree. Instinctively I covered my face and kept my legs together to prevent a branch coming up between them and splitting me in half. I crashed through small twigs and brittle branches. The sound was like gunshots. Suddenly the chute got caught and I landed gently on a thick limb. Nothing broken. Not a scratch.

Through the branches I spotted the recovery van speeding towards me. I was relieved to see help on its way. A small, spry man jumped out of the van and started up the tree. Hard featured, non-smiling, he passed me and scowled, "There had better not be any rips in the chute. It's worth 300-rand." (About $400). He didn't even stop to ask if I was hurt. So much for a caring crew.

From the treetop he called down, "You're lucky. It's not torn."

Back at the hangar I joined the three other first-time jumpers. No one had landed near the drop zone. One landed safely in a distant field. Another landed at 20 miles an hour, hurting his leg and hip. He had 'run with the wind' instead of turning his chute to face or 'hold the wind' when landing. The other landed near some demolished houses and hit two fallen concrete pillars. Fortunately, he wasn't hurt either.

The next day the *Johannesburg Star* reported: *'High winds caused a power cut in Springs. Trees were uprooted and a roof was lifted off a house.'*

Not mentioned was the crazy skydiver who was blown into a tree!

Malawi to Zambia

The witchdoctor's cure?

By road, Lilongwe (Malawi) to Lusaka (Zambia), April 1970
See map, page 12, B5

"Speaking as a medical doctor," George said, "I suggest the wart be removed surgically. But speaking as an anthropologist, I suggest you visit a witchdoctor and have him tend to it."

"A witchdoctor?" Trish said apprehensively. After all, it was her wart we were talking about.

Trish, 18, my younger sister – bright-eyed, slender and auburn-haired – was, like me, working in South Africa. We took advantage of the Easter holidays to hitchhike some of the southern African states.

In Malawi we were given a ride by George, a medical doctor, who invited us to stay in his home in Lilongwe, the capital.

We settled into comfortable sofas in the living room while George went to the kitchen to pour drinks. He was in his fifties, deeply tanned and hair greying.

For the umpteenth time, Trish examined the wart on her right index finger.

"It's awful. The wart must go."

I was sitting beside a bookcase full of medical journals and books with anthropological titles: *An Atlas of African History, Races of Africa, Primitive Religion,* and others. While I was leafing through them George returned.

"What can you tell us," I asked, "about witchdoctors?"

George's face brightened. This topic must be one he enjoyed discussing.

"Basically, a witchdoctor is a healer who practises traditional medicine. They often hold a respected position in a village. Don't be alarmed by the term 'witchdoctor.' It's a word coined by Europeans who thought the witchdoctors were practising devil worship.

"A witchdoctor has a variety of ways to cure people. He may tell a person to wear a lucky charm. Or, the witchdoctor may don a mask and perform a dance accompanied by drumbeats and chants. Or, he may prescribe a medicine made from a cow's fetus, lion dung or crushed-up monkey skull. On the other hand, he may offer something less repulsive like herbs and berries."

Then George asked where we were going next.

"Into Zambia. To Lusaka," I said.

"Good. I've met the witchdoctor who works in Lusaka. He has a two-roomed shack in the big open-air market. He's been there for many years and people say he's good."

"Going to a witchdoctor sounds ominous," Trish said. "What do you think he will do ?"

"He's an herbalist who probably has an ointment to kill the wart. Herbalists, medicine men, shamans or witchdoctors, call them what you may, are learned men and women with a knowledge of a large number of medicines concocted from a wide variety of plants. If you go to him, don't be perturbed by the paraphernalia in his consulting room. The bones, snake skins and masks are all to do with the African belief that if a person falls ill, it is because someone has bewitched him. The witchdoctor is also a diviner who can determine who or what caused an illness by 'throwing the bones' and interpreting them by the way they fall."

After overnighting at George's, we hitchhiked along a road that cut through undulating scrubland to the Zambian border. A car stopped, a stripped-down Hillman Minx driven by a skinny man with a cigarette dangling from his bottom lip.

"I run a tobacco plantation," he said, "and I don't see many hitchhikers on this road. Probably because of the rebels in the area."

I had heard of anti-government forces operating from Mozambique but I believed that the road we were on was a safe distance from any rebel activity.

We tossed our backpacks onto the back seat and were stepping into the car when the engine died.

The driver sighed. "It's hard to get spare parts for the car," he said as he fumbled under the dashboard and pulled up two wires which he pressed together. They sparked, the engine coughed, sputtered and the car surged forward.

We drove past village shacks built of branches and corrugated iron. Lines of laundry flapped in the warm air, and little boys waved wildly as we passed. In the late afternoon we reached Chipata in Zambia, a dusty, dirty town with one- and two-storey buildings flanking the main road.

"I am staying in Chipata to get the car fixed," the driver said, turning his head. "I can take you to the bus station."

At the bus station I approached the ticket seller.

"There's a bus leaving for Lusaka in two hours," he said, pointing to a dilapidated bus in the compound. "Takes about thirteen hours. Arrives early in the morning."

"Is it an express bus?"

"No, it stops at villages to pick up and let off passengers."

We bought tickets, then waited on a log bench and watched farmers arrive with gunny sacks of vegetables, mainly potatoes and cobs of corn. They hoisted them up to the baggage handlers on the roof who then tied them down, next to bags and bundles and our backpacks. One farmer rose up on his toes and heaved up two goats. They bleated their little hearts out. They definitely didn't want to go on a bus ride of no return. They kicked with all their might, but their legs were trussed. Meanwhile, the other farmers stacked their extra sacks along the aisle inside the bus and placed chickens, with their legs tied together, under the seats. The bus was scheduled to arrive in Lusaka in time for the market.

A woman food hawker sold us fried dough balls and boiled eggs for our supper.

Daylight disappeared with tropical suddenness. Departure time was imminent. We boarded the bus, scrambled over the sacks and squeezed into narrow seats. Comfort of passengers was secondary: men, women and children crammed together. Transportation of vegetables and livestock took precedence.

The bus rumbled out of the compound and joined the pitted road that led to Lusaka. The miles clicked by as the bus limped across the landscape like a runner with a cramp. I looked through our dirty window. All was dead calm out there, nothing but the silence of the bush.

Suddenly the bus stopped.

"Must be a village," Trish said. "I hope people are getting off, and not on. Can you see what's out there?"

I peered through the window into the blackness and got a jolt. "You won't want to hear this, but I can see a dozen or so guys with guns."

"What!" Trish slinked down into her seat.

I realized how vulnerable we were to the vagaries of armed bandits, rebels, hostage takers or whatever they called themselves.

Someone outside the bus barked an order and our fellow passengers shuffled along the aisle to the front door. My heart pounded. The other passengers, all local people, rifled for their identification papers. They showed them at the door as they spilled off the bus in various states of sleepy disarray.

Trish and I hesitantly pulled our passports from our moneybelts, but as we were about to show them I read the shoulder patches on the uniformed men. They were Zambian policemen. What a relief they weren't bandits. As we got off the bus a police officer explained that, because of rebels in the area, the police were making sure all people on board were *bona fide* passengers.

We stood beside the bus and watched the police board and shine their flashlights around the bus's interior. When no weapons were found, we reboarded and trundled along the road to Lusaka. Finally the sky lightened and the sun's rays penetrated the windows. I looked around me. The short-hop passengers had left us during the night, but the aisle was still crammed with farmers' sacks.

Fortunately for the farmers going to market to sell their goods, the delays were minimal. We arrived in Lusaka after a bone-shaking

375 miles. The bus stopped at the market and a farmer showed us to the witchdoctor's two-roomed shack, built from scrap lumber.

The first room served as a waiting room. Benches around a wall were occupied by two thin, sallow-faced men and half a dozen women with babies. The doctor had not yet arrived. A young boy beckoned us into the doctor's consultation room. He dragged two wooden boxes to the desk so we could sit while we waited. I felt embarrassed that we were taken ahead of the other people, and hoped they weren't annoyed. The boy left us. We stared at the animal parts that hung on the walls and cluttered the doctor's desk: bones, furs of small animals, snake skins, cow-tail whisks, skulls of birds and a wooden mask painted yellow and white.

My eyes wandered over shelves filled with numerous jars which, I imagined, contained ointments to heal a variety of ailments.

Presently a man with a dry, wrinkled face, like leather, ambled into the room. Probably in his sixties. His old pair of khaki shorts hung limply from his hips while his unbuttoned shirt displayed the bars of his rib cage. He perched on the edge of a box behind his desk and peered at us quizzically.

Trish held up her index finger and asked in slow, articulate English if he had a cure.

"Yes," he said, and in passable English added: "I can cure everything. I have been doing this job for forty-three years. My father and grandfather also did this work."

With that said he casually reached for a jar from the shelf, opened it, slipped his long bony finger inside and dug out some black goo. "Rub it on your finger three times a day for ten days to kill the root, then it will wither away. Have faith."

He put out his hand for payment. "Seventy ngwee, please." (About seventy cents.)

Trish faithfully applied the greasy ointment daily, as instructed. As the days passed she noticed three more growths under the nail of her index finger. They looked like white pinheads. More warts? She grew discouraged. Her faith in the witchdoctor waned; maybe her faith hadn't been strong enough. Something had gone horribly wrong with the cure. Maybe the doctor had grabbed the wrong jar.

By the end of the ten days the one wart had multiplied to four!

South Africa

Above the mountains

An unplanned stop in Mooi River, May 1970

See map, page 12, B6

My hopes rose when the station wagon approached, but it went right on by – another car with a family. Trish and I were hitchhiking the 390 miles from Durban to Johannesburg and had covered only thirty miles in the past two hours. We had already hitchhiked 600 miles from Johannesburg via Zululand to Durban and now we were headed back after an all-too-brief three-day holiday.

Trish was my sister, a spirited eighteen-year-old, slim and attractive with auburn hair. She was in South Africa to work and travel which is what I, seven years her senior, was already doing.

Being Sunday, most of the cars that passed carried Mum, Dad and the kids, probably on their way to the Valley of a Thousand Hills for a picnic. I felt discouraged as I watched the station wagon continue up the hill, but then unlike the others it stopped, turned and came back. A man with a smiling face, and a shock of fair hair flopping over his forehead, poked his head through the open window. "Howzit?" he said, and beckoned we get in. 'Howzit' was South Africa's most popular form of greeting.

"Thanks for stopping," I said. "Sunday's a hard day for hitching."

"We're going to Mooi River, about two hours away," the lady beside him said. She was a woman in her thirties with curly brown hair and a pleasant face. Trish and I slipped into the back seat of the station wagon, beside a young boy, and propped our backpacks on our knees. The boy was pinned against the door but he didn't seem to mind. I think he was intrigued by the experience of two hitchhikers sharing his space. The lady's name was Denise and she introduced her husband, Robin, and their young son Craig.

Conversation flowed easily. We mentioned that we visited Nongqai Fort, a British fort built in the 1880s. And we told them of our rewarding day in the Mkuzi Game Reserve, watching from a hide while warthogs, impalas, kudus and zebras came to drink at a water hole. It was late afternoon when Robin drove off the highway into the town of Mooi River.

Denise turned to face us. "We'd like you to stay the night. Can you?"

"Of course," we said. Then Trish added, "Maybe I should check my Appointments Book first."

We all laughed.

Meeting people is what travelling is all about. Being invited into a home is a bonus and privilege. Robin showed us around while Denise left us to prepare dinner. Their home was built on two levels with a large, landscaped, grassy backyard. One of the rooms was fitted with a bar and bar stools.

"What'll you have?" Robin asked, as he waved his hand towards his many bottles of spirits.

Trish and I opted for a beer.

"I'll have the same," said Robin.

As Robin sipped his brew he leaned forward enthusiastically. "I have an idea. I have the use of a Cessna. I'll give you a choice. I can either fly you from here to Johannesburg or take you on a sightseeing flight towards the Drakensberg Mountains."

I looked at Trish for her reaction. "The Drakensberg Mountains sound exciting," she said keenly. I agreed. We can hitchhike any time but the chance of a flight to see something different like the Drakensbergs doesn't come every day.

The clear sky the following morning meant a good day for flying.

"Denise and I have to go into town," Robin said.

He handed me a car key to their second vehicle, a Vauxhall. "Take the car for a drive-round. Denise and I'll be back in an hour."

I was surprised by his generosity and trusting nature to lend two strangers his car.

Trish navigated using a map she found in the car. We drove into undulating brown hills where maize fields lay fallow, and along the gently flowing Mooi River. Although the name meant pretty in Afrikaans, the river was a muddy-brown. "It'll be interesting to see all of this from above," Trish said.

Back at the house I heard Robin call, "Ready for the flight? We'll drive to Estcourt to the Flying Club – about 20 minutes away."

As we approached the airfield Robin pointed out the Cessna 172 parked beside the runway. He went to the office to file the flight plan while we waited at the aircraft – a high-winged, single-engined, four-seater plane. I felt just a twinge of concern at the single propeller.

Robin emerged from the office.

"It only has one engine," I said.

"Yah. Not enough room for two engines," Robin joked. Then he added in a serious tone, "Actually, the Cessna is reputed to be the safest light plane ever built."

His sense of humour and confidence made me feel better. Minutes later we took off and flew over brown fields at 120 mph. Trish was able to point out the roads where we drove earlier.

Robin aimed the nose west towards the Maluti Mountains in the Kingdom of Lesotho.

"The entire country lies above 3,300 feet," Robin said. "Some peaks reach 10,000 feet. Erosion is a problem. Much of Lesotho's food is imported. It's one of the world's poorest countries."

Robin banked the plane to the right. "I can't fly into Lesotho's air space," he said. "We'll go back the way we came and continue to the Drakensberg Mountains."

Rolling hills and green valleys passed below us, then the Drakensbergs loomed ahead. Robin pointed to a prominent group of peaks and bluffs in the Drakensbergs named the Giant's Castle. "If you use your imagination, you can see that the silhouette of the peaks and escarpment resemble the profile of a sleeping giant. There are many caves that hide thousands of hunting scenes painted by the San people. Most paintings are between 200 and 400 years old."

Trish leaned forward and pressed her camera lens against the Plexiglas window. "I want to remember this scene forever," she said, clicking the button. She peered ahead. "The mountains go on and on. The peaks look like a dragon's back."

"The mountain range is 120 miles long," Robin said. "But I don't want to get in too close. The wind is blowing at 15 knots. The downdrafts near the mountains could be deadly, or at least they could cause problems if we have to make a forced landing."

I could not imagine there being anywhere to land in the Drakensbergs.

I stared ahead at the spinning propeller. "How much fuel do you carry?"

"We have three hours of fuel but we'll only be up here for an hour."

All this time I was looking down and around, marvelling at mountain peaks and ravines. Who could have imagined that our slow Sunday morning of hitchhiking would lead to a flight over these spectacular mountains?

Robin banked the plane to the left. "Homeward bound," he said. "We'll fly over Mooi River and buzz the house to let Denise know we're on our way home. She's inside cooking roast beef for lunch – with all the trimmings." I watched for Denise to come outside and wave but it didn't happen.

"I don't go outside and wave any more," Denise told us when we arrived at the house. "I used to, but the novelty has worn off."

After we devoured the roast, we piled into the station wagon for the short drive to the Johannesburg highway. Robin and Denise waited in their car while Trish and I stuck out our thumbs to hitch a ride with an approaching vehicle. It was another station wagon. I felt lucky as it stopped beside us. We hopped in and waved to Robin and Denise. Robin cupped his hands to his mouth and bellowed: "Come back again."

Robin and Denise and I kept the spark of friendship alive by exchanging Christmas letters every year. Twenty-eight years later I wrote to say that my wife Penny and I would be escorting a tour group of fifteen people from Canada to South Africa. I said we would like to meet them at Mooi River when we passed by at lunchtime on September 18th. Denise wrote back to say Robin would be at the Esso station, the one with the Wimpy Restaurant, from noon onwards and that we were invited for lunch.

In the morning of September 18th I telephoned from Durban to confirm we were on our way. "We're travelling in a green safari truck with the name Drifters on the door," I told Robin.

As we approached Mooi River I announced to our tour group that they could eat lunch at the Wimpy Restaurant while Penny and I visited with friends.

Anthony, our driver, interrupted me. "There's a man at the petrol pumps jumping up and down, waving like a madman. Is that your friend?"

Sure enough, it was Robin wearing an oversized T-shirt with the word CANADA emblazoned in big letters across the front. He was waving his arms frantically.

I leapt from the truck to greet him.

"You're all invited to lunch," he said.

"But there are seventeen of us," I protested, "and our driver."

"I know. Follow me to the house. Denise is expecting us."

Denise most certainly was expecting us. The buffet table was groaning with food: curried lamb and rice, pizzas, salads and custard pies. The group was thrilled to have been asked into their home. They were touched by Robin's and Denise's generosity.

The Mooi River visit was a highlight of their trip. For me, it was as good in 1998, as it was in 1970.

Congo
(Democratic Republic of Congo, formerly Zaire)

Down the Congo River

By riverboat, Kisangani to Kinshasa, September 1970
See map, page 12, B4

Shafts of white light from the morning sun broke through grey clouds. As I stood on the high bank of the Congo River at Kisangani I hoped for fine weather for the six-day journey downstream to the Congolese capital, Kinshasa.

The boat I would travel on was the *Colonel Ebeya*, a double-decked motorized barge moored at the riverside dock. It was going to push another two-tiered barge which was divided into second class passage on the top deck and third class on the lower deck. When hooked together, the barges became a formidable riverboat able to carry fifteen hundred or more passengers.

It was my habit to always choose the lowest fare in order to stretch my dollars. At the ticket counter I asked for third class. A local man behind me in the queue spoke up.

"*Non, monsieur*. Don't go third class," he pleaded in French.

Other men in the lineup joined in. They implored me to buy second or first class because third was always dirty and overcrowded. Their earnestness convinced me. I bought a second class ticket for the departure in four days' time.

One of the men warned me that second and third class were often oversold and that soldiers without tickets regularly took over second class cabins.

"Go aboard early on departure day," one man suggested.

"You must keep your ticket safe until you arrive in Kinshasa," another man said, "and hand it in at the port gate. If you lose it, there will be trouble."

The fare included one meal a day. To stay healthy during my travels I always carried food rations for emergencies. I didn't want to excite any bacteria into a feeding frenzy in my belly by eating the food from a kitchen where hygiene was not a priority. I preferred to eat fruit and vegetables that I could choose at riverside markets.

I asked the clerk if I could buy a ticket that excluded food. *"Non,"* he said with finality. I shrugged. I guessed I'd have to use my precious dollars to pay for food I probably wouldn't eat.

I thanked my unofficial advisers in my fractured French. Use of the French language in the Congo was a legacy of the colonial days when the Belgians ruled the country.

Before my departure I had time to explore Kisangani. Once known as Stanleyville, the city was named after Henry Morton Stanley, the British-born explorer and *New York Herald* correspondent who uttered the words, "Doctor Livingstone, I presume?" upon finding the medical missionary on the shores of Lake Tanganyika, in 1871. In 1877, Stanley was the first white man to go down the Congo River, the second longest river in Africa, after the Nile.

Kisangani suffered during the Congo Civil War in the mid-1960s. The walls of many buildings were still pockmarked by gunfire, and their doors and windows boarded up.

But even so, the Hotel Stanley was open for business. I stopped by the beer garden for a bottle of *Stanor*, Kisangani's locally brewed beer, another legacy of the Belgian colonizers who ruled until 1960 when the country was granted independence.

"Excusez-moi, monsieur." The voice of a young boy interrupted my thoughts. I looked into a cocoa-brown face still pudgy with baby fat. He had a vervet monkey on a leash and asked me if I wanted to buy it. I waved him away. Why would I want a pet monkey?

On departure day, September the third, I arrived at eight in the morning and marched up the gangway with hundreds of locals who were chattering in Lingala, the local dialect. The women wore colourful, eye-catching, ankle-length, wrap-around skirts called *pagnes*. Matching head wraps were tied on their heads. Men wore slacks and shirts; they had long ago discarded their traditional toga-style clothing. Many of the passengers were travelling home to riverside villages, and carried their belongings in cloth bags and blankets, tied with rope.

Among the fifteen hundred people, there were traders hawking baskets of dried fish, bottles of palm oil, cigarettes, tobacco, sugar and fabrics. Others carried animals to sell for slaughter, to feed the passengers. I spotted pigs, goats, sheep, chickens, muzzled crocodiles, and monkeys. Maybe the young boy at the Stanley expected me to eat his monkey, not to keep it as a pet. The animals protested with grunts, bleats and squawks. I didn't blame them.

On the second class deck I found an empty bunk in a cabin occupied by three soldiers. I hoisted my backpack onto the mattress. The cabin, smelling of sweat and dirty clothes, was small and gloomy. The odour of rotting organic matter drifted out of one of the soldier's bags. The dingy den wouldn't win top honours for hygiene. Two of the walls consisted of thick wire mesh. It made me feel like a caged animal. It was hard to imagine I would be sleeping in this cage for five nights.

I padlocked my backpack to my bunk, my normal security procedure, and strode along the deck to watch the multitude of passengers swarm up the gangway. Among the sea of black faces, two white ones, of a man and a woman, stood out. I waited eagerly for them to board as I hadn't met any other travellers for four weeks. I hoped they spoke English. I was ready to give my high school French a rest.

The woman reached the deck first – a brunette with bright green eyes and a wide, friendly smile. Her companion was a ruddy-faced, broad-cheeked fellow with a relaxed manner. They introduced themselves as Ann and Ken. I was relieved they spoke English. Both were Canadian volunteer teachers on a two-week holiday from teaching English in West Africa. They were a cheerful couple and I looked forward to experiencing the river journey with them.

"We should get together," I said, "once you've checked into your cabin. Are you in second class?"

"No," said Ann. "We hadn't thought of second. We tried booking first class but it was full." With an embarrassed tone in his voice, Ken added: "We had to book deluxe class which was pricey but it includes three meals a day."

"Second class includes one meal a day," I said, "but I'm carrying my own food."

We agreed to meet later, after they had settled into their cabin.

A few minutes after midday *Colonel Ebeya's* horn sounded and a couple of crewmen pulled the gangway aboard. The engine of the mighty mechanical monster throbbed and shuddered, and belched black diesel smoke at the slate-gray sky. Early September was the end of the dry season and the beginning of the wet in this part of Congo. Farther downstream, in Kinshasa, the weather should still be dry.

I watched our progress from the second class deck. The flat, muddy-brown river carried run-off from the Congo's many tributaries that drained the huge forest basin. The terrain on both sides of the river consisted of low hills dotted with trees. Half-an-hour later, from the second class barge, I spotted Ken and Ann on the top deck of the *Colonel Ebeya*. I waved, then headed towards them, skirting around passengers sitting on the deck, and climbed the railing to first class. I passed the crew's quarters, galley, wheelhouse, dining room and deluxe cabins. The Canadians' cabin was furnished with two bunks, table, chairs and a private shower and toilet. I envied them.

The first class dining room was open so I booked to join Ken and Ann for lunch: kidneys and sweet potatoes. "Not my favourite," I said as I stabbed a kidney with my fork, "but I'm sure it beats the fish and rice served in second class. I heard via the grapevine that the meals left a bit to be desired. The fish often have worms."

A thought crossed my mind. "I wonder if I should ask for a rebate for not eating their meals," I said.

"It's worth asking," Ken said. "The captain probably speaks French. I can go with you as interpreter. I enjoy this sort of challenge."

I appreciated Ken's offer; he spoke fluent French.

"I have a letter which may help," I said. "When I was in Goma, in eastern Congo, I met the police chief who gave me a letter of introduction. The letter asks civilian and military authorities to help me with transport."

Ken looked intrigued. "How come he gave you a letter?"

"I had gone to the police station and asked if I could stay in a spare room. The chief agreed and I stayed for a few nights. At the bar next door I had a few convivial drinks with the policemen and the chief who offered to write the letter."

I dug it out of my moneybelt and laid it on the table. Ken and Ann pored over it. "This letter is amazing," Ken said. "With the page headed *Police Nationale Congolaise*, and the rubber stamp of the police detachment and the police chief's fancy signature, the captain should be impressed enough to grant you a refund."

We decided to pay the captain a visit the following day.

In the meantime the three of us explored the barges. Our feet made loud thudding sounds as we stepped down the iron stairway to the third class deck. The bottom deck resembled a village market. Traders, mostly women, stood at stalls selling manioc, papayas, pineapples, bananas, smoked fish, bread and biscuits, as well as mirrors, combs, soap and batteries. Animals let their presence be known. The stench of urine and excrement hovered in the air, trapped between decks. I was grateful to the men who persuaded me not to travel third class.

Congolese guitar music boomed at full volume out of amplifiers from the bar-room on the second class deck. Soldiers an d other passengers quaffed the popular *Primus* beer from Kinshasa at an alarming rate, judging by the number of empties piled up on the tables. The three of us found a table, bought beers and spent an hour shouting to each other over the music. The locals caroused and gyrated, wheeled and whirled to the up-tempo beat. My head throbbed. Congolese love to dance – anytime, day or night.

The late afternoon sun appeared briefly between broken clouds before it dropped over the western horizon. Darkness descended quickly as it always does near the equator. We went our separate ways, agreeing to meet the next day and speak to the captain.

To delay going to the airless prison-like cage I paused on deck and filled my lungs with the cool night air. As the boat rumbled downstream, a searchlight, held by a crewman in the wheelhouse, swept the trees along both sides of the river. The light lingered on thick, white arrows painted on tree trunks pointing towards the deep channels we were to follow. These navigational aids created a zigzag route down the river but enabled us to travel through the night.

I slept fitfully, listening to the amplified music until someone pulled the plug at three or four in the morning. The throb in my head started to subside. My room mates had not returned. I wondered if they were sleeping on the bar-room floor.

I rose at six, ambled to the bow and peered into the mauve-coloured morning haze. At that hour the river was as flat and clear as a pane of glass. The barge ploughed straight into floating islands of dark green hyacinths that slipped by our hull like some immense dark creature. The sky was grey with violet clouds but the sun was starting to peep through them. I expected another hot day. Gradually, the sun clawed upwards through the broken clouds and the air turned humid and heavy.

A village appeared on the port side at a bend in the river. The engine stopped and about twenty *pirogues,* canoes made from hollowed-out tree trunks, shoved off from the riverbank. They appeared to be attracted to the barges like iron filings to a magnet. The paddlers, both men and women, tied their canoes to the barges' railings then offered their fish and vegetables for sale to the passengers. Some of them hoisted crates of empty beer bottles onto the deck and bought full crates of beer from traders on the barge to take back to their villages. Other canoes served as taxis, ferrying passengers and luggage to and fro.

Two men stood out in the throng. With rapid strokes they paddled their canoe piled high with baskets of dried, blackened fish to the barge, heaved the baskets on board, then paddled quickly back to shore for more. On the deck, a short, barrel-bellied man with iron-grey, frizzy hair kept a tally of the baskets on his clipboard.

To enable passengers to disembark, the helmsman nudged one of the riverboat barges closer to the bank. A crewman lowered a gangplank, but it didn't quite reach hard ground. Passengers were required to roll up their slacks and skirts to slosh through the water and red-brown mud. Both Ann and I wanted to buy fruit in the market so we walked gingerly down the gangplank. I should have removed my sandals because the deep mud almost sucked them off my feet.

We clambered up the embankment to the village. The huts were built of sun-dried clay bricks, branches and palm fronds. At the market stalls, shaded with grass thatch, we filled our knapsacks with bananas, pineapples and papayas.

Ann and I returned to the barge and, like tightrope walkers, wavered and wobbled our way up the gangplank to join Ken on the top deck. After three hours at the village, the horn emitted its throaty sound, calling all passengers aboard and signalling village traders to paddle away from the barges.

At the same time I saw two men on the riverbank leap into a dugout canoe and paddle furiously *towards* the riverboat. They swerved to miss a canoe coming at them but thudded into another one loaded with bottles of beer. A crusty old woman screamed abuse as they quickly backed off. They dug in with their paddles and again surged towards the riverboat, yelling warnings as they forged through the twenty or so canoes that were leaving the barge.

I recognized them as the two paddlers who had rushed baskets of dried fish to the barge. One of them tossed a line to the short, barrel-bellied man on deck who previously was holding the clipboard but now clutched a fist-full of bank notes. He caught the rope but fumbled and dropped it in the water.

The panic-stricken fisherman in the bow of the canoe attempted to throw the line again but lost his balance. He tumbled backwards onto bunches of bananas. His partner in the stern leaned forward to help him up but he dropped his paddle in the river and lost control of the canoe.

The fast flowing current catapulted the flimsy craft towards another boat. The rogue canoe ricocheted from one canoe to another until it lurched out of the traffic jam. The river swept it sideways. The two men, crouching inside, gripped the edges of the canoe. It almost tipped over. The rushing water grabbed it and drove it towards the sprawling branches of a partly submerged tree trunk. The men ducked their heads. The canoe smashed into a branch, jerked sideways, careened towards the trunk and hit it head on. The canoe flipped. The men tumbled into the water, arms and legs flailing. The canoe took off, skimming down the river and around a bend.

The two survivors scrambled along the trunk, crawled over branches and twigs and struggled up the embankment to the village where they collapsed on the ground.

Had the canoe gone for good or did villages along the river have Lost and Found offices?

On the deck of the barge the barrel-bellied man put the money meant for the capsized fishermen in his pocket. With the excitement over, the whistle blew and the riverboat nosed into midstream.

Ken and I strode to the wheelhouse to see the captain about the rebate. We found him there, a heavily muscled man with a woolly Afro hairstyle framing a round, smiling face. Ken explained politely in French that I was requesting a rebate because I wasn't eating their food. I handed my precious, not-to-be-lost passenger ticket to the captain, quickly followed by my special letter. He took my ticket, read my letter without comment and gave it back. He thought for a moment then, in a gruff but friendly voice, said that he'd never been asked for a rebate before but the request seemed reasonable. He offered canned goods to the value of ten dollars. I accepted. It was more than fair. He called his quartermaster and, in rapid-fire Lingala, explained his decision.

The quartermaster was the short, barrel-bellied man with the clipboard. He led me to the padlocked storeroom. Shelves were stocked with numerous crates of beer, familiar looking baskets of dried, blackened fish and a variety of canned food. I selected ten dollars worth of cans: twenty corned beef and ten each of condensed milk and tomato paste. I planned to get cash for my cans by going down to the market on the third class deck and setting up a stall like the locals. But I was thwarted. The chief steward from first class – dark-faced, with chalky-white, shark-like teeth – made a full-price offer I couldn't refuse. Ten dollars. So I sold. Obviously, he could see his way clear to make a profit for himself.

I asked the quartermaster about the two capsized fishermen and their baskets of fish in the storeroom. He explained that the men were contracted to supply fish for the barge. "I'll pay them on the next trip," he said.

At night the riverboat continued its zigzag course down the river. The bar stayed open almost all night, music blared from amplifiers, men and women danced to records that occasionally jumped their damaged tracks, and people got drunk. Life on the river was continuing as normal.

In the daylight hours we stopped at villages but I didn't see any Lost and Found offices. Once a canoe got away, it was probably gone forever.

In the morning of the sixth day the riverboat docked at Kinshasa. I would be on my own again. Ken and Ann were booked to fly out of Kinshasa to Togo. My destination was Timbuktu in Mali which I expected to reach within a couple of months.

The Congo River trip was a unique journey enhanced by meeting Ken and Ann. But my Congo River experience had not yet ended. I still had to leave the wharf area.

The ticket collector was a burly chestnut-coloured man with a sullen, angry look on his face. He was collecting all the used tickets as passengers passed through his gate. I assumed his purpose was to catch stowaways who didn't have tickets. I searched my moneybelt for my ticket. It was missing! The captain must still have it. Should I explain how he got it?

I strode up to the ticket collector.

"Ticket," he growled in French.

"The captain has it," I said in English.

"You have to show me a ticket," he demanded loudly in French.

"I'm sorry, the captain has it!"

I marched on, hoping he wouldn't persist.

Again he bellowed at me.

I didn't catch the name he called me in French...and I didn't go back to ask.

Congo
(Democratic Republic of Congo, formerly Zaire)

Doing business...Congo style

Changing money in Kinshasa, September 1970
See map, page 12, B5

For six days I had travelled by steamer on the Congo River from Kisangani to Kinshasa. Because I was down to my last few coins of local currency, my first business of the day in Kinshasa was to find a bank to cash a travellers cheque. The second was finding a place to stay.

The morning sun bore down, heating the waterlogged air that hung over the river. Perspiration dripped off me as I left the docks and cut through a nose-twitching dump of rotten fruit and decomposing fish. I ploughed through a glut of roadside vendors, their tables brimming with pineapples, sweet bananas, coconuts and spices. The vibrant colours of the women's *pagnes* – clashing reds, oranges and purples – contrasted with the men's muted shades of dark blue, brown or beige slacks, and T-shirts.

After passing stalls with second-hand books, plastic sandals, woven baskets and ivory carvings of knives and masks, I arrived at a tree-lined avenue, Boulevard de 30 Juin. Trucks plied the road, puffing out black diesel fumes that left a revolting odour hanging in the air.

Modern European-style commercial and residential buildings, in various states of disrepair, lined the road. Farther on, I passed tired-looking grey and liver-brown concrete buildings, and billboards advertising motor scooters and skin-lightening cream. From behind a billboard, a mangy black dog crept towards me and growled. I apologized to the bitch for disturbing her, and shuddered. A bite from a rabid dog could have done me in. Thankfully, she just barked at me and slinked away.

I found a bank. Inside its spacious vestibule of varnished woodwork and polished brass railings, a sign pointed upstairs to the foreign exchange department. I stepped up to the teller. His pleasant, ebony face broadened into a welcoming smile.

"I'd like to change a ten-dollar travellers cheque," I said. A few minutes later he came back with three zaires. I had expected five.

"Where's the rest?" I asked.

"There is a standard two-zaire fee whether you cash ten dollars or 100 dollars."

"The charge seems too high," I said. "Is there some way you can lower it?"

"I'll get the manager."

The manager, a roly-poly European with a florid face, strode out of his office, leaned forward over the varnished countertop and, in a low conspiratorial voice said, "You will do better on the street, exchanging on the black market. You won't be charged the two-zaire fee, but be careful who you trade with."

This suggestion from a bank manager seemed most unusual. I thanked him and strolled along the boulevard. Presently two smartly dressed young men in dark trousers, yellow and blue shirts and sunglasses, their faces as black as their shiny shoes, sidled up and asked in French, the *lingua franca* of the Congo, if I wanted to change money. I suggested ten dollars. "Seven zaires for ten dollars," said the one who appeared to be the spokesman. His exchange rate was better than expected. He thrust out his hand for my travellers cheque but I held it tightly and asked to see his money.

"Let's walk down this side street," the spokesman said, "in case we are being watched."

The side street was open and bright so I agreed. I had been in similar situations before. The main unknown factor this time was whether or not they carried knives. I had a strong aversion to knives that weren't of the kitchen variety. If I had doubts about my safety I would've refused the side street.

Legally speaking, exchanging money was only permitted at banks so the government could collect strong currencies, like dollars and pounds, for its own use. Private transactions were illegal but widely practised because hard currency was needed by local businessmen for foreign purchases and travel. They couldn't rely on the State Bank for such funds. The zaire was virtually useless outside the country.

The spokesman raised his wallet close to his face as if to count his money but instead whipped out a business card with a flourish, flashed it before my eyes and yelled triumphantly, "Caught you!" His colleague, with less showmanship, flashed a card which, like the first, zipped by my face too fast for me to read.

The spokesman said in an authoritative voice, "Come to the police station."

My first thought was that they were plainclothes policemen trying to bilk me of some cash to supplement their low incomes, but my gut feeling told me they were just ordinary con men who had no intention of going anywhere near a police station. Deciding to call their bluff, I agreed to go with them to see how this encounter would play out. There was a point in my favour: I had not actually changed any money with them!

The three of us set off along the boulevard but had only walked a block when the spokesman made an offer. "Give us five dollars and we'll let you go."

"I prefer to go to the police station," I said with a smirk.

The concerned looks on their faces convinced me my response took them by surprise. I was getting the better of these minor con men. I suddenly remembered the letter in my moneybelt given to me ten days earlier by the police chief in Goma in eastern Congo. The letter requested that civilian and military authorities help with my travels through the Congo. The letterhead included the words *Police Nationale Congolaise*. This could be my trump card.

"I have a police document," I said as I fumbled in my moneybelt.

The spokesman looked puzzled. "Are you a policeman?"

I didn't answer. Instead, I extracted the page and unfolded it just enough to show the letterhead with the magical words *Police Nationale Congolaise*.

"You *are* a policeman!" the spokesman stammered. He grabbed my hand, pumped it vigorously and blurted, "Please forgive me." His pal also shook my hand. Then the two con men turned their backs and scurried down a side alley.

An hour later I encountered a Greek merchant who changed my travellers cheque. I was pleased with the six and a half zaires he offered me. And he didn't charge a two-zaire service fee!

Ghana

The slave castle

Outwitting officials in Accra, September, 1970

See map, page 12, A4

Without the courtesy of a “good morning” or other pleasant greeting, the burly, dark-faced man thrust his open hand towards me.

“Give me your film,” he demanded, his fingers wiggling at me.

“Why?” I asked. I was taken aback by his aggressive attitude and because he wanted my film.

“You took a picture of the castle.”

Along the 560-kilometre coastline of Ghana, formerly called Gold Coast, a sprinkling of trading forts and castles were built by Europeans after they arrived 500 years ago in search of gold and ivory, and later, slaves.

On the outskirts of the capital, Accra, stood Osu Castle which I wanted to visit. Formerly called Christiansborg Castle, it had an interesting history. Built by the Swedes in 1657, it was taken by the Danes in 1659. They sold it to the Portuguese in 1679 but bought it back in 1682. The British bought it in 1850. At present, it is Ghana’s seat of government and official residence of the President of Ghana.

Early the next morning was a good time to explore on foot because the light overnight rain had lowered the morning temperature to a moderate 23°C. To visit Osu Castle I ambled down to the sandy shore, breathed in the fresh salty air, unstrapped my sandals and strolled along the beach. Frothy tops came in on lazy waves as I passed. I couldn't see the castle from the beach. When I estimated I was close I climbed the rocky, shoreline cliff. By now the sun had risen, heating the land and increasing the humidity. In this waterlogged, tropical climate my shirt stuck to my back.

I was thankful when I reached the top of the cliff. There, across a field, stood the magnificent white monolith of Osu Castle. To photograph it I crouched behind a gnarled tree and used a branch as a frame for my photo. I was trying to be artistic but I felt like a spy lurking behind the tree. I pressed the button on my Yashica but there was no reaction. The film had finished. I put the camera in my bag and dug out my stand-by, a Kodak Instamatic, and took the picture.

I glanced up to see three local men headed straight towards me with purposeful strides. I quickly buried the Kodak in my bag, not wanting them to see I was carrying anything of value, and waited while they came closer.

All three men wore dark suits, white shirts and blank expressions. Probably government bureaucrats from the castle.

The first man to arrive barked: "Give me your film."

I could see no reason to do so. "Why?"

"You took a picture of the castle. It is forbidden because it is a government building."

His two drones buzzed around me menacingly, ready to relieve me of my film at the word from their leader.

I knew that many countries didn't allow photos to be taken of strategic installations like airports, military bases, bridges and port facilities. But Osu Castle? I felt adamant these men had overstepped the mark.

"You can't have my film," I said. "I want to speak to your boss."

We marched across the grassy field, through the open gates of the castle, up a flight of stairs and along a corridor. The place was solidly built. Clean with whitewashed walls. We stopped outside a closed door that had a sign, *Chief of Security*, screwed to it. One of the drones knocked and pushed it open.

A broad-shouldered hulk of a man sat slumped in a tilted chair. The drone explained why I was there. The *Chief of Security* leaned forward, his eyes penetrating and alert.

"Show me your camera," he ordered.

I showed him my Yashica and explained that I was about to take a picture of the castle but the film had finished. I pointed to the counter that indicated 36 exposures had been taken.

"Are you ready to have the film developed by us?" he asked sternly. I sensed he was bluffing. I was ready to bet he didn't have the equipment to develop the film.

I played along with his bluff. "Yes, you can have it developed if you wish, but you won't see a picture of the castle on the film."

The Chief appeared satisfied and slumped back into his tilted chair. "You may go," he said.

I was thankful he didn't order me to show the contents of my shoulder bag. The Kodak camera would have raised questions. And I felt relieved the Chief was more interested in relaxing in his tilted chair than he was in me.

That afternoon I wandered into a bookshop in Accra and flipped through some postcards.

Among them: Osu Castle.

Seventeen years later, in March 1987, I was again travelling in Ghana, this time with my wife, Penny. We were standing on the grassy median of a busy street in Accra, taking photos of the general life of the city. Suddenly I heard a shout. A policeman and a soldier were rushing towards us. I glanced over my shoulder to see who they were running after. It didn't take long to get an answer.

The policeman arrived first, panting and wheezing. "Give me your film," he demanded.

"Why?" I asked, surprised by this sudden order.

"You took a picture of the bank. It is forbidden. It is a government building."

The soldier arrived moments later and watched passively. He was probably a rural boy, still learning the opportunistic ways of the city. I had already suspected the policeman of having extortion on his mind.

Penny stepped forward. "Where's the bank?"

The policeman pointed down the hill to a collection of

buildings about three blocks away. "The blue building is the bank," he said. Penny and I could barely make out the blue gable of a building nestled between many others. He spoke again. "Give me your film or we go to the police station."

He was bluffing. He wanted us to pay him *dash* – a bribe – to let us go.

"All right," I said, calling his bluff. "Let's go to the police station."

Recalling my earlier experience I said: "I know the *Chief of Security* at Osu Castle. We should go there."

The policeman didn't move. To take into custody a friend of the *Chief of Security* would not bode well for the policeman. In a sudden conciliatory tone he said: "You need a permit to take pictures. Do you have one?"

"No."

He hailed a taxi and said to us: "You must get one from the tourist office which is a long way from here."

We left the policeman and the soldier standing on the roadside while we were whisked by cab to the tourist office. I asked the female desk clerk for a permit. "There aren't any printed permits, nor any brochures," she told us as she wrote a list of people and places we could not photograph: soldiers, police, power installations, broadcasting installations, the harbour, the airport and, of course, Osu Castle.

There was no mention of banks!

Mali

Timbuktu, where are you?

By boat and truck to Timbuktu, October 1970

See map, page 12, A4

I sweated and shivered, tossed and turned on the hard mattress. A fever in Mopti wasn't in my plans.

I suffered alone in a hut (stone walls, reed roof) rented for a dollar from the hotel next door. This fever could spell the end of the line for me. And I hadn't yet reached my objective – Timbuktu. My plan was to travel to the fabled city by riverboat along the Niger River. My route so far had been by train from Abidjan on West Africa's coast to Bobo Dioulasso in Burkina Faso, then by passenger-truck and bush-taxi to Mopti.

Mopti, in the West African Republic of Mali, is situated at the confluence of the Niger and Bani Rivers. It is dominated by a tall-towered mosque, an architectural wonder of sun-dried mud that dates back 800 years. One-storey mud-brick buildings lined the sandy streets.

Along the waterfront, brightly painted motorized *pirogues* (canoes) bobbed in the river. The riverside market bustled with people of different ethnic groups: Fulani, Tuareg and Bozo. They haggled over goats, sheep, fish, salt, brightly patterned fabrics, raw cotton, woven reed mats and baskets, and produce such as rice, sorghum, millet, corn and peanuts.

I had to get rid of my fever!

I flung the top sheet from the bed. My soggy, sweat-stained

clothes clung to my skin. I peeled them off and became as cold as an iceberg. I trembled. I wrested a dry shirt from my backpack and slipped it on, then pulled the sheet back over me. I struggled for breath, my mouth parched. I reached for my water canteen, gulped a cupful, then groped in my backpack for aspirin. I swallowed one, then another and hoped those magical white pills would break the fever.

Was it malaria, dengue fever, sleeping sickness, yellow fever, typhoid fever, blackwater fever, diphtheria, tick fever? I prayed fervently that I didn't have any of them. I was travelling alone and had no one to call upon for help. I dozed again and plunged into a nightmare in which I was an architect told to redesign Mopti.

"Knock down the hundreds of flat-roofed, mud-brick buildings," boomed a voice in my dream, "and replace them with skyscrapers built with stone blocks." I woke up sweating and shuddering, overwhelmed by the enormity of the task.

What had I eaten or drunk to cause this? Was it that bottle of questionable liquid I bought from a street vendor? Grave mistake! I should have popped a water-purifying tablet into the bottle.

I rolled off the mattress, stumbled to the door and pushed it open. Bright sunlight stung my eyes. I shut the door and flopped back onto the bed.

How long had I been down with the fever? I checked the date and time on my watch. Thirty-six hours!

I nibbled on crackers and rested for a few hours more. The fever began to break and I felt better. I pushed open the door and wandered outside, dazed and starving. On my way to the riverside vegetable market I heard someone call out, "Have you seen the other American?" In Mali, most foreigners are called American.

"No, I'll watch for him," I heard myself say weakly.

A double-decked riverboat, the *Liberté* – about one hundred feet long – was tied up at the riverside. The hull had oxidized. It looked like an old rusty tub. Which it was! I knew this was the boat that sailed along the Niger River to Timbuktu. I asked a crewman when it was leaving.

"In four days," he said.

I didn't want to miss my chance to get to the fabled city; it could be a week or two or even longer before another boat left. With the thought of finally reaching Timbuktu, I could feel myself getting better.

"The boat looks pretty old," I said to the shipping clerk as I forked over my fare for fourth class.

"It's long past retirement age," he said as he handed me a ticket for the 35-hour trip. Fourth class relegated me to sleep on the roof. Food wasn't mentioned on the ticket, unlike first, second and third classes. That suited me, because I carried my own rations.

By the departure date my strength and appetite had improved. I humped my backpack to the dock as the Saharan sun edged downwards, changing from sandy yellow to orange. It was dusk by the time I climbed the iron ladder to the fourth class passengers' roof.

I heard laughter and found half a dozen locals sitting in a circle, chewing and sucking on chunks of roasted meat. With them was a fair-haired man. I guessed he was the American. My spirits leapt. Someone who spoke English! He rose to his feet and greeted me with a firm handshake and a jovial smile. He stood tall and athletic and sported a mustache that drooped over the sides of his mouth. His name was Rick, a Peace Corps volunteer on vacation from his teaching job in Ghana. He was my age, late twenties.

He and the others had bought the meat from a dockside vendor. One of the Africans offered me a piece – it was goat – spicy and tough. My molars got a good workout.

The engine chattered and groaned and the horn sounded its farewell. Rick and I slipped into our sleeping bags while the Africans wrapped their blankets around themselves, from head to toe.

I looked up into the heavens. Innumerable stars sparkled like diamonds on black velvet. The magical charm of Africa washed over me. Then I drifted off to sleep.

I awoke when the sun's first rays started to gild the wide expanse of river. The water was high and overlapped the river banks, flooding the flat marshlands. The *Liberté* stayed a course that avoided marsh reeds poking above the water level. The morning was cool but I felt the temperature rising with the sun.

We stopped at a village where most of the women wore turquoise-blue cotton skirts. They waded out to the boat, balancing calabashes on their heads. From my vantage point on the roof, I could see that the gourds were full of sour milk, which they hoped to sell to the passengers. Some women carried baskets of dried fish to be sold to the quartermaster. Perhaps the main course for passengers in first, second and third?

We pulled in at other villages strung out along the banks of the broad river. A feature of each settlement was the minaret of the mosque that peeked over the rooftops. The homes of mud, sticks and grass were flat-roofed. Around them, in the sand, scrubby vegetation struggled to survive. Beyond the homes the land gradually surrendered fertility until everything was a brownish cream. *Pirogues* pitched and rolled gently at the water's edge. Men and women paddled to the *Liberté,* gathering like bees around a honey pot to trade their dried fish and sour milk.

Another night on the roof and thirty-five hours after leaving Mopti we docked at Kabara, the port for Timbuktu. The fabled city once sat on the bank of the Niger River, but decades of wind whipping across the Sahara pushed the river ten miles south.

Rick and I followed other passengers and piled into the back of a taxi-truck. We crammed together. With a sudden burst of acceleration the truck took off, spraying gravel before it hit the deep ripples and ruts in the road to Timbuktu. Desert surrounded us – a plain of yellowish white sand devoid of any landmark except the tire tracks we were following. The desert went on forever, receding into a sandy haze on the horizon. The vehicle's shock absorbers were useless so I reached up and grabbed a roof bar while Rick sat on his hands to absorb the bumps. I still felt slightly nauseous from the fever.

The other passengers were a mixed bunch. Beside Rick sat a copper-skinned woman. Her gold nose ring and dangling gold earrings, supported by a head strap, identified her as Fulani, a tribal group that specialized in raising cattle. She wore a long, multicoloured cotton skirt with a head wrap to match. Many Fulani had moved to towns, taking up sedentary occupations. It was believed they migrated from North Africa, as did the Tuareg, hundreds of years ago. Next to her sat a Tuareg, a tall, fine-boned man with tan-coloured skin. He wore a long, dark blue robe with a white turban wound around his head. Tuaregs depended on camel, sheep and goat herds for their livelihood.

Twenty minutes after leaving Kabara I spotted low buildings on the horizon. Timbuktu!

My pulse rate quickened. For years I had dreamt of visiting Timbuktu, the world's most famous oasis, the once-great city that now sat in the midst of sand.

The taxi-truck nosed along narrow streets to the town centre, passing a couple of wells where townspeople drew water for their homes. Donkeys carried bricks and sticks on their backs and goats foraged for anything edible. Timbuktu, with its low-rise buildings of sun-dried mud bricks, looked like Mopti's twin sister.

It wasn't long before a boy materialized, introduced himself as Mohammed, and led us to a restaurant proprietor who had rooms to rent. As the man showed us a room I suddenly ducked. Two black shapes streaked over my shoulder. Bats! I didn't like the idea of sleeping in a room with bats. They can carry rabies, the last thing I needed on top of a fever. The proprietor assured us they wouldn't come back while we were there. I glanced around the room. The walls, ceiling and floor were made of sun-dried mud, dusty to the touch. Reed mats covered the sandy floor. Two beds almost filled the room. Electric wires poked aimlessly out of a wall, but the biggest surprise was the modern refrigerator standing in the corner. I opened the door; the fridge was humming, making ice cubes.

Despite the bats and dust we took a chance and rented the room. The fridge made our decision easy and induced us to buy half a dozen bottles of *Flag Lager.*

The next thing to think about was lunch.

In the restaurant's dining area a hole had been scooped out of the sandy floor for a fire pit. The cook grilled shish-kebabs over charcoal, and boiled spaghetti. Sand and dust blew in from outside. It was relentless. It found its way into our ears and up our nostrils.

Although we couldn't see the dust it found its way into the food. We chewed crunchy kebabs and slurped slithery, gritty spaghetti.

Our young helper, Mohammed, came in to see us. "Can I show you around Timbuktu?" he asked in French.

"What will you show us?" I asked.

"Many things. But first a mosque."

We finished our lunch and followed him into the street where all was quiet. Nothing moved except the mercury in the thermometer. It had risen past 100 degrees. In the shade! Mohammed led us along dusty alleyways to the mosque built in the thirteenth century out of mud and wooden poles.

The poles protruded horizontally from the walls of the minaret, providing permanent scaffolds for the masons who slapped more mud on the walls after a rainfall.

We removed our shoes, as was customary, and entered. We encountered a white-robed *muezzin* who hurried towards us. Mohammed suddenly vanished. The *muezzin*, the holy man who called the faithful to prayer five times daily, would allow us to climb the minaret for an overview of the city. He said that Mohammed was an unlicensed guide who should not be receiving *baksheesh*, a tip, for showing us the mosque.

"But you can pay me," he said, as he thrust out his palm.

We climbed the spiralling stairs inside the minaret. From the top we looked down upon one- and two-storey flat-roofed homes, slapped together with mud bricks. Virtually all the homes were built around open-air courtyards, most of which were occupied by families going about their daily chores of cooking and laundering. A labyrinth of narrow sandy lanes snaked through the hodgepodge of homes. There didn't seem to be any plan to the city's crooked streets.

We reunited with Mohammed outside the mosque. He led us to the workshops of tradespeople. A woman in a purple *pagne* was selling clay pots she had made. They were used in homes and shops to store water. Nearby, a blacksmith hammered a piece of red hot iron into a hoe. A fellow blacksmith pounded an iron rod.

"What are you making?" I asked.

"A part for a Land Rover."

Over the years, adventurers had driven Land Rovers across the Sahara to Timbuktu. Blacksmiths learned a lot about those sturdy vehicles when asked to manufacture replacement parts for on-the-spot repairs.

Also in the workshops, we watched a Tuareg leatherworker hand-sew a scabbard for a 31-inch straight sword owned by a fellow tribal member. Tuareg swords and daggers were once the most feared weapons in the Sahara.

From roofed stalls in the open-air food market, vendors competed for customers for their millet, sorghum, corn, rice, peanuts, salt, hides and cotton.

The animal market enclosure was a moving mass of lowing cattle, and bleating sheep and goats. The odour of feces and urine, drying on sun-warmed pebbles and sand, floated in the dry air.

I savoured the sights, sounds and smells of the fabled city. I could hardly believe I was here. As a youngster I understood Timbuktu didn't exist, that it was only a figure of speech to denote a distant place.

We followed Mohammed along empty alleys. To escape the overbearing sun, people had taken refuge in their homes. The pace of life was slow for the 15,000 inhabitants, down from the 100,000 who lived here during its heady days 500 years ago. Around a bend we bumped into a woman who immediately greeted us with a cheery hello. Her accent was English. She held a clipboard.

Fiftyish and greying, she wore well-tailored khaki slacks and blouse and matching cloth hat.

I was surprised to see her in this narrow alley. After we introduced ourselves, I asked: "What do you think of Timbuktu?"

"It's dirty, dry and dusty, and I'm sure it has lost its spark. As an anthropologist, I think it's a fascinating place. It has an exciting history, being at the crossroads of different cultures."

"What are you doing here?" I asked.

"I'm sketching the routes of the alleyways. My specialty is urban-planning. It's more than a daunting task, it's a nightmare," she confided.

I felt a sudden kinship. She reminded me of my feverish nightmare. I told her about it. She laughed at the absurdity of the skyscrapers. We commiserated over the difficulties we faced, both real and imagined – hers of mapping Timbuktu, mine of rebuilding Mopti.

Under Mohammed's guidance we continued to explore the city that was founded by nomadic Tuaregs as a trading post in the eleventh century. We learned that a woman named Buktu used to water her camels at the *tim* – the well. The place became known as Timbuktu (Buktu's well).

By the fifteenth century, it had grown into a city and had become one of the most famous centres of Islamic scholarship in the entire Muslim world. Islam had flowed out of Saudi Arabia in the seventh century and spread like a brush fire across North Africa and south across the Sahara. West African traders who converted to Islam received favourable trading terms. When an African chief was converted to Islam, he would order his entire clan to be converted. Both actions assisted the spread of Islam.

The fabled city displays nothing of its former grandeur of the 1500s. Gone are the days when it thrived as a commercial centre with lavishly decorated homes of well-to-do merchants. Timbuktu was where the camel met the canoe. Arab camel caravans from the north crossed the desert with cloth, tea, spices, sugar, salt and weapons. African traders from the south transported their goods of gold and slaves along the Niger River. In the 1600s, when European nations started trading along the West African coast for gold, ivory and slaves, trade turned away from Timbuktu, causing its decline as a trading centre.

Rumours had been rife in Europe about a fabulously wealthy city in West Africa, thriving in the middle of nowhere. But, no one had been to Timbuktu to report on it. Explorers were eager to find the city, supposedly dripping in gold.

One of the first Europeans to try was Mungo Park, a Scottish doctor. He left Gambia in 1805 with a party of more than three dozen men. Most of them died of fever; others deserted. Park rafted along the Niger River but drowned before he reached his goal.

Next to try was another Scot, Major Gordon Laing. He crossed the Sahara from the north and arrived in 1826. He wrote in his journal he wasn't impressed with the city of mud buildings. Two days after leaving Timbuktu he was killed by desert tribesmen.

The third to try was a Frenchman, René Caillié. His journey took a year, five months of which he suffered with a fever. Poor guy! Life must have been hell. He also suffered foot problems. To rest and allow his foot sores to heal, he traded a pair of scissors as rent for a hut (mud walls, straw roof). Eventually, in 1828, he reached Timbuktu. He also wasn't impressed by the decaying city, as he recorded in his journal. He spent two weeks seeing the sights then headed home to write a book.

A German geographer, Heinrich Barth, was next in line. He crossed the Sahara from the north with two companions, Richardson and Overweg. They all suffered from fever, the scourge of West Africa. It seemed to be one of the prices to pay to get to the mysterious city. His two buddies died but Barth reached Timbuktu in 1853. He recorded in his journal he wasn't impressed with the city. Barth also made it back to Europe and wrote a book of his adventures.

I, too, wasn't impressed by the city of mud-walled buildings in their monochromatic browns and beiges. Or with the way dust and sand crept into food, clothes and nostrils, and the intense heat that sapped one's strength.

However, now that my fever had passed I could think rationally. Timbuktu's fame as a mysterious city had made it special but it exuded an atmosphere that was difficult to define. It could be described as full of decay and abandonment. I followed narrow, crooked lanes that went nowhere in particular. I got the feeling the city wasn't wanted anymore, that it had outlived its usefulness.

Because Timbuktu would forever hold a fascination for me, maybe it was time for me, like some others, to head home with my journals. To write a book.

Mali

Beyond Timbuktu

By camel into the desert, October 1970
See map, page 12, A4

Rick – six feet and tanned, brown hair and a mustache that drooped over the sides of his mouth – was my travelling companion. We had met on the *Liberté*, a riverboat that plied between Mopti and Timbuktu on the Niger River in Mali.

Rick and I took refuge in our hotel room from Timbuktu's afternoon sun, an orb of molten silver that glowed in the hazy, dust-laden sky. The dust had been stirred up by hot winds from the Sahara Desert.

A bonus that came with our room in Timbuktu was the refrigerator. As I reached into the fridge for a *Flag Lager* I heard a rap on the door. Mohammed, the teenager who led us to our hotel, sauntered in and asked if we wanted to rent camels.

"Where can we go?" I asked.

"Into the desert. You can visit a sheik and his wives."

A camel trek into the world's largest desert sounded challenging. "How much?" I asked.

"Eight hundred francs each." (About three dollars.)

We agreed, and met with Mohammed an hour later. In his beige shorts and shirt he blended well into the surroundings. He introduced us to Said (pronounced Say-eed), a Tuareg, a striking figure in a dark blue robe and indigo turban whose two camels were tethered to stakes near a well. At that moment the voice of a *muezzin*, a Muslim holy man, boomed over a loudspeaker from the minaret of the mosque, calling the faithful to prayer. Mohammed and Said excused themselves to pray, leaving us with an opportunity to get acquainted with the one-humped beasts of burden.

The dromedaries' humps were high, full of fat, a sign of good health. When food was scarce they could draw from their humps. While they were chewing thistles and grass, they displayed a row of strong lower teeth stained a slimy green. A good flossing was long overdue. They didn't have any upper front teeth which was normal in camels. Only a broad plate of hard gum. In the back were teeth used for grinding. The beasts needed a good mouth wash, or at least a squirt of air freshener to get rid of their foul smell.

About ten minutes later Mohammed and Said returned. Mohammed suggested we take a bag of sugar to the sheik and his wives as a gift. We bought sugar and put it in a pannier on my camel's flank and hooked a goatskin of water onto each saddle. Fortunately, we didn't have to worry about water for the camels as they can go without liquid for up to nine days.

The two camels, emitting noisy gurgles, sat sprawled on the sand. Mohammed said he'd give us a riding lesson before we left. As we mounted our steeds, they protested with deep-throated roars. We told them to cool it as we settled into our saddles on top of the humps. The underside of each wood-framed saddle was cushioned with a piece of old carpet to protect the camel's hump, while a sheepskin pad on top of the saddle made it comfortable for the rider.

My legs flopped aimlessly as my feet searched for stirrups, but there weren't any. A bit disconcerting!

Mohammed pointed to the base of the camel's curved neck. "Stretch your legs out and place your feet there," he said.

With my feet in position I held on to the front saddle-post and the low, wooden backrest to stop from falling. At a word from Mohammed I leaned forward, and the camel got the message to rise. It stretched its back legs almost fully. This manouevre threw me forward, forcing me to look directly down at the ground. With both hands I gripped the saddle tighter. The animal got off its front knees to stand. In doing so it jerked me skywards until I sat perched nine feet above the ground. I watched as Rick's camel thrust him into the air.

Mohammed continued with the driving lesson. To make it walk, I was to press my feet against the back of its neck. To stop, pull on the rein. To make it gallop, press hard against the back of its neck. I wasn't ready to gallop yet, if ever!

With all these instructions to confuse us, we were ready to go.

In mid-afternoon our party of four trekked north from Timbuktu into the parched landscape. Mohammed and Said each held onto a camel's single rein – a rope tied around its bottom jaw. Their holding the reins was imperative. They knew where we were going; we didn't. And we lacked driving experience.

Perched high on the hump, I was able to appreciate the immensity of the desert. I imagined I was in the Crow's Nest on my 'ship-of-the-desert' as it pitched and rolled across the sea of sand.

Our guides led the plodding camels up and over sand dunes and around thorny scrub to the rocky desert. I had a fleeting ambition to be a camel driver so I asked Mohammed to pass up my rein. To urge my dromedary forward I shouted highly motivational phrases like 'giddy-up!' and 'yee-haw!' Nothing happened until I pressed my foot against the back of its neck. It responded immediately – quicker than I expected. It loped forward, a mass of hooves, head and hump. Said also passed Rick's rein to him. As his camel barreled past mine, it leaned over and nipped my camel in the neck. Road rage? The last thing I wanted was a camel fight, with Rick and me teetering on top.

I felt a wave of motion sickness as I pitched and rolled out of control. Mohammed and Said sprinted after us, caught the reins, soothed the beasts, then handed the reins back to us. I waved mine away. "You lead the camel, Mohammed. You know the way." Rick did the same. Neither of us wanted another wild ride.

Ahead lay a panorama of never-ending shades of brown and yellow. I became aware of the sounds of the desert: the crunch of our guides' sandals on the pebbles and sand, the occasional squeak of the saddle, the whine of the wind as it blew around thorn bushes, the swish of the camels' broad, cushioned feet as they swept through the soft, hot sand, and a variety of hisses and gurgles that were probably our camels discussing the idiots on their humps. Desert travel was noisier than I expected.

After an hour lurching to and fro, little-used muscles started to protest. I had to stay alert, perched on my saddle in the sky. It was a long way down if I dozed and fell. We ambled by the sun-bleached skeleton of a camel, a reminder that the desert can be a killer.

The sun, a silver disc still glowing, beat down on us. A cold beer would be welcome but a cup of tea would be almost as good.

We plodded over a flat, rocky region then entered a scrubby area where goats roamed freely. A camel tethered to a stake uttered a short, roaring noise. A friendly greeting in camel-talk or a challenge? I wasn't sure. Our guides took no chances; they gripped the reins in case of trouble.

A man in a blue robe appeared. His leathery face, bristling with short grey whiskers, was etched with deep valleys from his years in the desert. Judging by his blue robe the man was a Tuareg pastoralist who herded his scrawny goats in the incessant search for vegetation. Goatskin bags made good water containers. He had about thirty future goatskin bags ambling and gamboling around. As for the meat, it was savoured on special occasions.

We followed him to his rustic home of palm-fibre mats draped over a framework of saplings. It was about six feet high and twenty feet long. When it was time to seek better pasture, the lightweight home could be dismantled and loaded onto his camel in just two hours.

We sat cross-legged on palm-fibre mats in the shade of acacia bushes that had struggled out of the sandy ground.

A woman in a black robe, the customary Tuareg dress for women, emerged carrying a pot of water. My eyes settled on the oldest face I'd ever seen. Her dark, leathery skin was lined as deep as a dry *wadi*. Milky cataracts veiled her deep-set eyes. Her wrinkled, skeletal hands struck a match under a few twigs in a fire pit. She added dried camel dung and within minutes water was boiling for tea.

Among desert dwellers, the etiquette was to offer tea first to visitors, then talk. The woman in black brought tea leaves, our gift of sugar, small glasses, and hot water in a brass kettle blackened by many years of use. She retreated into the home to leave the men to drink tea and talk. Our host cleaned each glass by pouring in a little hot tea then rubbing his long bony finger around the rim. I hoped my immune system was in working order.

We discussed the health of his camel and goats, and the loss of trees in the region for which he was partly responsible. I thought it amusing we all spoke in French, a language not one of us could speak properly. Rick's knowledge was limited, with mine on a par. Our host saved the day by suggesting entertainment. He clapped his hands towards the makeshift home. Six women emerged, one by one, all dressed in the customary shapeless black cloaks. Mohammed leaned towards us and whispered, "The sheik's women."

I didn't try to guess their ages. Their complexions had suffered wear and tear from the dry, desert air that aged their skin prematurely. They gathered in a line on the sand – the dance floor – and warmed us up with a short vocal, sung in high-pitched voices. "A love story," breathed Mohammed.

Their loud, shrill voices were hard on my ears and it was a relief when they ended their song. We clapped to show our appreciation.

The next offering was an instrumental, played by a smiling lady with beautifully slender fingers and a glorious set of broken teeth. She played an *anzad*, a leather-covered calabash strung with horsehair. She drew a bow across the strings, violin-like, and produced a whining sound. "Lost love," said Mohammed.

After a few bars of woeful music I thought she was going to call it quits. But no, she ripped into a bright, up-tempo number that got her pals jumping. They stomped barefoot in the sand, clapped their hands, swayed their hips and sang with gusto.

The sheik didn't applaud but I thought it was great. I clapped with enthusiasm and almost jumped up to give a standing ovation.

The women reverted to another high pitched, ear-punishing love song. I'd had enough. I caught Rick's eye. "How do we say 'No more, thank you'?"

"I think our clapping has been a signal for them to

continue singing," Rick said. "Let's not clap next time." It worked. They stopped.

The lull was broken by the arrival of a camel and rider. The visitor, resplendent in flowing blue robes and an ink-blue turban, dismounted, bid *salaam* (peace), unbuckled his sword scabbard and sat down on the mat beside us.

He slaked his thirst from his goatskin water bag, then accepted a glass of our host's tea. The women retreated into the humble home.

Conversation then became more difficult. The visitor didn't understand French and the sheik seemed frustrated trying to translate everything into the Tuareg language. Dusk was approaching, making it an opportune time to leave. We rose, thanked the sheik for his hospitality, shook hands and bid *salaam*. We left the family to get on with their lives. They all seemed content even though the sheik appeared to be camel-dung poor. It was not an existence I would choose for myself, but I was thankful for the peek into their way of life.

On our ships-of-the-desert we rocked and rolled our way back to Timbuktu, and to the refrigerator for a couple of cold ones.

USA

Coffee and doughnuts

Thumbing a ride, Virginia to Miami, January 1971

See map, page 11, B2

It was midday and a bone-chilling 40 degrees Fahrenheit – a far cry from the 100°F I experienced in Timbuktu three months earlier. Since then I had made my way to North America by plane, train and ship. Cold winds tormented me. I was standing on the shoulder of Interstate 95 hitchhiking from Virginia to the warmth of Miami, 900 miles to the south. I was relieved when a big, brown Dodge slowed to a stop. "Can you drive?" the man asked. I told him yes.

"That's good. Get in," he said. "I'm trying to make Miami by this time tomorrow. We can share the driving. Okay? The name's Howie."

Howie was a big guy, round-faced, fiftyish and overweight. From his rapid way of talking he gave the impression of authority. Howie was a man in a hurry. He hadn't shaved that morning. On the console sat an empty coffee cup and a half-eaten doughnut. My wish was to reach warmer climes as soon as possible. I was willing to share the driving as I didn't want him to fall asleep at the wheel.

I climbed in and brushed an empty doughnut carton from the passenger seat to the floor. I was thankful for the warmth from the heater.

Under the hood were more than 300 horses that carried us south through the Carolinas, Georgia and into northern Florida. Feeling saddle sore, we halted at an all-night diner for breakfast.

Howie ordered hot cakes – a short stack – while I chose eggs.

With her pen poised to write down my order the waitress asked: "How do you want them? Scrambled, fried, boiled or poached?"

"Fried," I said, to keep my order simple.

"How would you like them?" she asked, and rattled off the choices: "Sunnyside up, over easy, over hard or blindfolded?" These terms were new to me, a recently arrived Australian.

"Blindfolded," I said, without knowing what it meant. My two eggs arrived, sunnyside up with the two yolks a darkened yellow after having been basted, or blindfolded, with the cooking oil.

After we'd paid our bills, Howie strode straight to the take-away counter and ordered two coffees to go, and a dozen honey-glazed doughnuts. "My favourites," Howie said. "Something to eat while we're on the road."

Back on Interstate 95 we passed signs indicating turnoffs to Daytona Beach, Cape Canaveral, Melbourne, West Palm Beach. As we entered Miami I told Howie my plan was to find an employment agency. We drifted along some main streets, watching for signs as we munched on honey-glazed doughnuts.

"There's a sign," Howie said. "Stand-By Labor."

I felt elated that I'd soon be earning a few dollars.

Howie stopped in front of the office. He looked pleased. "We made it in 24 hours. There are two doughnuts left. You take them."

I protested.

"It's lunchtime," he said.

"They're your favourites," I said. "I'll just take one."

"Okay." We shook hands with sticky fingers.

I went inside the office and approached the desk clerk, a skinny guy with a sad mustache.

"I'm looking for work," I said.

"Let me see your Social Insurance card."

"I don't have one."

"I can't give you a job unless you have one. You should go to the Immigration office and apply."

I didn't feel confident but I went to the office and faked a Texan drawl to ask for an application form.

I filled out the basics: name and date of birth. When I got to "Place of Birth" I pondered awhile. If I wrote Melbourne, Australia it could ruin my chances of getting a card so I just wrote Melbourne, expecting the clerk to think Melbourne, Florida.

I dropped my form into the lady's IN basket and waited.

Ten minutes later she called my name. As I walked to the counter I realized that my immediate future was out of my hands. It all depended on what the clerk decided about my application.

"I need to see some ID," she said.

I handed her my International Driving Permit and passport.

"I see you're from Melbourne. Was that Florida or Australia?"

"Australia," I said meekly, believing my chance for getting a Social Security card was over.

"Take a seat," she said.

Five minutes later I heard my name called and I stepped up to the counter.

"Mister Jennings," said the lady, "here are your passport, Driving Permit and Social Security card. Have a nice day."

Elated, I bounced along the sidewalk to the employment agency. The clerk told me I could have a job that night sorting and stacking newspapers in the Miami Herald building. I often dreamed of working for a newspaper. Writing is what I had in mind, not sorting and stacking papers. My first newspaper job, however, was to start at the bottom of the ladder. With eight other part-time workers I laboured from eight-thirty p.m. to five a.m. with thirty minutes for "lunch" and cleared $10.68 after tax. Not a huge sum, but my co-workers told me about some inexpensive places to stay in Miami: the Salvation Army and the Miami Rescue Mission.

At four p.m. the next day I arrived at the Salvation Army hostel and joined a lineup for accommodation. One by one, men were allocated a bunk. I was next in the line but my luck ran out. To my dismay the hostel was now full, but, I had a Plan B: run to the Mission.

I hurried to the Miami Rescue Mission and stood in line. The man ahead of me told me the Mission could accommodate 120 men. He spoke with an articulate, cultured voice. Who was he? He had a ruddy complexion and his dark hair was tinged at the sides with grey. He wore a charcoal-grey double-breasted overcoat, stained and rumpled, a few sizes too big for him.

At the reception desk he paid a dollar for a bunk and trudged upstairs. He seemed to know his way around. The clerk at the desk asked me for ID. I showed him my passport and a Norwegian Seaman's identity card – a card issued to me when I worked my passage on a Norwegian freighter from Sydney to Oslo two years earlier.

"A foreign seaman," the clerk said in a patronizing but friendly tone. "We'll give you the first night for free." He handed me a slip of paper with a bunk number and I climbed the stairs to the spacious dormitory. On the bunk beside mine lay the familiar double-breasted overcoat. Its owner was sorting through an overnight bag. He looked up.

"Been here before?" he asked.

"No. I'm just passing through."

"You're lucky."

I searched his face and saw a blank look of defeat.

He told me his name was Max and that he'd been a lawyer. After his wife died his life went downhill, and with it, his law practice. On most days he was too deep into his wine to care about anything. He was only fifty-six.

At five p.m. a staff member called everyone to the Mission's large meeting room to attend a church service.

Dozens of men drifted in: young and old, tall and short, fat and thin, bearded and clean-shaven, talkative and quiet. They wore clothes in various states of disrepair: trousers with rope strung through belt loops, shirts with missing buttons, T-shirts and jeans, stained baseball caps, boots, sandals, and runners laced with string.

Some of the older men slumped in the many pews. Their heads lolled, mouths hung open, eye-lids drooped halfway. Gradually everyone in the room was seated in pews, on couches and in chairs that had been pushed against the back wall. I felt fortunate that to stay here was my choice, unlike many of the others who appeared destitute with few or any options.

Everyone faced the stage at the front of the room. A family of three sisters in their twenties sang a rousing "When the saints go marching in" with a fourth sister accompanying them on guitar. After the performance, the guitarist took the microphone and explained how her life had been meaningless until she found Jesus. The next people to perform were a black man and woman who sang foot-stomping spirituals and finished with a loud "Hallelujah."

The office manager stepped up to the stage, announced a 90-day Rehabilitation Scheme for Alcoholics, then said that dinner was ready in the adjoining room.

We stood at long, high counters to eat our dinner of stew-like vegetable soup and thick slices of brown bread. It was enough to fortify me until the next day. The meal was topped off with coffee and plain doughnuts.

I thought of Howie. He would've enjoyed the coffee. And the doughnuts. But only if they'd been honey-glazed!

Jamaica

Beyond the call of duty

By train and bus through Jamaica, January 1971
See map, page 11, C3

The nose of the Boeing 707 dipped in preparation for landing at Jamaica's Montego Bay airport. Next to me sat Steve, florid-faced, sandstone-haired, early twenties, on his first trip outside the U.S.A.

We had met a couple of days earlier when our backpacks almost collided as we skirted around pedestrians on a busy Miami street. After the usual backpacker questions of "Where have you been?" and "Where are you going?" we discovered we were both heading for the Caribbean. Over a cup of coffee at McDonald's, we sketched a route map on the back of a paper napkin. Deciding to team up, we set off for an airline office.

After a smooth landing we went through Immigration and Customs and started our walk to the town of Montego Bay. Suddenly, Steve felt his pocket. "My airline ticket's missing!"

He frantically dug into all his pockets and backpack. I checked my pockets without success.

"We've got to go back," Steve said. "I bet I left it at Immigration when they asked me to show an onward ticket."

Immigration didn't have it so Steve reported the loss to an airline representative. "It'll take two days to get permission to issue another ticket," said the rep.

As the more experienced traveller, I should have told Steve of my self-imposed rule. When leaving an office, restaurant, park bench or whatever, I always look behind me, to be sure I haven't forgotten anything.

In the cool of early evening we relaxed on the beach, poring over a map of Jamaica. We decided to visit Cambridge and Ocho Rios while waiting for his ticket to be reissued. Then we lazily watched the gentle waves lap the sand. An hour later, the orange sun slipped beneath the dark water.

As we sat on the beach, two local men in their early twenties swaggered towards us.

One with a knapsack slung over his shoulder told us they wanted to be our friends. An enigmatic smile fluttered on his dark lips. Steve quickly said "Sure" but then shot a sideways glance at me. My defence mechanism had already kicked in as the intruders flopped beside us on the sand. From past experience I had learned that young locals who say they want to be my friend sometimes have an ulterior motive.

We chatted with the Jamaicans, amicably but guardedly. They were edgy and laughed a lot, trying too hard to be friendly. After a while one of them left. The one with the knapsack stretched out on the sand, put his bag under his head to make a pillow, and appeared to be getting ready to spend the night.

Steve and I had planned to sleep on the beach, but I felt distinctly uncomfortable when I detected a sly expression in our intruder's beady, half-closed eyes. I didn't trust him, and sensed that Steve didn't either. We picked up our backpacks, said goodbye and crossed the beach road, looking back to make sure we weren't being followed. A trail led us to a grassy field dotted with low bushes. By lying down among the scrub we couldn't be seen from the road. I rolled up my jacket and placed it under my head as a pillow, slipped a backpack strap over my arm and another around my leg. Then I settled down for the night.

In the morning Steve discovered his backpack was missing. His spirits plummeted.

"No wonder I've been robbed. Look where I hung my jacket! On the bush! So everyone can see it." He was devastated. I felt sorry for him. I should have mentioned some basic security measures like attaching backpack straps to one's legs or arms.

"First, I lose my airline ticket, now my backpack. What else can go wrong?" Steve was not a happy camper!

"Let's search the area," I said.

Within minutes Steve found his backpack with the contents intact except for his camera, tent and travellers cheques. He was shaken. I tried to calm him. "Everything is replaceable. More importantly, we weren't physically hurt."

We visited the American Express office. "Two days to verify and issue new travellers cheques," the clerk said.

We reported the loss of the camera and tent at the police station. An Inspector by the name of Williams wrote down the details. He was a tall, lean, chestnut-brown man who listened sympathetically. I told him we were going by train to Cambridge to experience "small-town Jamaica." Inspector Williams' eyes brightened. "A good plan," he said. "You'll be travelling along the mountain range. Spectacular views. Our island was called 'Xaymaca' by the Arawak Indians, the original inhabitants. It means Land of Woods and Streams. You'll see why. By the way, give my regards to the police officers in Cambridge as I know them all."

We boarded the diesel train in the afternoon. The ribbons of steel curled around mountain sides, crossed trestle bridges, passed springs, waterfalls, coconut palms and banana trees, and snaked through forests. I was awestruck by the rugged beauty of the mountains that formed the backbone of Jamaica.

We disembarked at Cambridge. The beauty of the tangled foliage and deeply shaded ravines in the green hills impressed me. Bougainvillea in white, red, purple, pink and orange cascaded over garden walls while luscious green grasses rooted in whatever ground they could.

At the police station I passed on Inspector Williams' regards to the desk sergeant. He immediately radioed Montego Bay to establish our connection with the Inspector. Their old two-way radio crackled and popped, making the conversation difficult to understand. Good things must have been said because the sergeant asked us to stay overnight in the police barracks. A constable pointed it out to us: a single-storeyed wooden building with all its windows ablaze with light.

As we approached the sleeping quarters, the rhythms of a steel band exploded from inside the building. The music was so loud I expected the roof to lift off at any moment. I opened the door and was almost blown backwards by the vibrations bouncing off the walls. A large radio stood in the centre of the room, turned up to full volume.

Neither of us could ask the officers to turn down their music as we were their guests. A dozen beds lined the walls; three were occupied by policemen; we had a choice of the other nine. Steve and I flopped onto a couple of beds and tried to sleep. I slept fitfully, waking up continually to the loud music and the slamming of doors as men in uniform went in and out.

In the morning I opened the door to let in some fresh air and brilliant sunshine. Through half-opened eyes, I could see crimson bougainvillea cascading over a fence. Steve and I, half-asleep, staggered past the flowers on our way to the office to thank the desk sergeant.

"Where are you going next?" he asked in an amiable tone.

"Ocho Rios," I told him.

"Visit the police station and mention my name," he said. "I'm Sergeant Haywood."

Steve's spirits lifted. "What a novel way to travel a country, by staying in police stations. I don't have to worry about my safety."

Ocho Rios was a green, hilly region with plunging waterfalls, sugar cane plantations, coconut groves and beaches. When night fell we sought the police station. "You can sleep in the courtroom above the station," the affable officer told us. "No one uses it any more."

The officer led us up a stairway that squeaked underfoot, and pushed open a door whose rusty hinges had not seen oil for months, or even years. He fumbled on the wall for the light switch and flicked it on, bathing the entire courtroom in a ghostly white light. The room was furnished with dark-stained wood furniture but everything – the judge's seat, the witness box, benches for the jury and the visitors' gallery – was covered in a layer of chalk-like dust. Huge cobwebs draped from the light fixtures and ceiling fans. I was tempted to switch on a fan but feared it would create a fog of dust.

The officer looked apologetic. "I haven't been up here for months," he said. "If you want to stay I can give you a broom to sweep the floor before you put down your sleeping bags."

We swept the floor, dodging cobwebs as we did so. The officer bade us good night. We were overwhelmed by his friendliness and willingness to help.

In the morning we descended the creaky stairway to thank the officer who had helped us.

"Where are you going now?" he asked in a cheerful voice.

"Montego Bay," I said.

"Ah!" said the officer. "Go to the police station and ask for Inspector Williams. He likes to help backpackers. He'll take care of you."

After returning to Montego Bay we reconnected with Inspector Williams and asked if Steve's tent and camera had been turned in.

The officer shook his head and grimaced.

"I apologize for your loss," he said. Then, on a brighter note asked, "Where are you going next?"

"Kingston," I said.

"Ah! Let me give you names for Kingston."

Haiti

Voodoo in the Caribbean

Religious rituals In Port-au-Prince, January 1971

See map, page 11, C3

Four men, black as ebony, pounded rawhide drums with piston-like rapidity, their hands a blur. The drumbeats reverberated off the walls and permeated the night air.

In the middle of the main room of this voodoo temple in Haiti, fifty men gyrated to the drum beats, their bare torsos glistening with sweat.

Candles on the floor flickered, giving off an eerie light. Shadows whirled on the walls.

I was travelling with Steve, about 20 years old, sandy-haired with a sunburned complexion. We were island-hopping around the Caribbean.

The island of Hispaniola sat like an uncut emerald in the blue sea of the Caribbean. Discovered by Christopher Columbus in 1492, the island is now divided into two republics – the Republic of Haiti, the western one-third of the island, and the Dominican Republic which occupies the remaining two-thirds.

When Columbus arrived, Hispaniola, like other Caribbean islands was populated by man-eating inhabitants called caribs or canibs, names from which we derive the words Caribbean and cannibal. These people became extinct by the sword, musket and diseases of European colonizers who replaced them with slaves from Africa.

Steve and I arrived by air. As the plane descended I looked out the window and saw the orange sun already resting on the watery horizon of the Caribbean Sea. By the time we landed in Haiti's capital of Port-au-Prince and cleared immigration and customs, darkness had fallen. We were about to leave the airport building and walk to the city when a security guard rushed over and warned us not to go on foot. Because of political unrest – Jean-Claude Duvalier had just been installed as the new president – armed soldiers patrolled the airport perimeter to counter possible sabotage.

"You could be shot," he said, "if you are mistaken for saboteurs."

Shot? I stood bolt upright. The man had my full attention. I had read that not everyone was in favour of the new president who inherited the position from his tyrannical father Francois "Papa Doc" Duvalier, an ardent practitioner of voodoo. Many Haitians feared that Jean-Claude "Baby Doc" Duvalier would continue his father's undemocratic rule.

Steve and I didn't need to be convinced to hire a taxi. I asked a cabbie to take us to a no-star hotel. As we sped into darkness, I could see the armed soldiers outlined by the crescent moon. A shiver went up my spine.

An out-of-season rainstorm spattered the windshield and the wipers refused to work. The driver grunted, pulled off the road and wrapped a piece of tinfoil around a cigarette butt to make a temporary fuse. Quite ingenious. The wipers swished back and forth and he resumed a frantic pace, disregarding stop signs. We entered a residential district on the outskirts of the city. Old, grey, concrete buildings lined the street. He dropped us at a hotel partly obscured by overgrown bushes. Vendors milled around the gate, hawking cigarettes and candy. I bought a packet of cigarettes and handed them to the cab driver. "Enjoy these," I said. "Keep the butts; you'll need them."

Steve and I dodged the street vendors and checked in.

The room was furnished with a couple of squeaky beds and a chest of drawers. The insect screen on our window was torn and the ceiling fan so lethargic I feared each rotation would be its last. A cursory peek at the bed sheets convinced us to use our sleeping bags. The room had not yet achieved flea-bag status but was working on it.

Prior to visiting the Caribbean I read as much as I could about voodoo. A must-do, for me, was to attend an authentic voodoo ceremony. Some city hotels put them on for tourists but they were commercial ventures staged for a fee. I wanted to see the real thing. I needed to find a local person who could take us.

Outside the hotel Steve and I met Sonny, a man with a plum-dark countenance and white teeth that gleamed in the dark. He knew of a voodoo service being held that evening. What luck! "About twenty minutes away by foot," he said. "I can take you there." Fortunately he was blessed with a smattering of English. The gods were smiling on us.

Moonlight lit our way as we trailed Sonny along a paved road that climbed a hillside. We turned off and followed a narrow, muddy track bordered by lush, dank-smelling grasses and fern trees still dripping from the earlier rainstorm.

Drumbeats filled the air. Sonny looked back to make sure we had both heard them. My curiosity piqued.

At the end of the trail a flat-roofed building loomed into view. The whitewashed walls were illuminated by the moon that peeked like a voyeur over the wall of fern trees.

As we approached the open doorway my heart thumped with excitement. I turned to Steve. He looked nervous.

"Are you okay?" I asked.

"I'll be all right," he said. "I'm new at this sort of thing."

"That makes two of us!"

The drums thundered. An urgency in their sound signalled something was about to happen. Sonny led us through the doorway to the inner sanctum where more than fifty blacks gyrated to the pounding drumbeats. They gesticulated wildly and stamped the earthen floor with their big, splayed feet.

The room looked about the size of a volleyball court. The white, interior walls were painted with human figures in bold colours of red, black, yellow, blue and green. From what I'd read about voodoo, they represented Christian saints. Sonny leaned towards us: “We have changed the saints’ names to those of our gods and goddesses.”

About a dozen women, some clothed in white robes, others in colourful cotton dresses, stood around the walls. They clapped and chanted to encourage the frenzied dancers.

The drums worked up to a crescendo and stopped abruptly. Deathly silence. Dancers crumpled to the floor, exhausted. Into their midst leapt the *houngan*, or priest, clothed in a pair of dirt-stained brown trousers. His right hand clutched a machete, its long blade smeared with red paint. “It symbolizes blood,” Sonny said.

I tensed when the *houngan* brandished the machete and chopped erratically at the water-saturated muggy air. He stopped, rammed the machete into the earthen floor, poured liquid over it and lit a match.

Whoosh! Tongues of orange flame shot upwards and licked at the humid air. Excitement rippled through the crowd. The drums started a slow, pulsating beat; the men danced, their black bodies glistening. Women waved colourful, woven banners as they swayed and reeled in rhythmic motion. Some older women poured liquid from a rum bottle onto the floor – an offering to their deities. Other women lit candles and placed them at different points around the room. They appeared to be preparing for a special event. I watched, spellbound by all the activity.

Suddenly, the drumbeats grew more furious. The hairs on the back of my neck stiffened. The men and women withdrew to the edge of the room. The *houngan* again sprang into the middle of the floor. He pierced the air with a high-spirited, animal-like screech. His face twitched and his shoulders twisted.

His angular body leapt into the air, arms flailing as he jerked left and right. A moment later his legs buckled, his arms flopped uselessly by his side and he collapsed on the ground like a rag doll.

Sonny leaned towards Steve and me. “A spirit has possessed him. He’s in a trance.”

The women rushed to assist him to his feet and steer him to an adjoining room. “He’ll be back,” Sonny said.

A *mambo*, or priestess, draped in a white robe, bustled around organizing about ten people into a line. A couple of women escorted the *houngan* back to our crowded room and another handed him a bottle of rum. In a slow-moving, trance-like state he splashed rum over the head of the first man in line. It looked like a baptismal ritual. For the next person in line, a woman, he took a swig of rum and spat into her ear; to the third person in line he sprayed the rum from his mouth over the man's face and clothes. After the ten had been baptized in various bizarre ways, an assistant guided the *houngan* to greet each individual in the room.

All this time, Steve and I tried to be inconspicuous by staying in the background. Now, with the *houngan* being introduced to each person it would soon be our turn to meet him.

With outstretched, diagonally crossed arms, the *houngan* held both hands of each person. As I extended my hands for him to hold, I searched his eyes. They were wide open, fixed in a glazed, trance-like stare. He held my hands briefly and moved on to Steve. I felt he had looked right through me. I glanced at Steve. He looked uneasy.

At the end of these introductions, the drummers pounded a steady rhythm then quickened the beat.

Sonny moved away to meet with some friends on the far side of the room. Without his presence I felt a twinge of aloneness. Were we welcome here? Two white faces in a sea of black? Were we a type of voyeur like the crescent moon peeping over the fern trees into this other world? I didn't feel physically threatened; I just felt we didn't belong.

I whispered to Steve who was still by my side: "Are you ready to go?"

"Definitely," he said in a nervous tone. "I've been ready for a long time. From the moment we arrived. This place spooks me."

I politely carved my way through the crowd. Steve followed right behind me. I turned and saw Sonny with his friends and waved good-bye. Then Steve and I slipped out the open door.

"Phew!" Steve exhaled then caught his breath.

"What did you think of it?" I asked.

"It was mind-boggling. It's a different world! What's your take on all this?"

"It's the most bizarre religious ceremony I've been to. I've read a fair bit about voodoo, but nothing prepared me for what we just saw."

Drumbeats continued to fill the night air as we started down the hill.

"From what I recall," I said, "some people call voodoo a cult, but in Haiti it is an officially recognized religion. In the 1700s, this part of the island was snapped up by the French who wanted to set up sugar and coffee plantations. They needed labourers so they imported slaves from West Africa. The slaves brought their religious beliefs, or voodoo, which the French regarded as devil worship. They banned it. Anyone found practising it was thrown in prison, whipped or hung. So, voodoo went underground."

"Well," Steve said, "that would put an end to voodoo."

"Ironically," I said, "rather than stifle the religion it became more popular. Keeping it alive was probably a way the slaves had of snubbing their masters.

"The French taught Catholic beliefs to the slaves and were pleased to find that they were accepted. The white settlers weren't aware that the two religions shared some similarities. Both recognized a supreme being. Both had saints with specific responsibilities. For instance, St. Peter controlled the Pearly Gates and kept out sinners. Voodoo had *Legba* who was on duty at the gate between Earth and the spirit world.

"As time went on, the slaves painted saints on the inside walls of their temples. These images could be identified as either voodoo gods or Christian saints. As the slave masters became lenient, voodoo re-emerged. The combination of the two religions, Roman Catholicism and West African voodoo, produced Haiti's unique brand of voodoo."

Steve interjected. "What I'm curious about is what was happening inside the temple. Sonny mentioned trance and spirit possession."

I continued with what information I could recall from my reading. "A person, usually a voodoo priest, goes into a trance when a *loa* or spirit takes control of his body and voice-box. This is an important part of a voodoo ceremony. The ordinary man-in-the-street can then ask the *loa* directly for help in healing someone's illness, solving personal disputes or overcoming business problems. There's a lot more to voodoo than what I've just said. We'll have to see if we can find a book about it."

We arrived at the bottom of the hill to the familiar sounds of shouting, honking horns and tinkling bicycle bells. After a brisk walk we arrived at the hotel gates, slipped past the vendors and into the hotel. "Mission accomplished," said Steve. I agreed.

On the following day we watched a march in the streets by a hundred or so members of the people's militia. Dressed in their workday clothes, they were displaying solidarity to the new president, "Baby Doc" Duvalier.

Unlike the soldiers patrolling the airport, the people's militia appeared an unimpressive and dishevelled mob. Some toted rifles, others wore pistols in hip holsters. Some didn't have any weapons at all. They all marched out of step.

The people of Haiti may not take their soldiering seriously, but their voodoo, they do.

USA

Dust and grit

In a truckers' parking lot, Miami, January 1971
See map, page 11, B2

At 5:30 in the morning the truckers' parking lot along Miami's Biscayne Boulevard was quiet. I lay curled up in my sleeping bag under a semi-trailer that was parked overnight. In the early morning gloom I saw the outline of Steve's bulk in his sleeping bag a few feet away.

Steve – fair haired, short and stocky – and I, had just spent three weeks in the Caribbean and were now in Miami to earn a few dollars before heading north. The Stand-By Labor office was registering labourers for odd jobs, placing them with employers who came to the office looking for workers. We were lucky to get a day-long job unloading freight cars in a railway yard. Unfortunately, we were paid the minimum wage of $1.73 an hour – not enough to pay for food *and* a hotel. Food was more important than a hotel, so we settled on sleeping in the parking lot.

"Are you awake?" I whispered. As I spoke I realized my voice sounded croaky. "I think I'm getting a cold," I added. "My throat is raspy."

Steve grunted and said, "Mine is too."

We eased out of our bags and walked to the nearby Esso station to use the washroom before going to work. I swallowed a slug of water and, miraculously, my throat cleared. The same thing happened to Steve. Dust and grit from the parking lot had settled in our noses and throats overnight.

After we had worked our day shift we waited in the streets with our backpacks till eleven p.m. I hoped that the truck traffic had come and gone for the night as we headed for the truckers' parking lot again. Instead of stretching out on the ground under a semi-trailer we climbed into the back of an empty Toyota pickup truck. Hopefully, this would protect us from the wind and dust. I slept soundly until six when I heard a couple of growling dogs and the crunch of heavy footsteps on gravel. The footsteps and dogs came closer. I dared not peek over the edge of the pickup. The footsteps stopped near the truck and a voice ordered, "Up Butch, up Bruiser."

As I cowered in my sleeping bag, I was horrified to see two huge hairy dogs leap over the side of the truck and land between Steve and me.

"Hey, we're friendlies," I said gently to the panting dogs as I tried forcefully to push them away. The big, black one shoved himself against me and slobbered near my face. I cringed. It tried to kiss me with its salivating lips. Its teeth were long overdue for a flossing!

A man stared at us over the side of the truck. He looked amused. "Sorry guys. You're in their space. But they don't bite too hard."

I felt sheepish as Steve and I climbed over the side and dropped to the ground beside the owner.

He laughed.

We left. Nevertheless, we returned for three more nights. But we avoided the Toyota pickup.

USA to Mexico

Guns 'n' Gold

By road, New Orleans to Mexico City, February 1971

See map, page 11, B2

A cold February breeze was blowing as I shouldered my backpack along Camp Street in New Orleans. It was late afternoon and I wondered where I could stay during the upcoming Mardi Gras festival. Passing a bench I heard "Gidday, mate. I see you're from Oz." I turned to see a man in a dark, drab overcoat, fiftyish, with grey stubble, staring at the yellow kangaroo patches on the sleeves of my windbreaker.

"Are you arriving or leaving?" he asked in an Australian twang.

"Arriving," I answered.

"If you're looking for cheap digs I know a place for only ten bucks."

"Ten bucks a night is too expensive," I said. "I'll find something cheaper."

"Not ten a night. It's ten for a week."

That was more to my liking!

I followed him. Herb Williamson was his name. Originally from Melbourne, he was a seaman who jumped ship in New York many years earlier. Technically an 'illegal,' he could only work at odd jobs. His travels were restricted to Canada and Mexico where he didn't have to show a passport and visa at the border.

"Here's the place," he said, stopping outside a big, brown, wooden building. "1366 Camp Street. This is where I'm staying.

But I have to move every week or so because the cops come looking for illegals."

To reach the front door we navigated a maze of destitute men sprawled over the front porch, nursing their wine bottles. The proprietor, a wiry man with lizard eyes, handed me key number 9. The room was furnished with an ancient iron bedstead, table and chair, refrigerator, stove and washbasin. Perfect! The walls were cracked and the paint peeling, but the price was right.

Herb slipped into the room and startled me with a nervous chortle of "Heh, heh, heh!" I didn't quite know what to make of him. Nevertheless, he was a wealth of information. He told me where to buy food (at the supermarket around the corner) and where to get a cheap cup of coffee (for 10 cents rather than 15). Then he left, chortling "Heh, heh, heh!"

I foraged at the supermarket and found a great bargain – TV dinners on sale for 30 cents each. I bought ten and stacked them in the fridge. I was set for the week.

The Mardi Gras kicked off the next day at noon with a river parade on the Mississippi. Confederate flags, the Stars and Stripes, and colourful bunting flapped in the breeze as tugboats, launches and barges chugged down the river, whistles and horns blowing. Two hours later a parade of floats rolled along Canal Street. Crew members on the floats tossed silver- and gold-coloured plastic doubloons to roadside spectators who screamed with enthusiasm as they reached into the air to catch them.

It was easy to be caught up in the spirit of Mardi Gras as I joined the thousands of visitors who descended on the city for the 'Greatest Free Show on Earth.' I watched colourful, noisy parades with bands, marching girls, a sheriff's posse on horses and floats pulled by tractors. During some evening parades, flaming torches were carried through the streets. Revellers kept the bars of Bourbon Street open day and night.

During these festivities I decided to look for some short-term work to replenish my funds. I rose early and headed to an Employer's Overload office. It was five-thirty when I registered, then waited with twenty other hopefuls. By eight-thirty only five men had been given casual work. Discouraged, I left.

I bumped into Herb on his way to his 10-cent coffee fix. "Try Dutch Sibert's bar on Magazine Street," he said. "Dutch arranges jobs for seamen who aren't in a union – on ships that fly Liberian and Panamanian flags." I hadn't thought of working on a ship but I still carried a Norwegian seaman's card from when I worked my passage on the Norwegian freighter, *Triton*. I found the bar but Dutch wasn't there.

I saw Herb the next day. His worry lines had multiplied. "I'm running short of cash," he said. "I'm thinking of prospecting for gold in Mexico. Wanna come?"

I was enthused. "Have you prospected before?" I asked.

"No."

"Neither have I. I'll join you but let's wait a day or so. I want to do some research at the library."

I read that gold could be found near quartz and granite and that gold dust sometimes got trapped in the bends of streams. The equipment needed included a pick, shovel and panning dishes. With my new knowledge I felt I was ready.

Herb had his 1955 Oldsmobile serviced in the morning. We bought our prospecting equipment and left in the late afternoon, taking Highway 10 westwards. The car behaved well for its age. Sea air blew in through the open windows. After six hours we crossed the Texas state line and reached the outskirts of Galveston at two in the morning. Herb pulled off the road and we slept in the car.

I woke up to shafts of sunlight bursting through the window. Suddenly, Herb confronted me with an idea. "Let's buy guns in Galveston and run them into Mexico. We'll make good money selling them."

"You're crazy," I said. "That's illegal."

"I've done it before," Herb said defensively. "I know of a gun shop in Galveston."

"I don't care whether you've done it before, I don't want anything to do with it."

Herb fell silent and brooded.

I figured that if he was adamant about running guns I could go my own way when we got to Galveston. After all, I didn't owe him any allegiance. I hardly knew the guy. What shenanigans would he think of next? And what else had he done in the past that I wasn't prepared to do?

Herb needed cheering up.

"I have a suggestion," I said. "I'll go with you to the gun shop, then play it by ear as to what I'll do next."

In Galveston we stopped at the gun shop and wandered along the aisles, looking over the lethal hardware, until a sales assistant approached.

"I'm looking for secondhand .303 calibre rifles," Herb said in the phoniest of Texan drawls which in no way disguised his Australian accent. I turned away in embarrassment and saw the sales assistant raise his eyebrows towards a colleague, and smirk. I was surprised to hear Herb ask for a model that dated back to World War One. Why would he want such a rifle? Was it popular in Mexico and were bullets easily available?

"You have to be a resident of Texas to buy a gun here," the sales assistant said.

"I've bought here before." Herb sounded agitated.

"The law changed after the assassination of Senator Robert Kennedy," said the salesman.

Herb stood silent for a moment. I watched his face turn an angry crimson.

"I want quite a few guns. It'll be good business for you," Herb said.

"Sir, you still need to show proof of residency."

"I'll pay cash." Herb's voice rose, "No paperwork necessary."

"Sir, you don't understand..."

Herb seethed. He clenched his fist. Blue veins bulged on his forehead, his lips twisted into a snarl.

"Don't tell me I don't understand," he shouted as he thumped the glass top of the display cabinet.

The salesman instinctively leapt back a couple of feet.

I was surprised to see this aggressive side of Herb.

He leaned forward over the counter and shoved his whiskery

countenance into the face of the salesman. "Listen, punk, I want guns and I want them now."

The other salesman bounded over. "Is everything all right?"

"No!" Herb breathed venom into the air. "Your pal won't sell me any guns. My money's as good as the next man's."

"Sir, we'll sell you guns," said the second salesman in an even-tempered tone, "when you can show proof of residency in Texas."

I called out to Herb, "Let's go."

I was embarrassed, and couldn't get out of there fast enough.

Herb stood wringing his hands as if he was going to hit someone. Instead, he thumped the countertop again and stormed out. I had no idea Herb could be so unreasonable and possibly even have a violent streak. I was relieved he was thwarted from buying guns.

We followed the coastal highway which traversed flat land as dry as the dust blowing across it. The Oldsmobile rolled along, heavy and smooth, carrying us through Corpus Christi. We passed oil derricks thumping steadily into the arid land, pumping up precious liquid gold. At midnight we cruised into Brownsville near the Mexican border, slept in the car until six, then drove to the airport to clean up in the public washrooms.

The sun had already climbed into the tranquil blue sky when we crossed the Rio Bravo del Norte and entered Mexico. We followed the 101 across flat terrain, passing scores of adobe homes, donkey carts and horses.

A powerful stench wafted through the open windows. We rolled them up quickly as we passed the stinking carcass of a cow being gorged upon by vultures. "I'll be ordering 'vegetarian' tonight," I said.

I checked our map and suggested we stay at Ciudad Victoria, a town at the foot of the Sierra Madre Oriental range.

Herb glanced at the map. "Tomorrow we start prospecting. Heh, heh, heh!"

He was doing it again! A nervous chortle? Or something sinister?

After a night at the Hotel Casa Turista, Herb pointed the car towards the mountains. Our plan was to find a river we could pan for placer gold – gold washed down from higher elevations. We drove into the mountains to find that, unfortunately, streams had largely dried up. Nevertheless, we trekked into the tan-coloured hills where even cactus was in short supply. After half-an-hour of lugging our pick, shovel and panning dishes we reached the rim of a gully. A hundred feet below, a muddy river tumbled over boulders. We held our equipment tightly and skidded down the incline to a bend in the river where we hoped to find gold in cracks above the waterline. Herb shovelled sand into the pans while I sloshed it, keeping my eyes open for telltale flecks. No luck! After an hour, Herb grew impatient and disgruntled. To let off steam he grabbed the pick and ferociously attacked a rocky mound. Suddenly he hollered: "Hey, look at this."

I rushed over. Bright flecks shone in the sunlight. Quartz!

My hopes rose. If there was quartz there could be gold nearby. Herb grabbed the pick again and, like a maniac, smashed the mound of rock, clay and mud to smithereens. I panned it. Nothing! Herb continued to swing his pick like a madman. I moved fifty feet downstream in case he started to vent his anger on me.

"Heh, heh, heh!"

His nervous laugh, more like an evil cackle, unsettled me. I imagined the worst, that he was waiting to bash me over the head and steal my moneybelt. I made sure my back wasn't towards him when he used the pick or shovel.

We dug and panned separately, staying about fifty feet apart. Dust covered us. Our sweat turned the dust into mud as it trickled down the fronts and backs of our shirts. We perspired for another disappointing two hours without finding even a fleck of gold.

Maybe we expected too much too soon.

Herb bothered me with more maniacal cackles. Concerned that I was travelling with a psycho, I decided to quit our partnership. Back in Ciudad Victoria I told him so.

"That's okay, mate," he said. "I can make money running guns across the border. Heh, heh, heh! I'll figure out a way to buy them."

Herb and I had little in common except a need for the elusive dollar. I wished him well. We shook hands and parted as friends.

He got into his car and aimed it north, back towards Galveston.

I headed for the bus station and bought a ticket for the evening bus to Mexico City.

I never panned for gold again.

Mexico

The Matador's Secret

Bullfight in Mexico City, February 1971

See map, page 11, B3

Nighttime. Mexico City.

Floodlights illuminated the world's biggest bullring, Plaza Mexico.

The Plaza president and judges settled into their seats. The stage was set for the first of four fights. Trumpets sounded as the president waved a small, white handkerchief to start the event. I felt the excitement well up inside me.

In an instant, the gate of chute number five swung open and into the ring exploded a black, brawny beast with bulging muscles. Could the bull win the fight?

I had always been curious about bullfighting. Even though I didn't totally agree with it as a sport, it had been one for over 3,000 years. Its origins trace back to the Mediterranean island of Crete. From there the sport passed to Imperial Rome and subsequently to her domains, including the Iberian Peninsula now shared by Spain and Portugal. Centuries later, Spanish colonists introduced the sport to Mexico. The rules of bullfighting in Mexico, like those of Spain, decree that the bull be killed. The *aficionados* of the sport argue the bull is going to die anyway, so why not let it die fighting?

The bull that burst out of chute number five was a five-year-old, 500-pound fighting machine.

It lowered its bulky head, snorted and kicked up its hind legs.

It pawed the ground and careened around in circles as though confused and half-blinded by the bright floodlights.

It was the job of the *peones*, or matador's assistants, to tease and torment the bull, to encourage it to charge their pink and yellow capes. The bull's response enabled the matador, observing from the sidelines, to evaluate its fighting qualities so he could plan his moves for the fight to the death.

The job of a *peone* had its dangerous moments. Sancho Alvaro, a *peone*, stood in the ring shaking his cape. The bull snorted and charged. Alvaro sidestepped but snagged his cape on its horns. Defenceless without his cape, he wisely dashed towards the safety barrier – a wooden fence. The enraged bull shook free of the cape and pounded after his quarry. Alvaro glanced over his shoulder and saw the bull bearing down on him. Alvaro doubled his speed. His legs pumped up and down like pistons. The crowd stood and screamed encouragement; the excitement hit fever pitch. Just a few more steps to safety. Spectators jumped up and down, waving their arms in a frenzy. Suddenly, Alvaro stumbled. I shot out of my seat. "Get up," I bellowed. "Get up."

But Alvaro wasn't fast enough. The animal bulldozed headlong into his frail body, gored the flesh of his left leg and flipped the powerless *peone* into the air. He landed on the bull's head between the horns. Three other *peones* dashed in with their capes to rescue their comrade. The triumphant bull carried the bloodied, squirming body on its head for a few moments then belligerently dropped it into the dust and trotted away in defiance.

The other *peones* kept the bull from the unfortunate Alvaro, as stretcher bearers rushed into the ring to whisk him to hospital. There was more gore than I ever imagined and I hoped the *peone* would live.

I flopped onto my seat. All this action. And the fight hadn't even started! The bull was mean and tough. And fearless. Maybe there was a chance it could outsmart the matador and live, once the real fight started.

Meanwhile, the matador had been observing the bull from the side of the bullring. What was he thinking about the bull?

Into the ring cantered a *picador*. His horse wore heavy woollen padding over its flanks as well as a blindfold. The *picador's* job was to lance the bull in the back of the neck to weaken the muscles so it couldn't hold up its head. A barbaric act! A bull with a bowed head made it easier for the matador to insert his sword.

The bull charged the horse, and unwittingly thundered straight into the *picador's* sharp lance. It burrowed between his shoulders. But the bull kept advancing. Its momentum propelled it into the horse, pinning it and the *picador* against the wooden fence. The *picador* drove his lance into the bull's neck again, forcing it to retreat. I jumped up to boo the *picador* for using the lance, while the crowd booed the bull for retreating. I was definitely outnumbered. The chance of the bull beating the matador started to diminish in my mind. But if the bull knew the Matador's Secret, it had a good chance of survival.

The real fight was about to begin. The matador entered, resplendent in green and gold hand-embroidered breeches with matching bolero. His white shirt was trimmed with lace and he wore the customary pink stockings, black slippers and black velvet cap.

The bull charged. The matador entertained us with an impressive display of passes with his cape, twirling it above the bull's head. When the spectators rose in unison to applaud, I leapt to my feet and shouted *Olé* and *Bravo* along with them, giving the impression I knew what was going on.

The enraged bull stood panting, looking from side to side. The matador handed his red cape to a *peone* in exchange for two *banderillos* – wooden rods the length of his arm – wrapped in coloured paper. Steel harpoons, finger length and sharp, protruded at their ends.

The bull cast about for its tormentor.

"El toro, el toro," the matador hissed, holding up his two *banderillos*. The bull looked confused. *"El toro, el toro,"* the matador yelled. A few spectators shouted and clapped, alerting the bull that it was again the centre of attention.

The matador stood, feet together, arms raised, dangling the *banderillos* vertically, ready to thrust the sharp points down into the animal's brawny back to further damage its neck muscles.

The bull snorted, pawed the ground and lumbered forward. Its powerful legs gathered speed like a locomotive. The matador stood as still as a statue, *banderillos* held high as he waited for the precise second to sidestep the onrushing beast.

The moment arrived. The bull was almost upon him when the matador stepped sideways and leapt into the air to lend his full weight to plunging the spikes into the bull's back. Thud! The sharp metal pierced the hide. The spectators cheered. The maddened bull bellowed and kicked up its hind legs. The crazed animal twisted left and right to dislodge the harpoons in its neck muscles. A futile effort. Blood oozed from the wounds and spread out over its hide in a gory mess. The sight tore at my guts.

The matador took his red cape and silver sword from a *peone,* and with the bull before him ready to attack, continued to enthrall the crowd by twirling his cape, pivoting on his toes and dancing on his knees. All of this in front of the bewildered bull.

The wily matador manoeuvred his opponent to face him squarely with its feet together, head bowed. The *banderillos* and the *picador's* lance had done their job of lowering its head. Saliva dribbled from the bull's mouth. The matador shook his cape and aimed his sword, hidden by the cape, at the bull's head. The animal charged the moving cape – a fatal mistake – unaware of the sword. The matador lunged, driving the sword between the shoulder blades, cutting the aorta.

The bull, with *banderillos* in its back, gashes from the *picador's* lance, and a silver sword in its body, stumbled forward in a last effort to hold on to life. Then it collapsed, dying at the matador's feet.

The spectators roared their approval. I sat stunned, not wanting to believe that the bull was dead. I wondered if this was how the bull would have chosen to die.

The president waved two handkerchiefs. Both ears would go to the matador – a high honour. The matador raised his arms in victory and strutted in front of the judges. Admirers swarmed over the ringside fences, hoisted the matador onto their shoulders and paraded him around the ring. While the matador basked in the display of adoration, the lifeless bull was unceremoniously hitched to a pair of draft horses and dragged from the ring, enroute to the local butchery.

Where did the bull go wrong?

The bull paid with its life because it hadn't learned the Matador's Secret: *For a bull to have a chance of survival it must attack the man, not the red cape.*

USA

The hippie commune

The candle makers in Seattle, March 1971

See map, page 11, A1

It was mid-afternoon and I was fifty miles north of San Francisco, standing on the shoulder of Interstate 5, trying to hitch a ride northwards. In the midst of a steady stream of cars a van slowed down and stopped. It was a '53 Chevrolet completely painted in psychedelic colours. Heads of grotesque, feathered monsters swirled in hues of purple, yellow, red, blue and green.

I pulled open the passenger door and shot a glance at the driver, a thick-set overweight twenty-something man in a flowery Hawaiian shirt. He wore his long brown hair tied in a ponytail. I thanked him for stopping, heaved my backpack onto the floor on the passenger side and hoisted myself into the seat. All this time the engine throbbed and the van vibrated. Someone coughed behind me. I turned. Three guys in their twenties greeted me with a collective "Hi, man."

As the miles rolled beneath the wheels I got to know something of our driver, Alan. Originally from Rhode Island, he came to the west coast to find what he called action. He now lived in a house in Seattle where he shared a communal lifestyle with about twenty adults and four children.

"We want to be self-supporting," Alan said. "To do so, we run a candle-making business in the basement of the house. We want to remain outside mainstream society as much as possible, but it's not easy. The rural communes that grow their own food have a better chance of being self-sustaining."

"Nevertheless it sounds like an interesting place," I said, intrigued. "I've never experienced communal living."

After two hours of driving, Alan suggested we all chip in some money to buy food for a picnic dinner. When we all agreed, Alan took the exit ramp into Redding.

It was a motley crew that exited from the van at a mini-supermarket. I had learned that all were wanderers who had been hitchhiking together on Interstate 5. The first guy out of the back of the van was dressed in torn, frayed blue jeans and a purple, tie-dyed T-shirt. He wore a black dog collar with chromed rivets around his neck. Behind him crawled a sallow-cheeked thin man who didn't look healthy. His wild blond hair and straggly beard hadn't seen scissors for months. He wore Chinese peasants' black trousers and an oversized green shirt that draped loosely over his skinny frame. The third to emerge, a fair-haired, freckled, blue-eyed man with steel-rimmed glasses appeared nervous. He scratched constantly at either real or imagined itches around his rib cage. With my short hair and trimmed beard and fairly neat clothes, I was the oddity.

In the mini-supermarket we bought bread, cold cuts of corned beef, lettuce, carrots, a jar of coleslaw and a carton of milk. I was impressed by their choices. We climbed into the van and drove until we found a picnic table in a park, where we prepared and munched on our sandwiches.

"Where are you guys heading?" I asked the three.

"Oregon," said the skinny one. "We're going to pick shrooms."

."Shrooms?"

"Mushrooms. The magic kind."

"What makes them magic?"

"Something in them gives a sort of out-of-body experience. Makes you feel like you're dreaming when you're awake. A bit like being on LSD."

"Taking that sort of stuff doesn't appeal to me," I said. "I like my two feet firmly on the ground. What happens if you eat too many shrooms?"

"You could die, man. There are two kinds of magic mushroom

eaters – the smart ones and the dead ones. Even some of the smart ones are now dead. Mushrooms aren't addictive, you know; you can stop eating them whenever you want to. There are side effects. They can make you nervous. They can give you itchy skin and you can't stop scratching."

The sun, which had been shining warmly, retreated under iron-coloured clouds, and a cold wind whipped at our clothes. It was time to move on. The freckled guy with glasses continued to scratch himself.

The three shroom pickers left us in Oregon. Because Alan was eager to drive through the night he and I shared time behind the wheel. I learned more about Alan. He put all his energy into the candle business and occasionally suffered fits of depression. His commune colleagues had encouraged him to borrow the commune's van and go on a holiday. After having spent two weeks on California's beaches he was now anxious to return to Seattle.

We took turns napping and driving. After a pre-dawn nap I watched the sky begin to lighten. Alan estimated we would arrive in Seattle at three in the afternoon and he invited me to stay overnight. I immediately said yes. But suddenly I had misgivings. Would I be accepted by the other commune members whose lifestyle, I expected, was so different from my own? I had heard about the counter-culture's loose sleeping arrangements, drugs, strict vegetarianism, aversion to work and their distrust of anyone over thirty. I was 28, so surely age would not be held against me, nor the fact I wasn't into drugs.

The communal house was a ramshackle, three-storeyed wooden building built long ago. It was painted white with dark blue trim around the door and window frames. The roof was threadbare and swaybacked, the windows were streaked with dirt.

Alan showed me around the house. The main floor included a dining room with oak floorboards that squeaked. Adjacent to it, a kitchen. All other rooms were bedrooms; the attic space was also divided into bedrooms. The basement was used solely for the manufacture of candles.

Alan appeared to be the leader of the commune although he

wouldn't admit it. He asked me not to divulge the address of the house to anyone. "We are renting the house and we don't want the owner to know we are making candles in the basement. We use a lot of wax which is a fire hazard."

He mentioned that half-a-dozen of the commune members were going that evening to another commune house for a twenty-first birthday party and that I was welcome to join them.

At nine-thirty our small group set off to walk the six blocks to the other city commune. We ambled along a residential street of houses that ranged from decrepit to slightly better and arrived at the commune, a three-storeyed house cloaked in an aura of neglect. The sounds from an old Bob Dylan record pulsated through the windows that were partly covered with old plastic wrap. Meant to stop winter's chilly winds from blowing through the gaps in the window frames, the brittle plastic flapped limply, in tatters.

Climbing the front steps to the main floor, someone rapped on the door and pushed it open. We headed towards the music along a gloomy, carpeted hallway that exuded a cat odour flavoured with the musty smell of mildew. We entered a brightly-lit living room packed with forty or so hippies. Men wore tie-dyed T-shirts, beaded necklaces, loose cotton trousers, and sandals; the women wore long dresses of Indian cotton, silver anklets and beaded necklaces.

Towards eleven o'clock someone announced a toast to the birthday boy and everyone was handed a glass of champagne. As people drank their bubbly they started to drop like flies onto the floor. I suddenly felt a wave of fuzziness in my brain and I collapsed. Monsters and dragons swirled in my mind in bright psychedelic colours, like the ones on Alan's van. It took me over two hours to return to some type of normality. It wasn't something that I would ever want to experience again.

Alan, livid that someone spiked the champagne with an hallucinatory drug, mustered our group. Someone said the drug was Orange Sunshine, a form of the mind-altering drug, LSD. "That stuff's powerful," said Alan. "These guys probably put a micro dot of the acid in each champagne bottle."

We started back, albeit unsteadily, to our house. A gentle, misty rain fell. I couldn't feel it but I could see it as we ambled sublimely from one halo of light to another. A cone of illuminated drops spilled beneath each street lamp. It looked as if the lamps themselves were raining.

At the house, Alan suggested I sleep in a corner of the dining room. From somewhere, he produced a foam mattress pad to make the few remaining hours before dawn comfortable.

Morning arrived early for me because of a sound, like a whip being cracked. I opened an eye and saw bare legs stride past me. Again a whip crack, accompanied by loud squeaks. I realized the old oak floor was responding to the weight of the footsteps. I opened my other eye to see who the intruder was and glimpsed the back of a tall, thin woman with a tumble of fiery red curls cascading down her back, ending at her bare buttocks. Now my eyes were wide open. She turned to enter the kitchen, displaying a generous bust. I heard cupboards and drawers being opened and closed noisily. Probably in search of breakfast.

I rolled over and tried to go back to sleep, but that wasn't to be. The floorboards creaked again as she retraced her steps past my corner of the room and disappeared down the hall.

I dragged myself out of my sleeping bag and padded to the kitchen to investigate the food supply and discovered plastic containers of caraway seeds, peanuts and soya nuts. Was this what hippies lived on? I felt like an alien. I delved into my backpack and found a couple of Granola bars – my survival rations – and ate them for breakfast.

Hearing noises from the basement workshop, I walked downstairs and found Alan supervising students who had come to pour candles. "We pay them five dollars an hour," he told me, then proceeded to explain the operation.

"The candles are 36 inches long. To make a candle we hang a wick on a nail and attach a half-pound lead weight to the bottom to keep the wick taut. We heat paraffin in a five-gallon tin to 230°F on the electric stove, add wax hardener, dye and scents. With an old tin coffee pot, a worker dips the pot into the mixture and gently pours the wax down the wick. This will be repeated fifty or sixty times until the 36-inch taper has a diameter of one inch at the base." The smell of wax hung heavily in the air.

"We're getting orders from New York and San Francisco," Alan said. "A problem we have is how to wrap and pack the candles so they won't chafe, and thereby lose their sheen in transit. We're still looking for a solution."

Someone called out: "Lunch in fifteen minutes."

I thought of caraway seeds and peanuts. Lunch would be interesting.

I headed upstairs to the dining room and walked in on a round-table discussion about seeds and herbs. I wondered if they were talking about the lunch menu.

It occurred to me that they might be surprised if I mentioned the supermarket food that Alan ate for dinner the previous night.

One man's discourse was interrupted by what sounded like a pistol shot. The old floor again! As people walked across it, the floor boards protested with cracks and squeaks. I glanced up to see the woman with the fiery red hair. This time she wore a dark green Indian cotton skirt and blouse. A young girl and boy clung to her legs.

I was the only stranger in the room. The redhead introduced herself as Shea and added: "These are my six-year-old twins, Fiare Genie and One Free. Shea spelled her daughter's name for me. Fiare Genie had inherited her mother's red hair. It was tied in double ponytails so highly placed on her head that they looked like puppy ears. A man in his twenties entered the room and was greeted by everyone with "Hi, John." One Free, a freckle-faced bubbly boy with rust coloured hair, ran to greet the man, obviously his father. I wondered why these parents had inflicted such names on their children who would have a lifetime of explaining ahead of them.

I was told there were two other children living in the commune, Ocean and Skye, but they were away with their parents, picking shrooms.

There was a commotion at the dining room door. "Here comes lunch," someone shouted. My interest piqued.

I turned to see three of the hippies carrying in milk, a large jar of coleslaw and a big paper bag overflowing with french fries.

And, two huge cardboard buckets of *Colonel Sanders Kentucky Fried Chicken!*

Great Britain

The quest for lamb chops

An urban rustler in London, April 1971

See map, page 12, A2

"Wantcd. Room mate to share with two others. Three pounds a week. Come to 22 Penywern Road." I pinned my handwritten card on a notice board at the newsagency near the subway station. I felt optimistic that someone would respond within a day or two.

In London's suburb of Earl's Court, nicknamed Kangaroo Valley, I shared a flat with Andy, a fellow Australian. We wanted another room mate to share the rent.

In the late afternoon I heard a knock on the door and opened it to a short, stocky man with a ruddy face and a thicket of coppery-brown hair. "Gidday, mite," he said. "Me nime's Norm. I'm lookin' for a place to live."

I showed Norm our accommodation. One large room with a fourteen-foot-high ceiling, three bedrooms, a bathroom with a tub, and a small galley kitchen.

"Looks good," Norm said. "I'd like to move in now."

Norm didn't know how long he would stay. In fact, neither Andy or I knew how long we'd be in the flat. We were all travellers, out to see the world. I estimated I would stay for about three months, time enough to save money to travel overland through Europe and across Asia to Australia. Andy was working "just a little longer to save enough shekels to do Europe properly."

In the evening we introduced Norm to the King's Head, the local watering hole popular with Australians and New Zealanders living in the area. Norm entertained the patrons with his stories as a farm hand in Hanging Rock, New South Wales, particularly his exploits as a sheep rustler. He was in the middle of a story when the bar manager announced, "Time, gentlemen, please."Andy and I invited the pub's patrons to our flat where Norm could continue his tale about sheep rustling, how he would creep towards a flock, leap up, grab a sheep and cut its throat.

Ten people joined us for the walk to the flat in the chilly night air. Some were strangers; others we knew well. There was Blue, so called because of his red hair. Another was Dog, long and skinny like a greyhound. And Nightbeat, a journalist whose dark eyes glittered behind black-rimmed glasses.

Norm told us he was working at a temporary job, digging a swimming pool in Buckinghamshire, just outside London.

"I keep seeing sheep in the fields," he said. "They make my mouth water for lamb chops. Makes me homesick for Oz."

Dog chipped in. "Why don't you grab one?"

Blue got excited. "Yeah, Norm! why don't you?"

"Yeah, Norm! Why don't you?" the rest of us chorused.

Norm pondered for a moment. "I'll need a van to bring it back."

The room turned quiet. None of us owned anything bigger than a backpack. Nightbeat spoke up. "I know a Pommie with an Austin Mini van. I'll ask him."

At midnight we disbanded, deciding to gather at the King's Head the following evening to further our plans.

The next night the King's Head buzzed with excitement. A van was available. Norm had bought some large sheets of plastic. "To line the inside of the van," he explained. "There's going to be lots of blood."

"Where do you plan to kill it?" Nightbeat asked.

"In the field."

"How?"

"I'll slit its throat."

"Where will you take it?" Nightbeat sounded more like an investigative reporter than a journalist.

"To the flat," Norm said. "We'll string it up and let the blood drain. The best place is the bathroom; we'll hang it over the bathtub."

When the pub closed an enthusiastic mob strode to the flat. The group had grown to thirty, including the Englishman, Tim, who owned the van. I checked out the bathroom and reported that we could raise the shower curtain rod two feet higher. A sheep would fit. With Norm's plastic sheets we could cover the walls.

"I'm ready to go tonight," Norm announced.

We followed Norm and Tim outside into the cool air and walked them to the van. Norm had already lined the van's interior with plastic. We wished them good luck and returned to the flat to tape up the plastic sheets and sharpen the butchering knives.

"Isn't it illegal – stealing a sheep?" someone said.

The room fell silent. Nightbcat rose and suggested we compensate the owner. He would arrange a collection. We agreed.

The problem was solved lightheartedly as if sheep rustling were an everyday occurrence. I hoped there wouldn't be any repercussions.

Midnight passed. Then twelve-thirty. Whenever we heard a car in the street we leapt to the windows. Finally, just after one a.m. someone saw the van approach. I felt a rush of adrenaline. We dashed outside and stood anxiously by the roadside while Tim parked the van.

"Any luck?" I asked. By the way they walked, their shoulders down, I sensed disappointment.

"No," Norm said with his head bowed.

We returned to the flat, passed around cold cans of *Foster's Lager* and settled down to hear the story.

"We found a flock of about fifty or so," Norm said. "I climbed over the wooden fence and bellied my way across the field of grass and mud, towards the sheep. But, of course, they became skittish and shied away. I crawled after them but they headed towards the farmhouse about two hundred yards away. Then they started to bleat. What a bloody racket! The bleating alerted the farmer's dogs which barked continuously from the farmhouse porch. Fortunately, they were on leashes otherwise they would have been on top of me. Anyway, the dogs woke the farmer who switched on the back porch light and stood there, staring into the night. I froze, hoping the farmer wouldn't release the dogs. After a few minutes he switched off the light and went inside. But I stayed flat on the ground in case he was watching through the window from a darkened room. Eventually, I crawled back to the fence and – here we are."

Everyone expressed their condolences.

Nightbeat raised his voice above the others.

"Don't give up," he said. "On my way home from work yesterday, I passed a field of fat cows."

Australia

Homeward bound

Hitchhiking, Darwin to Townsville, November 1971
See map, page 13, C4

The red Toyota pickup truck hurtled past thousands of ball-shaped mounds of spinifex, a desert grass that thrived in the Outback's sandy soil. We sped by six-metre-high termite mounds and large tracts of scrub blackened by fire. "Lightning did it," the driver said, without taking his eyes off the road as he watched for potholes.

Joanna and I cringed with fright in the front seat. It was the first lift of our planned 6,000-kilometre hitchhiking trip from Darwin in northern Australia to Melbourne in the south.

Joanna was my youngest sister, eighteen years of age, nine years my junior. Long blonde hair framed her round face that lit up when she smiled. We had arrived in Darwin after four months of travel on the overland route from Europe through Asia to Australia by bus, foot, train and plane.

The land south of Darwin was desert-flat and the road, paved with bitumen, looked like a black boot lace stretching as far as the eye could see. We followed it into the harsh, inhospitable Australian Outback.

The Toyota driver, a man in a hurry, kept his foot on the accelerator pedal. He never lifted it even when he swerved to skirt a pothole or dodge a frightened lizard. I felt the muscles in my back and arms stiffen as I braced myself, with one hand gripping the back of the seat and the other pressing against the dashboard. After 360 kilometres at breakneck speed we landed in Katherine, in the evening, and skidded to a halt. We tumbled out of the car, grateful to have our feet firmly on the ground and thankful to be alive.

A road sign pointed to a caravan park. I peered up at the sky. No hint of rain. "Let's spread the ground sheet and sleep under the stars."

"Good idea," said Joanna as she cleared away small twigs.

The ground seemed harder than usual as I tried to get comfortable. Sleep didn't come.

The night wore on.

Joanna's voice floated through the darkness. "Are you awake? It's three o'clock. I haven't slept a wink. Do you feel like hitching?"

I agreed. It would be a relief to get off the ground and put some distance behind us. Within minutes we were standing beside the highway.

Many long-distance drivers preferred to drive in the cool of the night along The Track, the popular name for the Stuart Highway that linked Darwin and Alice Springs. I had hoped for an early morning ride but the sun was already up when a Holden utility pickup stopped beside us. Finally, some action. It would be good to be on the move again.

"Terry's the name," the driver said. "I'm going down The Track then turning off to do some business at the hotel at Mataranka Springs. Have you heard of the springs?"

"No," we both replied.

"There is a natural pool where you can swim. After that I'll drive farther south. Would you like to come?"

"Sounds great!" I said, speaking for Joanna as well who nodded her head vigorously.

It is a fact of life, when travelling, that some people pop up just when you need them. The heat of the day was so intense it almost debilitated us. A swim would be a godsend.

Terry, long and lean, often picked up hitchhikers, he told us. After driving 100 kilometres he turned off the highway and followed a narrow black-topped road to a lush tropical forest in the middle of the desert. I could hardly believe it when I saw a crystal-clear pool, the size of a volley ball court, ringed by pandanus and shady palm trees. The pool beckoned. Joanna and I kicked off our sandals and jumped in fully clothed. Warm water oozed and bubbled out of the earth. We wallowed in the shallow pool for over half- an-hour, climbed out into the 40ºC heat and in minutes our clothes were dry. We went in search of Terry in the Homestead, the adjacent hotel, and found him on a barstool talking business over a beer.

We left him to complete his discussion while we sat at a table, waving away flies and swatting others with a rolled up Women's Weekly.

Clean and refreshed, we got back into the Holden and Terry drove us down The Track to Larrimah, his final destination.

The sun beat down on us for six hours while we waited in vain for a lift out of Larrimah.

I glanced at Joanna. She appeared exhausted. I felt the same. Something had to be done.

"You wait here with the bags, Jo," I said. "I'm going to the hotel bar to ask if anyone is driving south."

A burly man with a bushy beard set down his beer glass. "I'm waiting for the sun to go down, then I'll be leaving. I can give you a lift."

"Thanks," I said appreciatively. "We'll be on the road in case someone comes by earlier."

"Okay. Good plan. I'll pick you up if you're still there."

I felt some comfort knowing we wouldn't be stranded. I watched the sun descend in the blue-grey sky and felt a refreshing, cool desert breeze cross my face.

A few minutes after sunset a big, white Mack truck crawled towards us, engine throbbing. A meaty arm waved us into the large cab. "Make yourselves comfortable," the burly one said. "My name's Bruce. I'm going through to Alice Springs."

"We're just going as far as Threeways," I said.

My map showed a turnoff at Threeways for traffic going to the east coast. Threeways was about 500 kilometres down The Track.

The driver talked long into the night, much of it about himself. He had been a stockman rounding up steers on cattle stations, a gold prospector, and a mine worker in the copper, silver, lead and zinc mines in Mount Isa. I believed he was pleased to have someone to talk to so he would stay awake.

The moonlight shone across the flat land, illuminating the clumps of spinifex grass. Occasionally a car glided towards us like a phantom with burning eyes. As time passed, both Joanna's and my eyelids drooped with fatigue. Bruce suggested one of us climb onto his bunk-bed directly behind us in the cab. In a flash Joanna hoisted herself onto the bunk. I closed my eyes, slumped in the seat and slept.

I don't know how long I'd been dozing but I awoke when I heard loud blasts of a horn. I glanced up and saw what looked like a train barrelling towards us down the middle of the highway, its lights flashing frantically.

"Bloody hell," Bruce muttered as he swerved from the bitumen to the shoulder. "Road train," he said, as the horn-blasting, lights-flashing, non-stoppable metal monster thundered past like a herd of stampeding rhinos. I felt the slipstream shake the Mack as three long trailers hooked in tandem to a truck-cab streaked past. The sound lingered as the stop-for-nothing road train roared into the night towards Darwin.

"My truck's big," said Bruce, "but I wouldn't want to tangle with that."

The Mack continued across the dark, barren plains and I dozed again.

Again, something woke me. We were turning off the highway. I saw the Threeways Roadhouse. My watch showed three-thirty.

"This is where we part company," Bruce said.

Joanna and I climbed down from the cab and thanked him. We watched as the wheels of his truck kicked up a fog of bulldust – dry, red powdery earth. Everything went quiet. The land, flat and dark, stretched away on all sides from the darkened roadhouse. Joanna found a patch of grass to lay our ground sheet on so we could catch up on some lost sleep. Two hours later we awoke to drops of rain on our faces.

At sunrise, the Roadhouse opened for business and the driver of a Holden sedan pulled up to fill his tank. We had heard from other hitchhikers that you could be marooned for days at Threeways.

"Here's an opportunity we don't want to miss," I said to Joanna. I sauntered over to the driver just as a few more drops of rain fell. The driver was a small man in his sixties with a tanned, leathery face.

"G'day," I said. He raised his head. "If you're going east would you have space for two passengers?"

He muttered something to himself. The raindrops were getting bigger.

"You'd better get in," he said.

The rain saved us. The drops were just enough to make the windshield greasy and the shoulders of the road slippery. The car had a barnyard smell and our driver, the horsy odour of a stockman, or cowboy.

He looked like an interesting man. Someone with a few tales to tell.

"Have you lived around here for long?" I asked.

"All my life," he said. "I work on a cattle station."

"You must have experienced some adventures."

"Yep."

"Do you have any worth telling?"

"Not really."

The conversation dried up. The rain abated. The grass tussocks, pale and moon-white, slid past the car window. The morning sky brightened as the sun tried to burn through the pale grey clouds. I watched a few rays shine through the breach. They illuminated the land that was arid and devoid of shade or water.

As we drove into desolate-looking beef cattle country a huge lump lay on the road ahead.

"A cow," said the driver, slowing down. "They like the warmth that radiates from the bitumen."

The cow made no effort to get off the road so he skirted around it.

"If it stays there, particularly at night when the big trucks roll by, it'll be hamburger meat before its time."

Buildings appeared on the horizon.

"Must be Mount Isa," Joanna said, looking at our map.

"It is," said the driver. "I'm stopping here but I'll drive you to the far side of town to make hitching easier." As if to welcome us, a flock of pink-breasted galahs, alerted by the sound of the car, took off from a gum tree and swooped and reeled, their grey tail feathers glistening in the early sunlight. They had been escaping the sun's rays by perching on the shaded limbs.

"Stupid galahs. You've gotta be careful if they're sitting on the road. They'll fly *at* your car, not away from it."

After passing through The Isa, as the town is called locally, we were dropped off on the eastern outskirts, near some grazing cattle.

The big disadvantage in cattle country is the cow dung. Bush flies breed in it. By mid-afternoon we had become the targets of swarms of flies. They annoyed us by crawling over any exposed skin to drink our sweat.

By late afternoon the blue sky above the sun had gradually turned yellow, then crimson, silhouetting the nearby windmill that loomed over the desert. A sight typical of the Australian Outback.

With the arrival of evening the bush flies disappeared. We decided to sleep under the stars but had concerns about snakes, ants, scorpions and spiders. Before laying down our ground sheet we checked for holes in the ground, potential critter nests, but found none.

"Something I learned in school," Joanna said, "is that of the world's 25 most deadly snakes, Australia is home to 21 of them."

"Hmmm. I think we should look over the ground again," I said, "just to be sure there are no snake holes."

After a thorough search we spread the ground sheet. Stars came out, rather faint and flickering. We scanned the heavens until we found the Southern Cross, then drifted off to sleep.

We awoke at sunrise – the same time the pesky bush flies decided to attack us. Murder was on our minds. We swatted furiously but they outnumbered us.

Back at the roadside, we perspired under a sweltering sun for seven hours. Not one car stopped.

I felt disgruntled but didn't want to show it. Joanna was more direct.

"I'm ready to expire," she said as she flattened a fly against her face. "What are we doing here?"

"Good question," I said. "I know we could take a bus, but hitchhiking is a challenge. We've come this far by thumb. You never know, the next car or truck may be the one that takes us all the way to the coast, to Townsville. It's about 560 miles."

"You've been away from Australia for too long, Russ. We've gone metric. It's 900 kilometres."

"I prefer miles; 560 doesn't sound as far as 900," I said. "I automatically convert kilometres to miles."

The summer heat and loneliness of the dry plain had started to get under our skin. It drained our energy and the continuous flat terrain taxed our morale.

"I'm homesick," Joanna said. "I've been away from home for six months and haven't talked to the family. When we get to Townsville, I want to call home."

"That's a good idea. I haven't spoken to them for three-and-a-half years while I've been travelling. We can let them know when to expect us." I paused to smack another fly, then added, "We'll soon be out of here and away from these accursed flies. Seven hours of this is enough."

"I love the Outback in spite of the flies," Joanna said. "But I need a change of scenery."

I laughed. "A change of scenery? It's all the same. Flat."

Joanna looked at our map. "There's a railway crossing about a kilometre down the highway. I think we should stand there. It'll give the illusion that we got a ride to a new location."

We tramped along the highway to the railway crossing where all vehicles had to stop before crossing the tracks. We stood there, thumbs out, throats parched and desperate for a lift.

It didn't work.

Most cars were full. Families on holidays waved and smiled as they passed.

We had to try something innovative to get a lift. In my backpack I carried a large, folded sheet of white cardboard to be used to write a destination. With a black felt-tipped pen I scrawled the words

"Going home to Mum." I hoped the words would tug at someone's heart strings.

A truck driver stopped at the railway tracks and called to us: "Where's Mum?"

Joanna answered: "Mum's in Melbourne."

The driver looked bewildered. "Is Mum a suburb of Melbourne?"

"No," Joanna said, "Mum is our mother. She lives in Melbourne."

He laughed. "Now I get it." He chuckled aloud as he changed gears to drive over the tracks, leaving us behind in his plume of diesel exhaust.

Our sign didn't work.

The setting sun glinted off the ribbons of steel and flooded the plain with yellow light. Still at the tracks, in the early evening, a family pulled up in a Chevrolet. The man said they had booked to stay in the nearby caravan park. They would be leaving the next morning for Townsville. "If you're still here in the morning we'll pick you up," the man said. "My name's Dan Tighe."

Great news! All the way to the coast in one lift!

Just as we were leaving the railway tracks to find a spot for the night, another car stopped. The driver called from the window: "G'day. Would you like jobs for five days on a cattle station? We're short of a cook and a yardman. Free accommodation, free food and ten bucks a day for each of you. You can start this evening. What do you think?"

It sounded tempting but we decided to keep moving.

"No, sorry," I said.

"No worries, mate. Good luck."

With that, he was gone.

At sunrise we rose from our camp spot near the tracks, hurried to the nearby caravan park, showered, and connected with the Tighe family. Dan was in his thirties, tall and lankily boyish with a quick smile. He introduced his wife, Margaret, a lean, compact woman with dark blonde hair. They were ready to leave with their two young daughters. Their 1961 Chevrolet pulled an eight-metre caravan and a Datsun sedan. It looked like a heavy weight for the Chev to pull.

The sun was well-risen when the multi-coloured metal creature crawled onto the highway.

Margaret turned in the seat to chat.

"I've never hitchhiked in my life," she said. "What's it like? Is it risky?"

"It can be risky," Joanna said. "You never know what the driver is like until you're in the car. Some months ago we hitched in Europe. Russ and I, our sister Trish and a family friend, Bruce, hitchhiked out of Paris to Greece. A truck stopped and the driver insisted that either Trish or I sit beside him while the other three would travel in a windowless rear section. Fortunately, Bruce noticed that the inside handle of the passenger door had been removed, thereby trapping the passenger."

"That was one ride wc turned down," I added.

"Sounds a bit scary to me," Margaret said. "You were lucky. Where did you sleep on that trip?"

"In hostels, hotels and vineyards," Joanna said.

"I don't worry about where to stay," I said. "My philosophy is that night comes and night goes, and you'll always find somewhere to sleep."

"Margaret or I wouldn't make good hitchhikers," Dan said. "We like to have our accommodation prebooked."

The weight of the Chev, caravan and Datsun restricted our speed to 45 kilometres per hour and caused the radiator to boil. After about eight hours of stops and starts to rest the engine and fill the radiator, Dan turned to me and asked, "Can you drive the Datsun?"

"I sure can," I said. Dan and I unhitched the Datsun. I topped up my water canteen and slipped behind the wheel. Progress was faster. The Chev's radiator didn't boil over, and we arrived at the caravan park in Hughendon at two-thirty in the morning, where they had a reservation.

"I meant to be here hours ago," Dan said, yawning. "I should have given you the keys to the Datsun much earlier."

The Tighes slept in their caravan, and Joanna and I, rather than be cramped in the cars, slept on the porch of the caravan park's shower rooms.

After we shared a breakfast of toast and fruit, Dan nosed the Chev onto the Flinders Highway that ran east across the plains of the Outback, over the low mountains of the Great Dividing Range and across the coastal plain to Townsville.

I was right behind the family when Dan drove into a car park on Townsville's ocean front.

This was the end of the ride with the Tighes. We waved as they headed north.

Joanna dug the map of Australia out of her bag. "Since leaving Darwin seven days ago," she said, "we have covered 2,500 kilometres."

I put my arm around Joanna's shoulders and gave her a hug.

"Let's call the family in Melbourne and tell them where we are."

Australia

Friends and strangers

Hitchhiking, Townsville to Melbourne, Nov/Dec, 1971

See map, page 13, C4

The city of Townsville, on Australia's northeast coast, hummed with holiday makers. The sky was clear, the sun burned down, cars were plentiful, hitchhiking should be easy. With my sister Joanna, I was about to hitchhike home to Melbourne, 3,500 kilometres south. But first, we needed to telephone the family.

"When do you think you'll be home?" Mum asked.

"Ten to fourteen days. Depends on the traffic," I said.

"Please, don't arrive on Saturday night, the 4th. Your father and I are going to a party and we don't want to miss your arrival."

I chuckled. "You mean, you don't want to miss the party?"

"That too." She laughed.

I laughed with her. I had been away from home for more than three years; another day or two before or after the 4th wouldn't make a difference. Joanna, who'd been away for six months, agreed.

Our first lift was with Ross, an Englishman on a two-week holiday from Mount Isa.

"That's a coincidence," I said. "We just passed through that town a few days ago. What do you do there?"

"I work as a jackaroo on a nearby cattle station."

"That sounds like an adventure," I said. "I understand a lot of English guys come to Australia to work in the Outback. I know a jackaroo is an apprentice farm hand but what do you actually do?"

"Lots of things. I fix fences that have been knocked down by kangaroos or fallen trees. Also, I help muster cattle on horseback then brand them, tag them and inject them."

"How long have you been doing that?"

"Three months. And I'm going back for another three."

"Jo and I were offered jobs for a few days on a cattle station near Mount Isa. Jo was to cook and I was to do yard work."

"Sounds like it could have been the same cattle station. They're always looking for workers."

We chatted while Ross drove. Sometime in the night his Simca coughed and died. Engine trouble. We discovered that three people sleeping in a Simca wasn't easy; it isn't a roomy car. In the morning Ross tinkered with the engine until it sputtered to life. We continued south, passing fields of sugarcane, pineapples and bananas.

When we reached the northern outskirts of Brisbane, in the evening, I asked Ross to let us out near a telephone booth. We found one outside a 'bottle shop' or liquor store. I checked my address book for the phone number of a family friend who lived in Ipswich, about 40 kilometres away.

"Bill," I said. "Joanna and I are in Brisbane. We'd like to visit you."

"Come and stay. And you're in luck, I'm having a pool party tonight."

At the bottle shop we bought a bottle of *Lindeman's* Chardonnay, put out our thumbs and after two lifts, were knocking on Bill's door. Bill lived in the wilds of suburbia. He was an imposing man of fifty-five, with a Nordic look. The party turned into a boisterous event with the fifteen inebriated partygoers leaping into the pool.

Three days later, we were on the road again. We travelled south along the scenic Gold Coast. At first through forests of highrise buildings. Later on, low green mountains flanked our right side while on our left, yellow beaches swept down to meet the waters of the blue Pacific.

In the early afternoon we arrived in Coolangatta, popular for its surf beach. After spending several hours on the beach and surfing in the seething foam we decided it was time to think about accommodation. The Coolangatta State School loomed nearby, overlooking the sea. We checked it out and decided to return later to sleep on the porch where we would be protected if it rained. Joanna thought for a moment. "I hope there isn't a night school course tonight."

We were lucky. The building was in darkness when we returned. Rain fell but it made only soft tapping sounds on the roof. A gentle wind blew, rustling the leaves in the school yard and in the surrounding gum trees.

At mid-afternoon the next day, exhausted but refreshed after more surfing, we stood beside the highway. Within ten minutes the driver of a Ford Falcon station wagon stopped. We were elated when Brett, the driver, offered us a lift all the way to Sydney, 900 kilometres south.

Late in the evening we stopped for the night. While Joanna slept in the station wagon, Brett and I slept in a park under a wooden picnic table to escape any overnight dew. The next morning we got up early to beat the traffic, but we hadn't gone far before we drove around a curve into a police road block.

"We're checking cars for defects," the constable said. "Keep your engine running." Then he prowled around the car.

"Cripes," exclaimed Brett in a worried tone.

The constable came back, slapped a Defective Motor Vehicle sticker on the windshield and said: "Two bald tires at the front and a defective exhaust."

"We're on our way to Sydney," said Brett. He sounded devastated. "Can I have the work done there?"

"Yes, you've got seven days to fix the problems."

I was relieved, not only for Brett but for ourselves as well.

We slipped away slowly, not wanting the exhaust pipe to sound too noisy.

Sydney's traffic during the afternoon rush hour was more chaotic that usual because of a strike by government bus drivers. The additional cars caused horrendous traffic jams. Joanna had a friend, Marlene, who lived near Sydney's popular Bondi Beach. We didn't have her phone number; we couldn't reach her by bus; a taxi was the answer. We decided to surprise her. Brett let us out when he saw an empty cab.

Thirty minutes later Joanna pressed the doorbell. Marlene's eyes widened. "I thought you were in Europe! Come and sit down."

We stepped inside. Marlene strode straight to the fridge and reached in.

"I've been waiting for a reason to open this," she said, as she unscrewed the cork from a bottle of *Penfold's* 1967 riesling, and poured the wine.

Two air mattresses appeared from a cupboard. "I'll blow some air into these," she said, stomping up and down on a foot pump. A blonde-haired human dynamo, Marlene took some chicken from her fridge as she turned to us with, "I hope you can stay a while."

Joanna told her about our not wanting to arrive home on Saturday night.

Marlene thought for a moment. "I'll drive you to the Hume Highway tomorrow, Saturday, so you can start hitching. You should be in Melbourne Sunday morning."

The next morning a car stopped and the driver took us 400 kilometres to Gundagai.

"If I could grant you a wish," I said to Joanna as we stood once again with our thumbs out, "what would you wish for?"

Joanna pondered. "Thanks to friends and strangers, we've been lucky so far. We're so close to Melbourne, just another 500 kilometres. I'd wish for a car to pick us up and take us right to our front door, arriving Sunday morning."

And that is exactly what happened!

Philippines

The faith healers

Psychic surgery in Baguio City, February 1974

See map, page 13, C3

Freddie was on the phone when I strolled into his travel agency in downtown Manila. Colourful airline posters promoting Taipei, Seoul, Hong Kong and Tokyo covered the office walls. A ceiling fan circulated the humid air. A few straw mats lay scattered over the concrete floor. Freddie was at his desk in the corner.

Freddie immediately put down the phone and rose to greet me with energy and enthusiasm. I had done business with him before. Of average height and weight, aged about thirty-five, he held an engaging smile. His telephone, the *Official Airline Guide,* a pen and paper – the basic necessities of a travel agent, sat on his desk. We discussed airfares and destinations in the Philippines, then I broached a topic that had been running wild in the back of my mind.

"Have you heard of the faith healers?"

"Of course. You're in the Philippines. Everyone here has heard of them."

"I'd like to see what they do," I said. "Newspapers around the world have reported how they were healing their patients in one- or two-minute operations with the use of psychic surgery. Do you know where to find these faith healers?"

Freddie confided he had often thought about visiting a faith healer to cure his chronic sinus problem. He had consulted four different doctors in Manila over the past few years without success. One of the doctors had suggested he visit a faith healer. "I was always too busy, and kept putting it off," Freddie said, "but now that you've brought it up, I'll do something about it. I'll call a friend, Claudio, who is an investigative reporter. He has written stories about the healers, both the good ones and the bad, for *Panorama* magazine. The bad ones are usually fakes who take advantage of foreigners."

Freddie dialled, spoke to his friend, mentioned me, discussed his sinus problem and arranged that Claudio pick us up in his car at the travel agency the following morning at nine.

"That was quick work," I said.

"Claudio said it was time to do another story about the healers. That's why he's ready to go so soon."

The next morning Claudio rolled up in a black Chevrolet. He was of slight build, bespectacled, with a constant smile. I got into the back while Freddie sat up front.

Claudio turned to me. "I know a few of the healers who live in and around Manila but there are some I haven't met. I have the address of a new one. Freddie and I want to see if he can cure his sinus troubles and we would like you to photograph the procedure."

That's exactly what I wanted. I had two cameras with me: a *Yashica SLR* for still photos and a *Canon Super 8* movie camera.

We drove along a narrow alley crammed with two-storey houses, until we found the number. Freddie knocked and spoke to a young woman. She retreated to another room where we could hear some activity, and returned to say Freddie would be helped. Then she added that I wouldn't be allowed to use a camera and that I couldn't watch the operation. Freddie argued with her briefly then said to me, "Let's go."

Freddie told Claudio what had happened. "They're trying to hide something," Claudio said. "Let's visit a couple of healers I've already checked out."

The next place was a small church-like building with crosses and pictures of Christ painted on the white interior walls. I estimated fifty people, including a dozen Westerners, seated on chairs, waiting to see one of the three available healers.

Freddie asked a healer if they allowed cameras.

"No, they can distract the healers. But you are welcome to watch the procedures, if the patients don't object."

I wandered freely and witnessed some amazing operations. A man hopped along on crutches to the operating table – a wooden table covered by a plastic sheet – and perched on the edge. The healer, a man in slacks and T-shirt, pointed his finger at the man's legs without touching them, and two incisions appeared. The healer removed long yellow strands of material that looked like dried spaghetti, from the knee area. Then the man got off the table and walked away, carrying his crutches.

Next, a woman lay on the table and the healer rolled back the woman's white blouse to reveal her midriff. With his fingers, he parted the skin of her stomach and removed diseased tissue which he tossed into a small bucket on the floor. I almost retched. I can't even watch a needle being injected into my arm. The sick woman's family and friends had gathered around the table as curious spectators and as helpers. They swabbed blood off the body with cotton wool and cotton towels.

Freddie and Claudio called me from the action. Claudio said that if Freddie was to have a sinus operation here, we would have a wait of about two hours because of the fifty or so people who were ahead of us. "Perhaps we should drive to Pangasinan province where there are a lot of healers," he suggested. "We could visit Josephine Sison, whom I have met before, and watch her operate." We agreed.

The drive north, along winding roads, carried us past rice fields and small towns consisting of wooden buildings with corrugated iron roofs. The late morning sun brought the temperature to thirty degrees Celsius, so we had the windows partly down to allow for air circulation.

I was sitting in the back seat. Claudio turned to me. "What do you think, so far?"

"I noticed that there weren't any instruments used to cut the skin. Do you know how it was done?"

Claudio explained there was energy around a healer's body, especially in the hands. When the healer touched the patient, the energy produced an incision by separating skin cells. Some healers were blessed with the ability to point the finger and make incisions from arm's length. After the operation the healer passed his or her hand over the incision and the cells knitted together, leaving no mark. Patients, conscious with their eyes open, stayed in their street clothes. This sort of surgery – psychic surgery – didn't hurt.

"Before coming to the Philippines," I said, "I read stories in newspapers and magazines that debunked psychic surgery, saying it was all a hoax. What do you think about that?"

He was quick to respond. "In some cases the stories are correct. Unfortunately, a few charlatans are cashing in on the fame of the true healers and, without proper direction, foreigners are being deceived. Some true healers may even use tricks to boost their reputations. Occasionally, a television crew from overseas will arrive to do a study and only concentrate on how the public can be fooled by using phoney blood and animal parts. That sort of reporting is one-sided and is done with one purpose – to sell a television show."

Claudio had a lot to say and seemed keen to answer my questions. He mentioned that sometimes serious investigators arrive from overseas, like the team of nine doctors and professors the previous year. They conducted extensive interviews with healers and patients and analyzed blood and body parts. Claudio had a copy of their published report with confirmation that the healings they investigated did not involve fraud, anesthetics were not used, the bodies were not opened with a scalpel or razor blades or other instruments, the operations took from one to ten minutes to perform, no special precautions were made to maintain sterile conditions, people could stay in their street clothes, the operations appeared to cause little, if any, discomfort and the patients were left without post-operative shock.

After a couple of hours we arrived in the town of Carmen where we bought some fruit for lunch. "It's not far now," Claudio said. We followed a side road into another village of wooden houses. Claudio pointed out a concrete building. "That's Josephine's sanctuary. It was built with donations from patients, mostly from overseas. The local people are too poor to contribute much money."

Claudio stopped at the sanctuary. Outside the building,

chickens pecked at grain and two pigs grunted as they foraged for food scraps.

Inside, about a dozen local people sat on benches. Josephine stood at a table administering to an elderly woman with a distended stomach. Claudio strode up to Josephine, a plump woman of about thirty-five, with a smiling, nut-brown face. He told her Freddie would like an operation and that I wanted to take pictures. She smiled, nodded her agreement and pointed to a book where Freddie could enter his name so he would be called up in turn. A man in his late thirties was in charge of the book. Josephine's husband, Claudio told us. He retired from the police force to help his wife because she worked long hours at healing and needed someone to keep her organized.

The three of us sat on a bench to await the calling of Freddie's name. I looked around to see a picture of Christ and signs saying: "Christ does the work; I am his instrument." "Pray to Jesus."

I turned to Claudio. "Is this mainly a Christian thing?"

"No. Psychic surgery was practised before Christianity was introduced to the Philippines. Because Jesus was a healer and teacher, the healers have faith in Him."

By this time, a young man was lying on his back on the operating table while Josephine worked on his groin area. "Does she have any medical training?" I asked Claudio.

"None. She's in a light trance. Her hands are being guided by a spirit who may have been a doctor when alive on Earth. The healers believe that God has given them a gift which allows doctors in the spirit world to work through them."

Suddenly it was Freddie's turn. I grabbed my movie camera and rushed after him to the table. He hoisted himself onto it and lay on his back. "What is wrong?" Josephine asked.

Freddie pointed at his nose: "Sinus."

Claudio asked her if I could film the operation and she said, "Yes. You'll need more light." She pulled the curtain aside and sunlight streamed in. I started the film rolling. Josephine went immediately to the left side of the bridge of Freddie's nose, and made an incision with her finger. Blood trickled out. She pushed some cotton wool into the opening. Then she opened the right side of his nose and inserted more cotton wool. Within seconds she was pulling the cotton wool out of his nostrils. An assistant wiped the trickles of blood from his face. Josephine closed the two incisions by passing her hand over them until there was no evidence that the body had been opened. Freddie swung his legs from the table after his two-minute operation.

"How do you feel?" I asked.

Freddie took a deep breath through his nose. "Amazing! This is the first time in fourteen years I've been able to breathe through my nose."

"Did it hurt?" I asked.

"I didn't feel a thing."

"I'm putting my name in the book," I said. And we sat down to wait.

I asked Claudio what ailments he had seen healed.

"I've seen tumors excised, different forms of arthritis and cancer treated, back-pain and tennis elbow alleviated, gall stones and kidney stones removed, just to mention a few. I've also seen a man's eye popped out onto his cheek, washed, and returned to the eye socket."

As the time ticked by I grew more curious.

When Josephine's husband called my name I strode quickly to the table. Josephine looked at me, surprised. I could read what was going through her head: Here's the one who needed to film the healing before he would believe.

"What's wrong with you?" she asked as I hoisted myself onto the table and settled down on my back.

"I don't know. Maybe nothing. Can I have a check-up?"

Josephine took a step back and scanned my energy field, or aura, for a break that would pinpoint a medical problem. I turned my head to Freddie. "Will you take a picture with my camera?" He grabbed the *Yashica,* but became confused by the dials and buttons. "Which button should I press?"

I didn't answer. Josephine had already lifted my shirt. She stuffed cotton wool into an incision she made in the right side of my belly.

After she passed her hand over the cut, the skin knitted and a whitish scar formed, then disappeared. I felt no discomfort despite the cotton wool being inside my body. I raised my head higher, rested on my elbows and watched Josephine move to my left side. She held her hand over my stomach and aimed her index finger. A gash appeared. With my eyes just six inches from it, I watched the cotton wool, now yellowish with body fluids, pop out of the incision, seemingly by itself. Claudio could tell I was amazed and explained that it was the same cotton wool that she had pressed into my right side.

Everything happened so fast, and Freddie was still fiddling with my camera!

To assist with the operation I reached for clean cotton wool and swabbed the blood oozing out of the gash. I watched my innards pulsate to the rhythmic beat of my heart. Josephine closed the incision by passing her energized hand over it to allow the cells to join together.

Then she looked around the room and said, "Next please."

"Wait," I said. "What was wrong with me?"

"You had too much acid in your stomach. You must have had stomach pains."

She was right. Over the years I occasionally took antacid tablets to relieve acute pain in my stomach. It was hard to believe what had just taken place even though I watched the procedure up close.

A hat for donations lay on a side table. The local people who came for healing were subsistence farmers. They left a few cents worth of pesos in the hat, to help maintain Josephine's family. Healers, like Josephine, relied on overseas visitors, like me, to boost the donations.

During the drive back to Manila I asked if many foreigners visited faith healers.

"Thousands," Claudio said. "For example, tomorrow a Jumbo jet from Rome arrives with 300 visually-impaired Italians.

"Over the years many healers have moved to Manila so they can be more easily accessible to those who need help. As a result, they earn bigger gratuities. In fact, Josephine was asked to relocate but she decided to stay in her village with her friends and family."

Eight months later I wrote to Freddie about his sinuses. He felt good, he replied, but at Claudio's suggestion had gone back to Josephine six months later to make sure the sinus trouble was fixed once and for all.

I was able to tell Freddie that I had no recurrence of stomach pains.

And I told him I would return to the Philippines if I had a medical ailment in the future.

Thirty-two years later, when living in Canada, I jetted to the Philippines with my wife, Penny. I had told her of my experiences of observing healers in action. It was time for another check-up. Penny had an open mind and was willing to go along with my venture.

A number of books had been written about the 'faith healing' or 'psychic surgery' phenomenon. Ten years earlier I had bought a book written by Dr. Donald McDowall, a chiropractor from Canberra, Australia. *(www.chiroclinic.com.au)*. He witnessed and assisted at numerous psychic surgeries. His accounts of what he experienced bolstered my belief in what I had observed.

Before flying from Vancouver I searched the Internet to update my knowledge of the healers and to decide which one to visit. I learned that Josephine had died about 1988. I e-mailed Dr. McDowall who by now had written five books on the topic. He provided three names of healers in Baguio City, a city north of Manila where I preferred to go because of its pleasant temperature.

I also e-mailed Jaime Licauco, a businessman and author in Manila who had observed more than 2,000 operations and had written fifteen books on the subject. Originally a sceptic, he changed his mind after observing the healers at work. Like the doctor, he gave the names of three healers in Baguio City: Jun Labo, Placido Palitayan and William Nonog. Both McDowall and Licauco wrote that their information could be outdated.

After arriving in Manila, Penny and I flew to Baguio City where I planned to telephone the three healers. Unfortunately, the airport offices were closed and there were no public telephones in sight. The situation looked grim until a cab driver approached and asked: "Are you looking for Placido?"

"Yes," I said. I felt hopeful. That was one of the names on my list.

"Placido is on Mindoro Island, doing healing," he said. He then told me that of the other two healers on my list, Jun Labo was healing in Germany and William had left Baguio without saying when he would be back.

"But you can visit Laurence Cacteng," he said, " I can take you to him."

My antenna went up! Was he a faith healer or a fake healer? I'd not heard the name Laurence before. But, of course, there were many healers I hadn't heard of. We took the cab to his house where we saw a short, stocky man in his sixties standing on the sidewalk.

"That's Laurence," said the cabbie.

Penny and I shook hands with Laurence and followed him into his house, to a large room lined with sofas. It was his healing sanctuary. Religious paintings, including one of Christ, hung on the walls.

Laurence asked about my health concerns but, before I could answer, he pointed to my lower back and said, "You have a sore back." He was right. For years I felt pain in my back after a walk of only forty minutes. I added I had Parkinson's disease which caused my legs and arms to tremor. Laurence admitted immediately he had not been successful in alleviating the symptoms of Parkinson's disease, nor had his departed grandmother who had also been a healer. "But maybe, after I have treated you, I will have slowed the progression," he said hopefully.

"Do many people come for healing?" I asked.

"Twenty-one local people were here this morning, and I have a group of French people arriving tomorrow. Sometimes I am invited to other countries like France, Germany and South Africa to give healing."

I found Laurence to be a pleasant, humble man who was easy to talk to. He had been a healer since the age of seven.

I also had a faulty heart valve, I told him, plus spondolothesis – degeneration of the spine in the small of my back. I felt a bit embarrassed; he must have thought of me as a walking medical disaster. Something I forgot to tell him was my tendency to lean to one side when I walked.

After half-an-hour of chatting, he suggested he could start work on me immediately if I wished. It all seemed rather sudden. After all, we had only landed in Baguio an hour-and-a-half before and hadn't even checked into a hotel. Nevertheless, I agreed.

Penny asked if she could take photos. "Yes, of course," Laurence said as he directed us into a small private room. It was just big enough for a seven-foot-long wooden table covered with a plastic tablecloth, and working space for Laurence and his wife, a retired school teacher, who was to assist. A painting of the Nativity hung on the wall. On a small table sat a plastic basin for washing his hands and on the floor at his feet was a plastic bucket for disposing of diseased tissue. A yellow towel for swabbing blood lay on the table. I slipped off my shirt, hoisted myself onto the table and lay on my back.

So, here I was, after the passing of many years, on a healer's table again. Was I really doing this? I was concerned that I might have an anxiety attack but, instead, I felt calm. My life was now in the lap of the gods, or God.

I waited to be opened up.

Penny recorded the session with her camera and told me later what she witnessed.

With his hands resting on my head, Laurence recited a prayer and went into a light trance. He immediately parted the skin in my stomach area with his fingers, and put two fingers into the gash to stem the blood flow. He pulled out what looked like small blood clots, each the size of a pea. (Later he explained he withdrew diseased tissue.) He held the plum-coloured tissue so Penny could take a photo, then plopped it into the plastic bucket on the floor. He did this procedure to several parts of my upper body including my heart and neck, while his wife wiped the blood away with the towel. He washed his hands in the basin each time he moved from one area of my body to another. I had not felt any pain, nor was I aware of where he was operating on my body, unless I looked.

"Please turn over. I'll work on your back," I heard him say.

I wondered what he was going to do but knew that I would see the photos. He ministered quickly. The session lasted fifteen minutes.

Penny and I left his healing sanctuary, agreeing to be back at 5:30 p.m. for another session. We walked in silence, each absorbed in our own thoughts.

Penny broke the silence saying "Do you think he is legitimate?"

I cast my mind back over the years. "His operations are similar to what I saw in '74. I know it is difficult to accept 100% because there are many unanswered questions as to how it works. I've no doubt he is genuine."

Penny said she remained surprisingly calm and was not put off by the sight of blood.

We checked into the Pines View Hotel, not far from Laurence's home, then spent the rest of the day sightseeing, on foot. I didn't experience any post-operative stress or pain.

Over a four-day period I had eight treatments with Laurence.

After I assured Penny that I hadn't felt any pain during the treatments she asked for a check-up. She told me of a cold-as-ice, split-second sensation when he opened her stomach. Otherwise, she felt nothing. I watched him remove a dark red globule and drop it into the bucket. He concluded Penny's check-up by telling her she was healthy.

After my healing, I realized that my back didn't hurt after many hours of walking and that I didn't have a sideways lean any more. The lean was the problem I had forgotten to tell Laurence about. I considered it a bonus to walk straight again. There was no way of knowing if he slowed the progression of the Parkinson's disease. I'd like to think he did. I knew that keeping a positive mind, and having faith in the healer, could help the healing.

Because Laurence was in a light trance throughout the healing sessions, and because his hands were guided by spirit, as he put it, he wasn't always aware of the area of the body he was treating.

Before leaving Laurence's house, I compensated him for his time and thanked him for the healing.

"Don't thank me," Laurence said, and pointed over his shoulder to a painting of Christ. "He did the healing."

It wasn't until after we arrived home from the Philippines that we looked at our photos and wondered which internal organs he had worked on. We recognized the external parts of the body where he had ministered: head, neck, back and feet, but had to call upon a friend, Judith Ann, a registered nurse, to explain other photos and identify the internal organs Laurence had attended: liver, pancreas, heart and stomach.

Controversy still surrounds the question as to whether faith healers, or psychic surgeons, can or cannot really open a body and cure an ailment. To argue the point knowledgeably, one must travel to the Philippines and experience healers in action, or better yet, climb onto the table for a check-up. Give it a go.

Japan

In and out of hot water

Bathing, Japanese-style, May 1975

See map, page 13, C2

Travel-stained and feeling grimy, I longed for a shower. I checked into a *ryokan*, a Japanese inn, for my first night in Japan. I was in Nagasaki on the island of Kyushu. I found the bathroom easily; I smelled the steam. I expected a room with shower stalls but instead found a room with six sets of hot and cold taps, and six short milk-maid-style stools. Beyond this room I saw a large tub of hot water about twenty feet long and ten feet wide. Ten men stood in it with small, white towels perched on their heads.

I retreated to my room to study the brochures on bathing, Japanese-style. I was lucky. Directions were succinct: Strip off, sit on the low stool, face the hot and cold taps, pour water over yourself, rub on soap, wash it off, rub yourself down with a small, white towel, drop into the hot tub, place the towel on your head, and relax.

I returned to the bathroom in the rubber thongs which the inn provided. I hoped I had remembered all the directions in the proper order.

After washing I lowered myself into the hot tub. Phew! It was hot. Steam rose all around me. I was tempted to clamber out but I persevered.

I greeted the other men with “hi”; they nodded and grunted friendly acknowledgements. The man near the taps spoke to the others. When a few of them answered with a nod he turned on the hot tap and steaming water gushed from the spout. They luxuriated in the hotter water while I felt as if I were a lobster boiling in a pot. I took the towel from the top of my head and wiped away the perspiration dripping down my face. A few men climbed out, soaped and doused themselves and got back in. I did the same. I concluded that the bathing ritual provided an opportunity for the men to socialize and discuss business.

The next day I continued my travels to the hot-springs town of Beppu. At the Youth Hostel I heard about the Suginoi Hotel – a hotel with a complex of baths fed by hot water from underground springs. The hotel promoted a Dreamland and a Jungleland. Men and women alternated between the buildings. I was curious.

The day I arrived was the men's day to use Jungleland. I decided to check it out.

I paid a modest entrance fee at the hotel counter, walked to the changing room and stripped off. I placed my clothes in a locker, sat on a now-familiar low stool, soaped and doused myself and headed towards the door marked Jungleland.

I stepped through the doorway into another world – a tropical wonderland – where palm trees loomed over large-leafed exotic plants in various shades of green. Trees and shrubs bordered the pathways which led me to steaming pools, about 10 feet in diameter.

Along the way I passed other patrons meandering along the footpaths, modestly holding their small towels over their privates. They slipped into the steaming pools. I did the same and I learned that the denser the steam, the hotter the pool.

Jungleland resembled an aircraft hanger because of its arched roof. See-through ceiling tiles allowed in natural light.

The first pool I went into had warm, murky, mustard-coloured water with a stench of sulphur. It was only lukewarm so I slipped into a hotter one. My body was becoming accustomed to the higher temperatures so I pushed on to the sandpits.

Each of the two sandpits was roughly twenty feet by ten. I followed the example of other bathers who went to the brown sand pit, and dug a shallow body-length trough with a shovel. I felt like I was digging my own grave. Lying in the trough, I dragged sand over my prostrated body until only my head and one arm were visible, and started to cook. Natural heat from below penetrated my muscles. I perspired; salty sweat rolled down from my forehead. With my small white towel I wiped my face. Through squinting eyes, I could see other men burying their friends up to their necks. What a crazy way to spend an afternoon!

As the heat became unbearable, I dragged myself out and washed off the sand under a shower near the pits. Judging by the grimaces on the men's faces, the other pit, with black sand, was obviously much hotter. I backed away from additional torture.

Instead, I headed for a large slab of stone placed over a bed of hot sand. Thermal heat from under the sand kept the stone continually hot. The idea was to lie on the slab and absorb the heat. I lay down for all of two seconds and was almost scorched with second degree burns. I fled to the cold showers.

Once I was cooled off I noticed another challenge: the massage chair. I sat in the chair and suffered while little rubber hammers relentlessly pounded my back.

After being boiled in water, baked in sand, fried on a stone slab and pummelled with hammers, I decided to leave Jungleland behind me. *Sayonara*!

Samoa

The leaky faucet

A village experience at Sitivi's, March 1976

See map, page 14, B2

When I stepped from the air-conditioned comfort of the jet onto the tarmac of Faleolo airport in Samoa, a thick wall of humid air took my breath away. Polynesian Airlines had landed at 2 p.m., the hottest time of the day.

I had been given the names of two places to stay by a traveller who had visited the island. The first was a guest house in Apia, the capital, nineteen miles from the airport. The second, the home of Sitivi Tupou who lived in Leulumoega village, three miles away.

In the airport terminal I picked up a pamphlet that described Samoan customs. With interest I read the following rules.

- Do not address your Samoan hosts in their *fale* (home, pronounced far-lay) while standing, if they are sitting.
- Sit down cross-legged on a straw mat and then talk.
- If you are tired while sitting cross-legged, you may cover your feet and legs with a mat and then stretch them.
- Do not eat while standing in a *fale*, or when walking in a village.
- Do not enter a *fale* while a family is offering prayers; a visitor should wait outside until prayers are finished.
- A visitor must remove footwear before entering.

I chose Sitivi Tupou's because I wanted to experience village life. Sitivi welcomed guests for a dollar a night, the other traveller had told me.

I boarded a little, old, blue bus for the short run to the village. The roughly paved, twisting road followed the coastline. On my left side, gentle white-capped waves twinkled in the blue sea. On my other side, groves of tall coconut palms curved upwards on the island's green hills. We passed banana groves, cattle, horses, a game of cricket played by women using baseball bats, and a couple of tall, stone-built churches. There was also a sprinkling of small boxlike homes built of timber and tin.

When I got off the bus I saw that the homes in Sitivi's village were traditional *fales* – spacious, oval-shaped, open-sided, dome-roofed huts. Some young village boys led me to Sitivi's *fale*. It was about sixty feet long, larger than most of the others. I guessed that Sitivi must be affluent, because the roof on his home had corrugated iron sheets, whereas others were covered with less durable palm leaves. The *fale* sat on a raised platform built of white coral, reinforced with black stones.

A stocky, toffee-coloured man standing inside beckoned to me. I kicked off my sandals, walked across a sea of reed mats that covered the entire floor, to meet the man.

"I'm Sitivi," he said, then introduced me to his wife and three teenaged daughters. All three girls had inherited their mother's good looks: thick, wavy, black hair framing bronze, oval faces with big, grape-dark eyes and brilliant smiles. They were dressed in the *puletasi,* an ankle-length wrap-around skirt and blouse of colourful, flowery cotton – the popular attire among island women. One daughter was holding two young girls. "She's married to a man who works in New Zealand," Sitivi said. "We all hope to emigrate there one day."

When I asked why he wanted to live in New Zealand he answered with 'better education and jobs.' He added that many Samoans had already settled there, as well as Tongans and Cook Islanders.

The *fale* consisted of one large room. I was shown to the end where a mosquito net hung from the roof's crossbeams. "The mosquitoes become active at night and are simply a nuisance," he said. "They do not carry malaria."

Sitivi led me outside and left me to explore.

A patch of green-leafed taro, half-a-dozen banana trees and two papaya trees grew in the yard. Water was gushing out of a faucet on top of a six-foot high galvanized pipe. Someone must have left it on by mistake. I reached up to turn it off but the faucet continued to leak. It must be missing a rubber washer. I promised myself that if ever I returned to Samoa, I would bring some washers.

In the evening, the aroma of roasted meat twitched my nostrils. Sitivi invited me to join the family for dinner. I looked forward to sharing a traditional meal with them. Laid out on the floor mats were wooden bowls heaped with food: roasted chicken, sliced pork, boiled taro and breadfruit, a bunch of bananas, papaya and tea. We sat cross-legged around the bowls of food, and reached forward with forks to spear portions for our china plates.

After dinner I strolled through the yard. One of Sitivi's daughters had already started to wash the dinner dishes under the leaky faucet. She told me that the family scrubbed their clothes and showered under this never-ending stream. What a waste of water! The small island was susceptible to water shortages. I reminded myself that I mustn't forget rubber washers if I ever returned.

I wandered past the village's open-sided *fales* and saw families talking and eating. Blinds of woven coconut leaves were presently rolled up but could be lowered to form walls to keep out rain and wind.

At five to ten I heard the clang of a bell.

"What's that?" I asked half-a-dozen teenagers who were striding past purposefully.

"The curfew bell," said a girl. "We must be home by ten or we will be fined 10 *sen*."

I decided to respect the curfew, too, and hoofed it back to the *fale*.

As I lay on a mat under the protective mosquito net, the overwhelming charm of the South Pacific islands crept over me. Chickens scratched at the ground and the family pig sniffed and grunted as it foraged for food scraps. To these barnyard sounds, I drifted off to sleep.

Morning came early when snorts from the porker woke me. A

couple of roosters started warming up their vocal chords to greet the sun. Dogs barked and chickens squawked. Someone revved a motor bike which, I'm sure, woke up the entire village.

Sitivi and I chatted in the morning. I learned he was a politician. He was waiting for a bus to take him to the *Fale Fono* (Parliament House). He invited me to go with him. Samoa, he said, was a democracy. It had a prime minister elected by parliament from its ranks. There was also a ceremonial head of state chosen from the native chiefs. Parliamentarians were expected to adhere to a dress code. Sitivi wore a white shirt and dark tie and a *lava lava* – a calf-length wrap-around skirt – the local equivalent of trousers, and a wide belt and sandals.

The government building was of a beehive-shape, designed after the traditional *fale*. All the members' seats were arranged in a semi-circle, facing the Speaker of the House. I sat in the Visitors' Gallery while the politicians debated. English was the language of business and administration but Samoan was the official language.

I listened to a debate about imports and exports. Concern was expressed that the value of imports was six times that of exports. I left the Visitor's Gallery, hoping that one of their imports would be rubber washers.

Ten years after my 1976 visit, my wife Penny, and I, stopped in Samoa. In a little, old, blue bus we bounced our way to Leulumoega village with photos I had taken during that first visit. I recognized the *fale* but not the stocky man standing in it. "I'm Sitivi Tupou's brother," he said.

I showed him the photos. "They've changed a lot," he said. "They've all settled in New Zealand. A few years ago I was living in New Zealand; that's why you and I never met."

I glanced around. Pigs and chickens roamed the grounds. The taro patch was smaller but there were more banana and papaya trees. The brother – a Born-again Methodist, he told us – spent his evenings preaching in the villages. He invited us to have some taro and tea and to stay overnight. We settled on a cup of tea. He got water for the kettle from the outside tap, the one that was six feet above the ground.

I was pleased to see the tap had stopped running incessantly – because I had forgotten to bring rubber washers!

Fiji

In search of the idyllic island

Visiting Vatulele Island's masi makers, March 1976

See map, page 14, B2

I was on a self-imposed mission to find an idyllic island in the South Pacific. I checked into the Coconut Inn for my first night in Fiji. Reed mats lay strewn over the concrete floor of the lobby. Seated cross-legged on a mat was a big-boned, brown-skinned man wearing a blue wraparound skirt and a white T-shirt.

"Welcome to Fiji," he said. "My name is Jacob. Please sit with me. I am preparing *yanggona.*"

In front of him was a wooden bowl half-full of water. Beside it lay a couple of handfuls of crushed tree roots. "They are from the pepper tree," Jacob said as he placed them in a cloth bag. He dunked the bag of roots into the bowl of water, then massaged and squeezed it until the water turned a mud-brown.

At that moment two backpackers who were staying at the inn stopped to join us.

"This is our national drink," Jacob said. "In Fiji we call it *yanggona* but some other Pacific islands know it as *kava.*"

Jacob dipped a half coconut shell into the brown liquid and turned to hand it to me.

"Before you drink," he said, "you must clap once. It is an old Fijian custom. After drinking, you clap three times."

I clapped, took the cup in both hands and drank some of the bitter brew. I grimaced as my lips and tongue experienced a numbing sensation. Following Jacob's instruction, we all clapped three times in unison.

"It relaxes you," Jacob said as he scooped another cupful from the bowl. "Our custom is to drink and clap until the bowl is empty."

Knowing that, I summoned my courage, and with my fellow backpackers, downed several more cups of the distasteful liquid until, thankfully, the bowl was empty. It wasn't a drink I would want to try again.

Jacob told us *yanggona* was consumed at social occasions such as births, weddings, funerals and at meetings of village chiefs.

His mention of village chiefs prompted me to ask for a suggestion of a village to visit.

"Vatulele Island," he said. "Go to Korolevu Beach and wait for the boat from the island to arrive at 8 am."

I stood in the bow of the open boat headed for Vatulele Island and tasted salty spray whipped up by the wind. Elijah perched on the seat in the stern and held the tiller firmly. He was a bearded Fijian with legs and arms of iron, and two rows of teeth that looked strong enough to crack a human thigh bone. I'd read that the last foreigner to be eaten by Fijian cannibals was the missionary, Reverend Baker. But that was in 1868.

The 15-foot boat, powered by an outboard motor, rose and fell in the choppy sea. As the wind blew stronger, the sea grew rougher and the craft reared and plunged like a bucking bronco. I plunked myself down on a bench in the bow and gripped the edge of the boat. I looked around for a life vest but couldn't see one.

With each new swell the boat slid down a long incline like a surfboard rider, until confronted by another cresting wave. Bubbling foam splashed away from the bow. Elijah smiled broadly as he gripped the tiller, his upper arm muscles bulging. "I like this," he shouted, waving at the sea. He wore a bright, confident smile that filled his face.

Just an hour earlier I had been standing on Korolevu Beach on the south coast of Viti Levu, Fiji's main island, waiting for the village boat from Vatulele Island. It was supposed to arrive with a cargo of *masi* cloth made by the women of the island, then return to Vatulele.

The cloth would be sold in the tourist shops in Viti Levu. I had asked the boatman, Elijah, if I could go to the island with him.

After a two-hour trip over the choppy sea we arrived at Vatulele, a raised coral island dotted with coconut palms and paper mulberry trees. We nosed through a break in the coral reef and entered a quiet lagoon with a white sandy beach of old coral. Village huts lined the edge of the lagoon.

I had come here to satisfy my curiosity: Was there such a place as an idyllic South Pacific island? Surely if there was one, it would be amongst the 320 islands that made up Fiji.

On Viti Levu I had met friendly Fijians who welcomed newcomers with a wave and an exuberant *bula* (hello). I looked forward to experiencing island life on Vatulele.

I had no idea where to stay and was unaware of any guest houses or hotels. I tended to play things by ear and face challenges as they arose. Night comes and night goes and I always find somewhere to sleep: on a beach, beneath a bush or under a roof.

When I asked Elijah about accommodation he offered a room in his home. But, he told me, I should give a gift to the village chief to allow me to stay on the island. Two dollars would be sufficient. Elijah called out to a boy of about ten to deliver the gift. Thirty minutes later the boy returned from the chief's compound with a few words of thanks written on an old scrap of paper. Villages are still run by hereditary chiefs but their prestige is waning. Rich chiefs are respected. Poor chiefs are not. I didn't ask the chief for his Financial Statement!

Elijah led me to his home, an L-shaped structure with walls of thatched coconut palm leaves and a roof of corrugated iron sheets.

It had a wooden floor of rough-hewn planks covered with reed mats but had no furniture, electricity, running water or inside toilet. A well in the yard, with tin buckets scattered around it, provided fresh water. Half-a-dozen banana trees and a couple of coconut palms grew in the yard.

Elijah's wife, a thick-set woman wearing a blue blouse over her multi-coloured *sulu* or skirt, was working with other women beneath a shade tree. Using a wooden mallet, she was pounding a piece of *masi* cloth against a flat board to make it stretch wider. When I approached, she stopped and broke into a broad, welcoming smile. The continual banging sound of mallets reverberated through the village. It seemed as though every woman was involved in producing *masi* cloth for the tourist trade. *Masi* cloth, called *tapa* cloth on other South Pacific islands, was made from the bark of the paper mulberry tree. It was worn as clothing in earlier times, and sheets of it were hung as privacy curtains in village huts.

When lunchtime approached, Elijah's wife and another woman set off for the house to prepare food. Men, women and children trickled into the home. "Relatives," explained Elijah. The five men who arrived, all bare-chested and wearing shorts, had round faces, flat noses, frizzy hair and mustaches.

On the large reed mat in the middle of the room the women placed wooden bowls of fish, yams, taro and cassava. I had watched two men catch fish from a rowboat in the lagoon that morning, so I knew the fish was fresh. Fish and vegetables were standard fare for the islanders; all families had their own vegetable plots. A self-sufficient island is how I imagined paradise.

I sat cross-legged on the floor, in a circle with eight adults and five children. Two of the women waved cloth towels over the food to keep away the flies. We spooned small portions from the bowls onto plates cut from banana leaves.

The diners used their right hands as utensils to stuff food into their mouths. Then they quickly chomped it down. It seemed a bit messy but I followed their example. No one spoke; eating was a serious business. We washed down the food with cups of black tea.

After lunch I watched some of the women making *masi* cloth. With their mallets they hammered the long, four-inch-wide strips of white bark until it stretched to six inches. A woman asked if I would like to buy a piece and have it painted in traditional colours and designs. We agreed on six dollars for a piece twenty inches wide and eight feet long. To make the cloth that size they overlapped the six-inch-wide pieces and hammered them again to force the fibres to entwine, then glued them with breadfruit juice. The cloth was placed on the ground, to be dried by the sun.

I explored the village in the afternoon. The dominant sound was the tap-tap-tap of the mallets pounding the bark. I strolled past the thatched *bures* (homes) and stopped to watch fishermen tending their fishing boats and mending nets. Everyone seemed happy and relaxed – another requirement for paradise.

That night, as I lay in my sleeping bag on the floor, I listened to the waves washing the shore, and the wind rustling the fronds of the coconut trees.

The following morning my *masi* was painted with geometric designs. In earlier days, the women cut stencils from leaves of the pandanus and banana trees but these days they cut them from cardboard. The shapes included squares, crosses, rectangles, wavy lines and rosettes. The colours remained the same: red and black. Red was derived from clay found on the island while black was obtained from charcoal.

The job of painting was shared by various women and girls. When friends came by to gossip, they picked up a cardboard stencil and a cloth moistened with either red or black paint and stencilled the design onto the cloth. The *masi* had the texture of rough cardboard.

In the early afternoon the village exploded with children released from the schoolhouse. Their laughter and shrieks cut through the humid air. Some played on boats in the lagoon, some fished, and others chased each other in and out of the water.

I entered a boat-building shed covered by a roof of palm thatch. Half-a-dozen men were sitting on their haunches playing cards. Each one looked up, smiled and said, *"Bula."* The eldest man, the one with a round, deeply creased face and a crop of hair like steel wool, said they were playing 'twenty-one' and started making room for me. However, I said I wanted to look over the boat they were building. It was in the beginning stages. The keel had been shaped with adzes and they were now hewing planks for the hull. With the construction interrupted by card games I expected the work would be slow. But then I thought, 'What's the hurry?' The men had time on their hands. They could enjoy their days without alarm clocks and deadlines and stress.

I moved on and discovered vehicle ruts that followed the

coastline. I caught up with an old red farm tractor hauling a trailer load of skinny tree trunks about eight feet long and two inches in diameter.

The driver saw me, waved and greeted me with a loud *"bula."* I waved back.

The trunks were of the paper mulberry tree, destined for the village women who would peel off the bark to make their *masi* cloth. I followed the tractor to the edge of the village where the driver dumped the load.

As much as I enjoyed this laid-back island I decided to leave the next morning to continue my travels.

It was the custom in Fiji that *sevusevu* (a gift) be offered to the lady of the house. It could be tea, coffee, a T-shirt or money. Because I was travelling lightly I could only offer money. It was gracefully accepted. I joined Elijah at the lagoon where he was stashing *masi* in the boat.

During the two-hour boat trip back to Korolevu Beach I thought about this island where life was so simple. I knew that I would soon have to deal with the challenges of urban living whereas these islanders were not reliant on electricians, plumbers, policemen, lawyers and a host of other professionals to keep their society rolling along.

Idyllic island? I believe I found it.

About the Jennings

Penny hails from Vancouver, Canada; Russell is from Melbourne, Australia. They work as a team and could be called entrepreneurs. They have presented travel slide shows in Vancouver for thirty years, a result of their independent globetrotting that included four months in Central and South America, fifteen months in Asia and East Africa, nine months in West Africa and Europe and multiple travels in Australia, New Zealand and the South Pacific islands. They also have given night school courses on various travel themes: archaeology, anthropology, budget travel.

Their book publishing business started when they were managing a travel agency in Vancouver. In 1981, China opened its doors to independent travellers. The Jennings went to China in 1982 to gather first-hand information for their clients. Their new-found knowledge led them to publish a guide-book, appropriately called *China On Your Own*, that sold internationally.

They gave slide presentations to promote the book, but many people preferred to join a tour rather than endure the difficulties of travelling on one's own. This prompted the Jennings to plan and escort a series of tours to China.

After touring China, clients requested other destinations. The Jennings then planned and escorted tours to many of the countries they had travelled independently.

Tour planning required a knowledge of weather patterns and the best time to visit a country. The World Meteorological Organization in Geneva, Switzerland supplied them with 30 years of data. After additional research they published a 432-page definitive tome, *Travel Planner's Weather Guide*.

Two books of personal travel tales followed: *Around the World in Sandals*, and *Timbuktu, where are you?*

The Jennings live in Vancouver when they aren't travelling.

Resources

Travel Planner's Weather Guide
by Russell and Penny Jennings
Second edition, 2003, 432 pages, Cdn$24.95 or US$24.95

This quick reference weather guide suggests the best time to visit over 200 countries and island dependencies.

The guide contains:
- Weather tables for hundreds of cities showing temperatures, rainfall, days with rain and hours of sunshine.
- Weather descriptions for every country, region by region, and season by season when necessary.
- More than 240 maps.
- List of name changes of countries and cities.
- When to cruise, ski, trek, go on safari, dive, climb mountains, and visit national parks.

The guide also warns of seasons of strong desert winds, cyclones, monsoons, snowy conditions, freezing temperatures and searing heat.

The authors compiled the weather tables from thousands of pieces of raw data gathered over past decades by the World Meteorological Organization in Geneva, Switzerland. The tables, therefore, can be considered reliable.

Explanations of the effect of global warming and the ozone layer are included.

This easy-to-read guide is an essential source for vacationers, business travellers and travel agents.

Around the World in Sandals
by Russell and Penny Jennings

Published 2005, 288 pages. Cdn$14.95 or US$14.95
Includes the authors' stories of personal encounters during their off-beat journeys which included four months in Mexico, Central and South America in 1975, fifteen months in Asia and Africa in 1978 and 1979, one month in China in 1983 and nine months in West Africa and Europe in 1987.

Warning: Be prepared for adventure.

- Visit the hill tribes of northern Thailand
- Journey along the White Nile in Sudan and the Ucayali and Amazon in Peru.
- Stay with Berbers in Morocco's Atlas Mountains
- Trek by donkey cart to Dogon villages in Mali
- Explore archaeological sites in Mexico, Egypt and Sudan
- Encounter tribal groups: the Kochi of Afghanistan, the Jivaro of Peru, the Afridi of Pakistan, the Tamberma of Togo
- Meet these fascinating characters:
    - Doctor Dako the witch-doctor
    - Gerard the eccentric
    - Padre Crespi the archaeologist
    - Pauline the psychic
    - Gordon the wheeler-dealer
- Be inspired by generous passersby:
    - Ahmed, Mr. Po, Jimmy, Hussein, Faizullah, George, I'mande, Hassan and others.

Book prices

Travel Planner's Weather Guide
Second edition published in 2003, 432 pages.
Cdn $24.95 or US$24.95

Around the World in Sandals
Published in 2005, 288 pages
Cdn $14.95 or US$14.95

Timbuktu, where are you?
Published in 2008, 256 pages.
Cdn $17.95 or US$17.95

Postage and handling:
Charges are subject to change

- **Travel Planner's Weather Guide**

Postage and handling for one book

	Surface	Air
Canada	12.00	12.00
USA	12.00	15.00
International	15.00	30.00

- **Around the World in Sandals**
- **Timbuktu, where are you?**

Postage and handling for one book

	Surface	Air
Canada	10.00	10.00
USA	8.00	10.00
International	10.00	16.00

ORDER FORM

(see opposite page for book prices)

- ***Travel Planner's Weather Guide***
- ***Around the World in Sandals***
- ***Timbuktu, where are you?***

How to order:

E-mail orders: jennings@worldweatherguide.com (We accept payment by VISA and Mastercard.)

Fax orders: 604 734 1586. Send this form.

Postal orders: **Open Road Publishers, 3316 West 8th Ave., Vancouver, BC, V6R 1Y4, CANADA**

Books are mailed within 24 hours of receiving payment.

In this space specify quantity, add postage and handling, and calculate the total payable. For book prices, see opposite page.

Book	**Quantity**	**Total $**
Travel Planner's Weather Guide	______	__________
Around the World in Sandals	______	__________
Timbuktu, where are you?	______	__________
Postage and handling	______	__________
5% GST (Canadian addresses only)	______	__________
Total	______	__________

Please send books to:

Name ____

Address ____

City ______________ Province/State ________________

Country ______________ Postal/Zip code ______________

Phone ______________ E-mail ______________________

How to pay:

Pay by money order or check to Open Road Publishers drawn on a Canadian or US bank, or pay by VISA or Mastercard.

Canadian orders: Pay in Canadian dollars.

U.S. and International orders: Pay in U.S. dollars.

If you are paying by VISA or Mastercard we need the following:

Exact name on card ______________________________

Card number ____________________________________

Expiry date __________ Signature ________________

www.worldweatherguide.com